Politics Is about Relationship

A Blueprint for the Citizens' Century

Harold H. Saunders

First published in 2005 by
PALGRAVE MACMILLAN™
175 Fifth Avenue, New York, N.Y. 10010 and
Houndmills, Basingstoke, Hampshire, England RG21 6XS
Companies and representatives throughout the world.

PALGRAVE MACMILLAN is the global academic imprint of the Palgrave Macmillan division of St. Martin's Press, LLC and of Palgrave Macmillan Ltd. Macmillan® is a registered trademark in the United States, United Kingdom and other countries. Palgrave is a registered trademark in the European Union and other countries.

ISBN 1–4039–7145–5

Library of Congress Cataloging-in-Publication Data

Saunders, Harold H.
    Politics is about relationship : a blueprint for the citizens' century / Harold H. Saunders.
        p. cm.
    Includes bibliographical references and index.
    ISBN 1–4039–7145–5
        1. Civil society. 2. Political planning. 3. Peace. I. Title.

JC337.S28 2005
323'.042—dc22   2005049187

A catalogue record for this book is available from the British Library.

Design by Newgen Imaging Systems (P) Ltd., Chennai, India.

First edition: December 2005

10 9 8 7 6 5 4 3 2 1

Printed in the United States of America.

To Carol, my beloved wife,
who knows that the message of this book is seared on my soul and
who enriches and brightens my every day

To my children and grandchildren
and those near and far of all generations, races, classes, cultures, religions
who can make this truly
The Citizens' Century

CONTENTS

ACKNOWLEDGMENTS

The early foundations for this book took shape in the mid-1980s. The experience that provided the materials reaches back years earlier. My debts are countless.

They include numberless colleagues in a dozen countries: participants in over a thousand hours in nonofficial dialogues; scholars in whose classrooms I have taught; students with whom I interacted; authors I read in conflict resolution, mediation and negotiation, international relations, political psychology, and related fields. I cannot name them all; a few are acknowledged in the notes. My debt to all is heartfelt, though much of it is unknowable even to me.

During my government years, we created "peace process" by conducting a uniquely intensive, flexible, and imaginative form of diplomacy and mediation. Flying in 1974–1975 on the "shuttle" with Secretary of State Henry Kissinger, who conceived and implemented the strategy under Presidents Richard Nixon and Gerald Ford, and then working with President Jimmy Carter and Secretary Cyrus Vance virtually seared on my soul the power of a disciplined political process to change relationships. Each of them shaped my thought in his own way.

Among colleagues flying on the shuttles, I deeply valued my relationships with Under Secretary of State Joseph Sisco, Assistant Secretary Alfred L. "Roy" Atherton, Jr., and Robert Oakley, a Princeton classmate and career diplomat who succeeded me on the National Security Council (NSC) Staff when in July 1974 I become deputy assistant secretary of state for Near Eastern affairs. The professional team at Camp David in 1978 with President Jimmy Carter, President Anwar al-Sadat of Egypt, and Prime Minister Menachem Begin of Israel included Atherton, by then ambassador-at-large; Samuel Lewis, ambassador to Israel; Hermann Eilts, ambassador to Egypt; William Quandt in my former position on the NSC Staff; and myself, now assistant secretary. We worked closely, effectively, rapidly, sometimes almost without needing to talk because we sensed what needed to be done and who could do it best. We learned from each other. I owe a tremendous debt to each one both personally and professionally—each an incomparable professional and a wise and giving human being.

High among those whom I can identify in my post-government years are David Mathews, president of the Kettering Foundation, and the

Foundation's Board of Trustees, who since 1982 have given me—first as an associate and since 1991 as director of international affairs—freedom to develop the theory and practice of Sustained Dialogue and to publish what I have learned. In July 2002, David proposed incorporating the independent International Institute for Sustained Dialogue (IISD) to concentrate that work in one place and to promote the conduct and teaching of the process through established nongovernmental organizations around the world. For this most generous support and expression of confidence, I am grateful beyond words. This book stands as my tribute and contribution to the twenty-fifth anniversary celebration of the Foundation's commitment to the deliberative process.

During the later 1980s, Robert F. Lehman, then vice president and general counsel of the Kettering Foundation, later president now chairman of the Fetzer Institute, introduced me to readings about twentieth-century physics and to Martin Buber's writing on relationship. Buber's *I and Thou*[1] is a continuing source of discovery and reverence for relationship. Rob encouraged me persistently in my focus on relationship. He also took me to meet with David Bohm.

After I left government in 1981, my principal laboratory as a Kettering Foundation associate for learning through experience the process of a dialogue sustained over time was the Dartmouth Conference Regional Conflicts Task Force. I am particularly grateful to Philip D. Stewart who, as executive director of the Dartmouth Conference for Kettering, introduced me to the art and practice of developing a relationship of mutual respect with our Soviet partners for much of two decades—Yevgeny Primakov, Gennady Chufrin, Vitaly Naumkin, and Irina Zviagelskaya. Phil also serves on the IISD board.

That task force in 1993 started the Inter-Tajik Dialogue within the Framework of the Dartmouth Conference. It provided the first serious test of the five-stage process of Sustained Dialogue. In March 2000, Dialogue members formed the Public Committee for Democratic Processes, which became our primary laboratory for experiencing the uses of dialogue in peacebuilding—the engagement of citizens in experimenting with their own forms of democracy. Ashurboi Imomov, Abdunabi Sattorzoda, and Saifullo Safarov as leading board members and Parviz Mullojanov as executive director have been prime movers. I deeply value their wisdom, commitment, and friendship.

As the work in Tajikistan developed and as we responded to opportunities presented by creation of the IISD, Randa Slim as vice president and a board member has become an alter ego in advancing this work. She is one of the finest professionals of her generation in this field and a close friend whom I respect enormously and learn from constantly.

Ramón Daubón, vice president of the Inter-American Foundation, associate of the Kettering Foundation, and IISD board member is a friend and colleague of more than a decade. His creativity in seeing the relationship between the citizens' political engagement and economic development, in which he has spent his professional life, has enlarged my perspective greatly. His friendship is a constant joy.

From 1996 to 2000, I was privileged to serve as an alumni trustee of Princeton University. Apart from my assigned duties, that experience provided the opportunity to immerse myself—to the extent possible for any semi-outsider—in the culture of a research university. Two experiences are relevant.

First, the Secretary's office arranged more than three dozen in-depth talks with faculty about multidisciplinary research and resistance to it in the natural, physical, and social sciences. This provided an unparalleled opportunity to test my ideas in an academic setting.

Second, I began more than six years of work with students who use Sustained Dialogue to improve racial and ethnic relationships on campus. The IISD's Sustained Dialogue Campus Network, formed in 2003, has helped start this program on more than a dozen high school and college campuses as of this writing. Among the several hundred students who have engaged in Sustained Dialogue, I name only those who have worked directly with the Campus Network Management Team: Teddy Nemeroff, founder at Princeton, and his closest colleague, David Tukey; Jessica Munitz, first fulltime program director of the Network after a year as head moderator at Princeton; Priya Narayan Parker, cofounder at the University of Virginia and the second program director of the Network; Samar Katnani, also at Virginia; Tessa Garcia, founder at Notre Dame and associate program director of the Network; and Clark Herndon, third Network program director. I owe special thanks to Tessa for designing the Network's logo and for her permission to adapt it for use in this book. Their enthusiasm, effectiveness in making things happen, and wisdom in strategizing the building of a network have provided insight into what causes young citizens to participate in building an engaged public. They are an "awesome" group.

In my research for the second half of this book, I am grateful to the many in South Africa, West Virginia, and China who spent hours with me in taped interviews. Many are named in later chapters. I also am proud to call Parviz Mullojanov and Phil Stewart coauthors of chapters seven and nine for which they provided drafts. I also thank the many participants in the China-U.S. Dialogue and citizens in Russia and the United States whose words in public forums I quote without knowing their names.

I must also thank those foundations, in addition to Kettering, that have supported either my writing or the living laboratories in which I have learned. In the late 1980s while at The Brookings Institution, I received grants from the MacArthur, the Ford, and the Ira and Miriam Wallach Foundations and from the United States Institute of Peace. In the 1990s, the Charles Stewart Mott Foundation supported our work in Tajikistan for six years; the William and Flora Hewlett Foundation will have supported our projects in Tajikistan for a remarkable 13 years; the United States Institute of Peace has provided two separate grants for different phases of a project in Tajikistan; the Foreign Ministry of Switzerland has supported two projects in Tajikistan and the first year of our Arab–European–American Dialogue; the Foreign Ministry of the Netherlands is supporting the second year of that Dialogue; and the Compton Foundation supported our work in South Africa. I am extremely grateful to all for nourishing the experience that has given this book substance.

Throughout my years at the Kettering Foundation, I have been blessed to have the assistance of a sequence of graduate students, most of whom worked with me while earning their degrees. Those who have helped in so many ways with great enthusiasm, patience with me, and effectiveness with the research and preparation of this book are Bryan Kurey, Katharine Wheatley, Loreene O'Neill, and Manuel Mendoza. In addition, I am deeply grateful to Phillip Lurie who has generously supported me in so many ways.

I must also express warm thanks to David Pervin of Palgrave Macmillan for his enthusiastic support and encouragement in producing the best book of which I am capable and to Assistant Editor Heather Van Dusen; to Production Manager Donna Cherry and to Maran Elancheran for their gracious and thoughtful care in seeing the book through production; and to Asha Boaz for her meticuluous but unintrusive editing. I am grateful to Rebecca Francescatti for her thoughtful indexing.

I owe special thanks to Alexander Knapp for his sensitive and genial work in producing the photo portrait for the cover.

No words exist to thank my wife, Carol. She has been a superb editor in the fullest substantive tradition of the word. Even more important, she has been unstintingly supportive of my commitment to Sustained Dialogue well past what used to be called normal retirement age and in my devotion of the time from our vacations together that this book has absorbed. In so many ways beyond description, she has been what Anwar Sadat called a "full partner" in this work and in life—more so than I have any right to ask or expect. It has been an act of love, which I reciprocate as fully as I can.

Finally, I must state that the views expressed are mine alone and not those of the International Institute for Sustained Dialogue nor the Kettering Foundation.

PREFACE: A PERSONAL ESSAY

This book turns out to be the third in an unintended trilogy on peace process. When I started down this track in 1985, nothing was further from my mind than writing three books on this subject.

My experience had begun 11 years earlier as a member of the National Security Council Staff flying on the Kissinger shuttles after the 1973 Arab–Israeli war. Having left government in 1981, I wanted to conceptualize the Arab–Israeli peace process in a way that might be useful both in the Middle East and in other conflicts. Experience by experience since, my thinking has broadened and deepened and produced books on three levels of the multilevel peace process.

In 1985, I published *The Other Walls: The Politics of the Arab–Israeli Peace Process*.[1] I was writing about the official peace process through the lenses of a former diplomatic member of the U.S. government team under Presidents Nixon, Ford, and Carter and Secretaries of State Kissinger, Vance, and Muskie that mediated five Arab–Israel agreements in six years, 1974–1979. I was writing for those who were then conducting the official peace process, but I was urging them to reach beyond negotiating issues to pay more attention to the human obstacles to peace.

My title was drawn from Egyptian President Anwar al-Sadat's historic speech to the Israeli Knesset in November 1977. In his peroration, he referred to the "other walls between us"—the "seventy percent of the problem" that he called "psychological." I would say "human." "If I ever forget that I am dealing with people in pain," I had said to myself at one particularly difficult moment in 1974, "I will not be doing my job as a diplomat."

I characterized the peace process as a series of agreements between governments but embedded in a larger political process. It was in that process that relationships changed. It was the interaction between the official and public levels that we on the Kissinger shuttles in early 1974 intended to capture in coining the phrase, "peace process," in contrast to our earlier phrase, "negotiating process."

Beginning to probe the human dimension of the peace process, I wrote a chapter on each of the central parties to the Arab–Israeli peace process to illustrate how focusing on human obstacles might enrich the official peace process. At the same time, I published an article, "We Need a Larger Theory of Negotiation: The Importance of the Pre-Negotiating Phases,"[2] emphasizing steps in the often long periods before negotiation that could overcome human obstacles to negotiation. This was often work done in the non-governmental arena, where I was gaining experience.

Over the next half-dozen years, I wrote a number of papers, articles, and chapters developing a new paradigm that would include citizens outside government in the peace process. I had concluded that until leaders and citizens could see the world around them through lenses appropriate to the changing world, they would not act differently. I shaped a concept of relationship to give analytical and operational rigor to transforming the dysfunctional relationships that often blocked peace. In 1991, I began to think of dialogue sustained over time as developing through a discernible progression of experiences in which relationships were transformed.

In the mid-1990s, I began to speak of the "multilevel peace process" to include both the official and the public processes but also to recognize the key role of what we were by then calling "civil society." A precipitating moment came in 1996 in a dialogue among participants from different factions in the civil war in the former Soviet republic of Tajikistan. One participant, then a member of a joint (government and opposition) commission to oversee cease-fire agreements, described in the dialogue how the commission had worked with field commanders, local notables, and municipal authorities in negotiating a regional cease-fire. After his account, another participant reflected: "The reason cease-fires have broken down is that they have been negotiated at the highest political level without reference to local citizens with the guns and the interests at stake. What we need is a multilevel peace process that connects the local and the official levels."[3]

On a related track, I had been associated since 1982 with the Kettering Foundation in Dayton, Ohio, and Washington, DC, which focuses on the politics of citizens outside government dealing with their communities' problems. During my government years working for five U.S. presidents since 1961, I had become vividly aware of the necessary sensitivity of a president to what citizens regarded as important. This was a level of politics that reached beyond parties and legislatures—although obviously closely connected. That level of politics led me to the first subtitle of my book on the official peace process, *The Politics of the Arab–Israeli Peace Process.* As I got to know the Kettering Foundation in the 1980s, I saw in their work on citizens' politics a concept of politics that resonated strongly with my own experience.

In 1999, after almost two decades of intensive participation in nonofficial dialogues, I published *A Public Peace Process: Sustained Dialogue to Transform Racial and Ethnic Conflicts.*[4] This, in retrospect, was the second of the trilogy.

I conceptualized the "public peace process" as a five-stage process of systematic dialogue over time among citizens enmeshed in "deep-rooted human conflicts." I presented this as the instrument of citizens ouside government—Sustained Dialogue—for dealing with conflicts not ready for formal mediation or negotiation. It is the citizens' counterpart to the formal instruments of statecraft—diplomacy, mediation, negotiation. Participants are members of what I called "the policy-influencing community"—members of groups that could influence policy and the course of events.

This is a book about "whole human beings in whole bodies politic." It states the need for a conceptual framework—a paradigm—for the study, teaching, and practice of politics that includes all levels of the multilevel political process, including citizens at the "grass roots." To repeat, only when leaders and citizens have lenses that bring events into focus will they act effectively. The prevailing paradigm for the past two generations or more has focused on states and governments; it left out most of the world's people. This book suggests a wider angle lens—a broader paradigm—to recognize citizens outside government as political actors. I call it the relational paradigm.

The concept of relationship has been central to my thinking since the late 1980s. Experience demonstrates that focusing on relationship enlarges the frame for policymaking and action—whether by officeholders or citizens outside government. I have tried to enlist the help of scholars in probing the dynamic process of continuous interaction within, between, and among groups—their relationships—as a focus for research. Rarely have I found readiness to tackle *inter*action—relationship—as something happening *between* the parties to an interaction and worthy of focus in its own right. Yet, intensive experience in the Arab–Israeli peace process in the 1970s and in sustained dialogues since taught me that it is possible to conduct that process of *inter*action so as to change conflictual and dysfunctional relationships. I am told that the winds of change are blowing in the social sciences. I hope this book will bring forward some allies.

My purpose is to introduce the relational paradigm and to offer evidence that it makes a difference in the lives of citizens. I invite readers to explore this proposition with me.

One further personal comment is necessary. The more I recognized my purpose as introducing a new political paradigm, the more I needed to understand how a paradigm shift takes place.

Since a major shift had taken place in physics at the turn of the twentieth century, I read Thomas S. Kuhn's *The Structure of Scientific Revolutions*.[5] Most exciting for me was that physicists as well as biologists were replacing the precepts of the worldview rooted in Newtonian and Enlightenment thinking with principles very close to those that had emerged from my experience in the Arab–Israeli peace process and subsequent nonofficial dialogues. Since the broader cultural worldview is more likely than a political paradigm to affect how citizens act, I felt it essential to devote a chapter to "a proper world view, appropriate for its time."[6] It turned out to be the perfect introduction to the relational paradigm and the concept of relationship that are central to this book.

In including that chapter, I risk flak from all directions. A rigorous analyst–practitioner I try to be, but not a scientist. At the same time, since our worldview underlies how we relate to each other, it seemed important to be explicit about the worldview that lies behind the relational paradigm.

I also found it affirming that insights I had come to through experience seemed parallel to insights from a quite different realm of experience.

In taking this step, I found comfort in the words of physicist and Nobel Laureate the late Richard Feynman in a public lecture in 1963: "In talking about the impact of ideas in one field on ideas in another field, one is always apt to make a fool of oneself." Then he plowed ahead as a "citizen-scientist" to speak about "how society looks to me."[7] Perhaps that is humanity at its most authentic—speaking from experience, both personal and professional.

Let us—citizens all—now turn the pages.

Harold H. Saunders
International Institute for Sustained
Dialogue and the Kettering Foundation
Washington, DC
July 19, 2005

INTRODUCTION

Meeting the Challenges of a World in Crisis: Engaging Whole Bodies Politic

"What is it that the poor reply when asked what might make the greatest difference in their lives? They say, organizations of their own so that they may negotiate with government, with traders, and with nongovernmental organizations. Direct assistance through community-driven programs so that they may shape their own destinies. Local ownership of funds, so that they may put a stop to corruption. They want nongovernmental organizations and governments to be accountable to them. . . . These are strong voices, voices of dignity."[1] These words introduce a courageous World Bank study titled *Voices of the Poor: Can Anyone Hear Us?* These are the voices of citizens outside normal power structures reaching for political engagement.

The challenges of our troubled world require political—not just technical—responses. In this book, I present an approach to political life that taps humankind's greatest untapped resource—human beings themselves, the citizens of our world. Its organizing insight is that some things only governments can do—negotiate binding agreements, enforce laws, provide for the common defense, fund public projects and programs. But some things only citizens outside government can do—transform conflictual human relationships, modify human behavior, change political culture.

The prevalent approach to the study and practice of politics has been to focus on the structures of power and their elites. Power has been defined as control or the ability to coerce. I suggest ways for citizens outside those structures to think about political life, peace, and sustainable development that enable them to find dignity and the capacity to change what they need to change. I offer a human framework for citizens to use in naming their problems and engaging fellow citizens in tackling them. I describe instruments within their reach. These are the essence of democracy.

The conceptual lenses we use to understand events determine how we act. Achieving a fresh way of understanding the world around us requires new conceptual lenses to bring a rapidly changing world into focus. Thus we must spend some time reflecting on how we think about politics. Please bear with me. Finally, you will see the world through these new lenses and will have new tools in your hands.

People ask why I as a political practitioner write about such things as worldviews, paradigms, concepts, and political instruments. These are not so strange to us as they may sound; they are tools we all use daily to make sense of what happens around us; we just do not use those names. Working with five U.S. presidents and other world leaders convinced me that the conceptual lenses that leaders wear determine how they act. So it is for every citizen.

To act more productively, we must change our way of understanding how our public world works—a world that is falling behind in meeting its challenges. Helping each of us see the world through new lenses and demonstrating that these can change how we act are this book's aims.

The Challenges

Five challenges top the human agenda at the beginning of the twenty-first century. You may add your own. Responses to all depend on citizens outside government as well as on the governments *they* constitute.

First is whether and, if so, how people of different racial, ethnic, cultural, historic, and economic backgrounds can coexist peacefully, justly, and productively. Can they live and work together, or must they segregate into different social and political entities? Large multiethnic units have greater populations, land areas, resources, economies of scale, and energy from diverse traditions. More homogenous single-ethnic units offer comfort zones where people live with others like themselves. Peoples in the twentieth century made vastly different choices, ranging from Yugoslavia's breakup to South Africa's transformation and the anxious but glacial consolidation of the European Union. Whatever the specific arrangements, the choice is between a productive peace and dehumanization and destruction. How such choices are framed, made, and executed is the essence of politics.

Second, the gap between the rich and the poor widens—both within and between countries. Governments frame solutions in economic and bureaucratic terms, not in political and human terms. Instead of collaborating to channel the resources turned loose by globalization, demonstrators simply rail against it, and managers do not see beyond their own gain. Societies are increasingly fragmented, crime-ridden, and violent; we neglect the power of citizens to build whole bodies politic worthy of defining their identity. Countries clash, and we talk in diplomatic language, not as citizens who care and want to try to change. Sustainable and just economic development requires building productive relationships within and across polities.

Third, ideological gulfs within and between societies widen and deepen. The attacks in New York, Washington, and Pennsylvania on September 11, 2001, in Israel, Indonesia, Spain, and a mounting number of other countries demonstrate that alienation, hopelessness, ideological extremism, and anger can be expressed in devastating ways by tightly organized, committed, and marginalized individuals. Why do people become terrorists? While often well-educated leaders pursue their own ideological fanaticism, those who face this question daily say young people are drawn into extremist groups by loss of hope—hope of meaningful work, hope of a voice in their future, hope of dignity, inclusion, and purpose. The challenge to polities is political—creating an environment that offers dignity and realistic engagement to all. A violent response alone cannot make the world either more peaceful or more just.

Fourth, we are taxing the earth beyond its ability to sustain us. Since 1972, periodic global conferences have placed the environment on the global agenda and urged multilateralism to protect it. Their cry: "Protection of the environment is a noble endeavor in itself. But the survival of the environment is also the strategic basis of human survival. . . . The protection of Earth must go hand in hand with measures to fight poverty and enhance human dignity and security. Development and environment are interlinked."[2]

Reports leading up to the Johannesburg summit in 2002 posed the challenge:

> Given current trends in production and consumption, social and environmental strains threaten to derail development efforts and erode living standards unless we design better policies and institutions. . . . If we stay on the road we are on, the signs do not appear very encouraging. By 2050 the world's annual output of carbon dioxide will have more than tripled, while 9 billion people—3 billion more than we have today and mostly living in developing countries—will be tapping into the earth's water, adding more stress on an already strained water supply. Food needs will more than double. . . . Globally 1.3 billion people already live on fragile land—arid zones, wetlands, and forests—that cannot sustain them.[3]

The Rio summit in 1992 led to widespread national commitments "to protect one of the planet's most valuable natural resources: the tremendous variety and diversity of plant and animal species." Since, ". . . humanity is squandering this biological bounty at such a high rate that scientists describe the current era as the greatest period of mass extinction since the period of the dinosaurs."[4] Enough to say that the challenge is without adequate response. Technical remedies may meet some challenges, but we lack political capacity to right the balance.

Fifth, some see the new century as a crossroads for humankind, but governance falls far short of the challenge. In the words of Czech President Václav Havel: "It is not that we should simply seek new and better ways of managing society, the economy, and the world. The point is that we should fundamentally change how we behave."[5]

The global project of the twenty-first century is political: to engage citizens in and out of government in whole bodies politic in responding to these challenges. With some leap of faith, I have called this "The Citizens' Century." Only citizens can change political culture. Only citizens can decide to work and relate in different ways. Only by engaging the resources of whole bodies politic can we as citizens meet our challenges. Bodies politic that exclude or ignore much of their populations are not whole, nor are they engaging the full richness of resources they need to meet the challenges of this new century. Engaging whole bodies politic is both a practical and a moral imperative. This book is for all who feel compelled to engage in this project—beginning in our own communities.

Hear the words of United Nations Secretary General Kofi Annan when he accepted the Nobel Peace Prize in 2001: "In the 21st century I believe the mission of the United Nations will be defined by a new, more profound, awareness of the sanctity and dignity of every human life, regardless of race or religion. This will require us to look beyond the framework of states, and beneath the surface of nations or communities. We must focus, as never before, on improving the conditions of the individual men and women who give the state or nation its richness and character."[6]

If we are, in Havel's words, to "fundamentally change how we behave," we must begin by seeing the world—and politics—differently. We must change how we relate to others and deepen how we think about relationships.

Whole Bodies Politic

We need a way of understanding politics that embraces citizens both inside and outside government since each have work that only they can do. If we see them as parts of a whole dividing the labor, the challenge to each group is to enlarge their own capacities—and then to stretch those capacities by learning to work together to build *whole* bodies politic.

Concretely, governments face more and more problems both internally and across borders that no government can deal with alone. Internally, they need new cooperation with and among their own citizens. Across borders, problems such as global warming, drug trafficking, disease, terrorism, global trade and investment, and environmental degradation require intergovernmental collaboration and the contribution of international nongovernmental groups. As a corollary, citizens outside government increasingly influence the policies of their governments and the interaction between bodies politic. The challenge is to find more effective and fairer ways of conducting relationships within and between bodies politic. The challenge is to develop, enrich, and sustain the relationships needed to deal with problems that no one group, government, or country can deal with alone and to overcome differences—often violently expressed—that would undercut their efforts.

Western democratic thought has evolved along two lines of concept and practice—not just one. One has focused on the machinery of democracy: principles such as one person/one vote; free and fair elections; protection of the fundamental civil rights of citizens; free and responsible media; checks and balances among units of government; independent judiciary. The second tradition focuses on the citizen as political actor—the citizen out-side the structures of governmental power. It starts with a simple human proposition: "We have a problem; let's talk about it." It has roots in the forums of ancient Greece and Rome. It comes to us in the United States through our early town meetings and to peoples in other cultures and civilizations through their own traditions of dialogue.

In the late 1980s, as a new wave in the ongoing democratic revolution began, many of the political transformations resulted from citizens working together—from the "vote no" campaign against Chilean military dictator Augusto Pinochet to the demonstrations in Wenceslas Square and then a decade later in Belgrade. But rather than building political practices from that experience, these citizens—many of whom had never known a free and fair election—understandably turned to the machinery of democracy. They focused on written constitutions, political parties, parliaments, elec-toral machinery, respect for basic human and civil rights, and rule of law. This was understandable and important.

The great eye-opener of the mid-1990s, however, was the insight that one tradition without the other will not work—that both traditions must work hand in hand. Barely five years after the installation of demo-cratic methods, we began to hear plaints such as the following from a woman who had played a key role in the "vote no" campaign in Chile: "When we had Pinochet, we as citizens could work together against him. But when we elected and installed a democratic government, those citizens went back to pursuing their own interests and their own competitions with each other. Then they discovered that the government was not solving their problems. How can we bring the citizens back into the life of the country?"[7]

This book weaves these two threads of democratic thought into one tapestry depicting whole bodies politic. It starts from the second—citizens organizing to meet their challenges—but it certainly does not exclude government. It enters politics through an old but recently neglected door— the principle that citizens constitute government. This was the founding principle of the democratic revolution.

Whole Human Beings in Whole Bodies Politic

The only form of politics that will meet the challenges we face is one that engages *whole human beings* in all their complexities in whole bodies politic.[8] Too often over the past two centuries we have thought of human beings only in terms of part of who they are. First, we separated the rational and the emotional or intuitive, glorifying the former. Then we studied them as voters, consumers, managers, welfare recipients, workers, politicians joust-ing for power, or members of one ethnic group or religious persuasion.

Citizens are whole persons with multifaceted identities and interests. They have within them the capacity to commit the noblest acts and the most horrible atrocities—sometimes rational and calculating, sometimes far-seeing and compassionate, sometimes self-centered, narrow-minded, irrational, and bestial. They pursue interests integrating the material and the spiritual. We must focus on the politics of these whole human beings in and out of government interacting to meet life-and-death challenges to the whole body politic.

The new wave in the democratic revolution is slowed by two shoals. A purpose of this book is to help free that wave to realize its potential.

First, we do not have a large enough conceptual framework to bring together the two main lines of Western democratic thought in the right balance—the practices of democratic government and the potentially powerful capacities and energies of whole human beings outside government. In thinking about politics, people commonly focus heavily on institutions and organizations struggling for power—not on whole human beings as political actors or on the collaboration among these whole human beings outside and inside government.

Second, we are suffering a crisis in the conduct of relationships. Neither government nor civil society is strong in its own right because citizens in and out of government are not conducting their relationships in productive ways.[9] They wrestle over competing interests rather than building relationships to meet their challenges. The 9/11 Commission spotlighted the failure of intelligence agencies to cooperate fully; in my view this was a failure of human beings to relate—not primarily a structural problem with structural solutions. Relationships involve whole human beings with multiple and even conflicting interests, who nevertheless are willing to seek and find bases from which to work together for the public good.

Some scholars have turned their attention to human motivation and basic human needs and, eventually, to the implications of these for resolving deep-rooted human conflict in political life. Psychologist A. H. Maslow in the 1940s, for instance, called attention to basic human needs such as physiological (food); safety; love, affection, belongingness; self-respect and the esteem of others that grows from capacity and achievement; and self-actualization (self-fulfillment).[10] From the late 1960s, John Burton, an Australian diplomat turned scholar, brought that focus on basic human needs—rather than sole attention to interests—into the budding field of conflict resolution as he and others developed processes of dialogue to probe the human roots of conflict and enable conflicting parties to transform their relationships.[11]

It is time to integrate the human dimension—whole human beings—fully into the study of whole bodies politic. The study and practice of politics today does not yet reflect the full range of thought and practice humanity requires to survive and to improve quality of life for all. The present practice of politics—mostly through institutions—has alienated citizens outside these institutions in country after country. Citizens too often do not relate peacefully or productively. This is a human or political—not a structural—problem.

While this chapter was being drafted, a remarkable op-ed piece appeared in the *International Herald Tribune*. It was written jointly by the president of the World Bank, the chairman and chief executive officer of Conservation International, and the head of the Global Environment Facility under the title, "How Biodiversity Can Be Preserved if We Get Smart Together." Three extracts underscore my point:

> . . . overall we are failing to stem the lethal dynamic of chronic poverty and growing population, which is destroying species a thousand times faster than ever before. . . .
>
> . . . for poor people in the developing world . . . conserving biodiversity is not just about long-term welfare. It is about survival, because so many of them depend on the habitats that support biodiversity for their daily needs.
>
> If we are to make a real difference, we must involve poor people and communities more centrally in the management of their lives and the stewardship of our shared natural resources.[12]

To paraphrase in the terms of this introduction, institutions alone will not solve the problems of humanity; only if the human beings whose lives are at stake become involved is there a chance of resolving them.

In the same *International Herald Tribune*, three of the six main front page headlines were: "A Tamil Guerrilla's Story, Starting at Age 7," topping a picture of an attractive fourteen-year-old girl; "Digging for Roots of Youth Racism in Eastern Germany"; and "American TV's New Stars: Rapists and Murderers." These in one of the world's outstanding and responsible newspapers dramatize the violent dimension of failed politics.

A Conceptual Framework for Whole Human Beings in Whole Bodies Politic

To repeat, the approach to the study and practice of politics prevalent for two generations at the end of the twentieth century has focused on government and other political institutions such as political parties and interest groups—the structures and wielders of power. In internal affairs, the mantra has been "politics is about power" with power defined as control or the ability to coerce. In international politics, we have spoken of the "realist paradigm" or "power politics model" focusing on states pursuing objectively defined interests in zero–sum contests of power with other nation-states.

This book presents new conceptual lenses—new assumptions about how the world works, a new political paradigm, and an operational concept with a practical instrument for putting that paradigm to practical use. The paradigm and the assumptions behind it are the starting point for changing how we act.

The proposed paradigm: *politics is a cumulative, multilevel, and open-ended process of continuous interaction over time engaging significant clusters of citizens in and out of government and the relationships they form to solve public problems in whole bodies politic across permeable borders, either within or between communities or countries.* This focus on a *multilevel process of continuous interaction among citizens* contrasts to the traditional focus on a linear sequence of actions and reactions among institutions as in a chess game. Continuing *inter*actions are the essence of that process. What is important are the interplay and interpenetration between entities—not just the action by one on another.

To capture this process of continuous interaction, I have used the human word *relationship*, carefully defined in terms of five components. It is a diagnostic tool because it enables practitioners to organize the elements of complex interactions for analysis. It is an operational tool because practitioners can get inside each component of relationship to change it.

This paradigm and the concept of relationship bring human beings— citizens outside as well as inside government and related institutions—into the study and practice of political life. That does not denigrate the importance of states and governments. I spent twenty-five years in government and am proud of many of our accomplishments. Government remains one of the most important instruments that citizens can build and use in solving their problems. By itself, however, government is not enough. Citizens need their own instruments. The paradigm, the concept of relationship, and the instrument of dialogue broaden our focus to include the rich resources of whole bodies politic.

I am not alone in the search for a new paradigm. Underneath the surface of the old paradigm, many social scientists and practitioners have been working their way toward a new conceptual framework, building from the realities they encountered and often instinctively using language resonant with the paradigm proposed here.[13] Listen to a few of the actors whom you will meet in later chapters:

A citizen of Tajikistan, the poorest of the former Soviet republics: "The government has neither the capacity nor the resources to put every town in our country on its feet economically. If anyone is going to do that job, the citizens of the towns themselves will have to do it."[14]

A strategist of the resistance to apartheid in South Africa: "There was a picture of change made up of more than just who sits in power. There was a complex understanding about what the nature of change would be. If you see your objective as dismantling one system and replacing it with another, change is of a holistic order. In the first instance, yes, you have to have access to political power; in the second instance, that access would allow you to have the resources, the authority, and the legislative means to introduce other changes; third, that would have to be underpinned by changes in the economy; fourthly, there would be a social element to this change which involved a change in relationships—the development of a nonracial culture, reconciliation of sorts between black and white, introducing a new set of values which would enable people to respect each other, to accept each other as equals, etc."[15]

Or a citizen of West Virginia: "When people come together for the common good, power springs up there."[16]

This book is written with the hope that we can find common purpose across this spectrum of scholars and practitioners in meeting the challenges humankind faces. The success of our attempt depends heavily on recognizing that there is nothing more authentic than the experience of whole human beings tackling their most difficult challenges in whole bodies politic. Experience nurtures a different way of knowing. I have had a career in which analytical rigor was demanded of me—writing options papers for five presidents, drafting disengagement and peace agreements between governments that parliaments ratified, and working in sustained dialogues with those whose groups have hated, dehumanized, and killed each other. I know of no fuller way to understand political life than to plumb the complexity of human experience.

The formulation of a new paradigm reflects a broadening of approach that embraces important thinking from the past; it does not reject past concepts. It responds to new problems not earlier addressed. Albert Einstein and his fellow physicists did not reject Newtonian physics; they discovered that—while it remained accurate in addressing the visible world—it did not explain the subatomic world. So today, past thinking about institutional politics provides much insight into that part of political life, but it is not broad enough to embrace whole human beings in whole bodies politic.

The Line of March in This Book

To develop these ideas, I pursue a progression of questions in this book. These questions shape the three parts through which the book now develops:

Following this Introduction's posing of the challenge, chapters one and two describe *our starting points*. Given the challenge, what is the thinking that has shaped our responses? In chapter one, how have scholars and citizens outside government thought about politics? In chapter two, how have other thinkers—especially physical and life scientists—shaped an alternative worldview?

Chapters three and four explain *the new paradigm and the concept of relationship* through which that paradigm reveals itself, is studied, and can be put into practice. They are a conceptualization of experience in the last third of the twentieth century. They offer the new lenses that I believe are essential to ways of relating that are necessary to meet the challenges of this century.

Chapters five through ten respond to the inevitable questions: *What difference does it make to think this way? How is dialogue appropriate to this new way of thinking?* Chapter five lays out a framework for analysis built around the concept of relationship and identifies instruments of change that citizens uniquely use within the relational paradigm and the concept. Chapters six–ten test the paradigm and the concept of relationship against a range of significant recent experiences to suggest both a systematic way of organizing analysis of real-world situations and ways of using that analysis to change relationships.

The final chapter presents closing thoughts in reflecting on exactly *what makes this difference* and on the effect of "a different way of thinking— another way of relating."

Because words such as *worldview, paradigm, concept,* and *instrument* are often used in different ways, I want to explain the simple meanings that I assign to them.

Our *worldview* determines how we instinctively think about experience. It is the collection of assumptions about how the world and human inter-action work that most of us absorb in childhood and carry through life in our minds, almost without recognizing them. It is the mental filter that helps human beings organize and give meaning to their experience. It shapes our way of thinking about—interpreting—experience. It lies behind the habits, customs, rules by which we conduct our lives together. Often, we think of it as the culture that surrounds us. Do we see the world as a series of discrete actions and reactions, each to be analyzed? Or do we see a complex of interactions? Do we see a whole as a collection of parts or as more than the sum of its parts? Because it reflects our view of what is and what works, it shapes our view of truth. It provides a benchmark for judg-ing what is effective and what is right. Chapters one and two describe the prevailing Western worldview at the end of the twentieth century along with the elements of an alternative worldview that is the starting point for the paradigm proposed in chapters three and four.

A *paradigm* is a statement intended to provide a starting point for further analysis and more effective practice in a significant area of research and human life. What is the focus of research? What do we need to understand more deeply in order to act more constructively? As one historian of sci-ence suggests, it "defines the legitimate problems and methods of a research field" and is "sufficiently open-ended to leave all sorts of problems for sub-sequent researchers to resolve."[17] For citizens, it can be the guide in their minds to where it will be most useful to apply their energies to achieve their goals. Research could suggest more effective political practices for cit-izens, or citizens' experience could pose perceptions of how politics works that call into question the starting point for scholarly analysis. The paradigm presented in chapter three suggests a starting point for research that would relate it more directly to the world that citizens experience and a way of interacting to make the most effective use of citizens' energies and capaci-ties. It is conceptualized from this experience and continuously tested in it.

A *concept,* as used here, is a carefully defined idea that captures the essence of a paradigm in practical terms and provides a framework for analyzing complex experience or data and for acting in relation to them. The concept

of relationship presented in chapter four—the centerpiece of this book—
is laid out in human terms that citizens can use to understand everyday
situations.

An *instrument*, in this discussion of political life, refers to possible ways in
which citizens may organize themselves and their work to effect change. I
think, for instance, of the Citizens' Political Process and the process of
Sustained Dialogue, which are described later, as political instruments
uniquely available to citizens.

With these words of introduction, we now turn in the next chapter to a
fuller discussion of the traditional thinking about politics that the new
paradigm seeks to enlarge.

Our Starting Points

A grove of aspen trees is said to be one of the world's largest organisms. Above ground, we see individual trees. Below ground, they are connected through one ever-spreading root system.

First glancing at the image above, we see a sturdy trunk carrying nourishment from those roots through the limbs to the leaves above, which in turn cleanse the surrounding atmosphere. On second look, we see that the lines defining the trunk also profile the faces of two persons in dialogue—a source of nourishment for social change. Aspens are often called "quaking aspens" because their leaves move constantly in the slightest breeze. One could imagine this motion as the energy and excitement of dialogue.

Our experience in the perceptual shift from trunk to faces is similar to the shock and struggle of shifting from one paradigm to another. We will see the network grow as we read more deeply into the paradigm shift. At the end, we will have trouble seeing anything but faces—dialogue.

CHAPTER ONE

Politics Is about . . . ?

If we are to talk about a new paradigm, scholars and practitioners together need to define our starting line—the prevailing paradigm's contributions and shortcomings and its underlying assumptions. As Thomas Kuhn says about paradigm shifts in science: "The decision to reject one paradigm is always simultaneously the decision to accept another, and the judgment leading to that decision involves the comparison of both paradigms with nature *and* with each other."[1] Starting points for thinking about the character of politics have varied widely. It is worth taking a few moments to situate the paradigm presented here in that larger spectrum.

On one side of the spectrum have been scholars of politics understandably concerned to define the study of politics as an academic discipline. Their need was to define their field rigorously so as to make research manageable and to distinguish it from others. As noted in the introduction, the prevailing mantra has been "politics is about power" with power defined as control or coercion. This approach led to a focus on institutional politics. Others in the field argued for a broader approach. Many in the field have defined problems in terms amenable to mathematical analysis.

Across the spectrum have been some political and other social scientists, philosophers, practitioners, and citizens at large who felt that the capacity of citizens outside the structures of power to relate constructively has been neglected, yet it is critical to human survival and progress. They have relied more on description and conceptualization of experience than on quantification.

I dare to suggest that the mantra of the second group might be "politics is about relationship," of which power is one component—only one and frequently not the most important. But this is the subject of the dialogue I hope this book will stimulate.

My own deep concern is that focus on the structures of power leaves out most of the world's citizens. Yet many of today's conflicts and problems are beyond the reach of governments acting alone. Power as traditionally defined—whether the power of office or the power of a gun—has proven itself a deadly principle around which to organize politics. It is divisive, exclusive, and too often destructive.

That politics is a key to survival is captured elegantly by biologist John Moore: "Human beings are now making such extraordinary demands on the environment that the natural cycles can no longer provide a seemingly unlimited supply of resources. . . . And the waste products of civilization now exceed the ability of the environment to deal with them effectively. . . . Very difficult decisions will have to be made if we are to have a sustainable human society in a sustainable environment."[2] The character of politics will determine whether and how those "very difficult decisions" will be made.

All of us have an interest in conducting human affairs more productively. To engage in dialogue about a new paradigm, we need to lay out the assumptions about politics that underlie these two approaches. They are capsuled below.[3]

Politics Is about Power

This was the prevalent paradigm for much of two generations in the last two-thirds of the twentieth century. Listen to the giants in the field:

Hans J. Morgenthau: "Domestic and international politics are but two different manifestations of the same phenomenon: the struggle for power."[4] Or: "The political actor seeks power, that is to say, he seeks to reduce his fellow man to a means for his ends."[5] Or still another: "When we speak of power, we mean man's control over the minds and actions of other men."[6]

Harold D. Lasswell: "The experiential data of political science are acts considered as affecting or determining other acts, a relation embodied in the key concept of power. Political science, as an empirical discipline, is the study of the shaping and sharing of power. . . ."[7] Or: "The study of politics is the study of influence and the influential. . . . The influential are those who get the most of what there is to get. . . . Those who get the most are *elite*; the rest are *mass*."[8]

Bertrand Russell: "In the course of this book I shall be concerned to prove that the fundamental concept in social science is Power, in the same sense in which Energy is the fundamental concept in physics. . . . Love of power, in its widest sense, is the desire to be able to produce intended effects upon the outer world, whether human or non-human."[9]

The political scientist differs from the practitioner partly in needing to define a field of study distinct enough from others to allow rigorous study, whereas the practitioner focuses on human relationships and practical problems. Even Hans Morgenthau cautions: "By making power its central concept, a theory of politics does not presume that none but power relations control political action. What it must presume is the need for a central concept which allows the observer to distinguish the field of politics from other social spheres, to orient himself in the maze of empirical phenomena which make up that field, and to establish a measure of rational order within it."

Morgenthau's distinction between economics and politics shows the scholar's need to define disciplinary boundaries in focusing research: "As economics is centered upon the concept of interest defined as wealth, its accumulation and distribution, so political science is centered upon the concept of interest defined as power, its accumulation, distribution, and control. A central concept, such as power, then provides a kind of rational outline of politics, a map of the political scene. Such a map does not provide a complete description of the political landscape as it is in a particular period of history. It rather provides the timeless features of its geography distinct from their ever changing historic setting."[10]

Toward the end of the twentieth century and beyond, some scholars—often outside the mainstream of U.S. political science—defined power more broadly. Listen to these different voices:

Kenneth Boulding, "an economist and a Quaker" with interests reaching beyond any discipline: "My own interest in the problem of power goes back to a very early interest in the integration of the social sciences and the deep conviction that they are all studying the same thing, which is *the total social system*, from somewhat different perspectives. . . . In social systems and human behavior there is a larger concept of power: To what extent, and how, can we get what we want? Within this there is a smaller concept of power, somewhat beloved by political scientists, which is our capacity to get other people to do things that contribute to what we want [emphasis added]."[11]

Erwin A. Jaffe in a book with the human title, *Healing the Body Politic*: ". . . many Americans—including journalists and scholars—equate power with control or domination or influence. . . . I do ask the reader, however, to set aside the formula 'power = control' and consider an earlier one: 'power = the ability, capacity, or faculty to do, to act, to accomplish something.' . . . The initiation and foundation of a polity depends upon recognition and acceptance of human beings' connections to one another. . . . 'Political power' is what human beings generate when they operate together to get things done as choosing, selecting, evolving, transforming beings."[12]

In the early 1990s, Joseph Nye coined the phrase "soft power": "What is soft power? It is the ability to get what you want through attraction rather than coercion or payments. It arises through the attractiveness of a country's culture, political ideals, and policies. When our policies are seen as legitimate in the eyes of others, our soft power is enhanced."[13]

Anne-Marie Slaughter citing Lani Guinier: "From 'power over' to 'power with' is precisely the transformation from hierarchy to network, from hard power to soft power."[14]

Other political scientists moved across a spectrum in arguing for an even broader approach in defining their field of research. For instance: "While the academic discipline of Politics tends in general to focus on the narrowly 'political' institutions of government in a manner that may be more analytical, it nonetheless leaves out *most* collective human activities *within* modern states as well as in historical and contemporary non-state societies," wrote British scholar Adrian Leftwich in 1984.[15]

In the field of international politics, scholars have concentrated on state sovereignty, on government, and on power narrowly defined. For two-thirds of the twentieth century, events surrounding two world wars, a great depression, and the Cold War between nuclear superpowers supported this thinking. Even democracies increasingly relied on big governments to solve countries' social and economic problems. Elsewhere, authoritarian and totalitarian governments dominated.

The traditional paradigm in international affairs—the "power politics model" or "realist paradigm"—could be captured in a formulation like this: *leaders of nation states amass economic and military power to pursue objectively defined interests against other nation states in a zero–sum contest of material power.* The metaphor was the strategic chess game.

Three assumptions have been central to the realist paradigm. In the words of Robert Keohane: "(1) states (or city-states) are the key units of action; (2) they seek power, either as an end in itself or as a means to other ends; and (3) they behave in ways that are, by and large, rational, and therefore comprehensible to outsiders in rational terms."[16]

As Keohane notes, an important thread in this approach to politics has been the theory of the "rational actor" or "rational choice." As one scholar puts the point: "Rational choice is a simple idea: Actors do what they believe is in their best interest at the time they must choose."[17] Argument over how actors determine their best interest, what actions might support that interest, what the consequences of those actions might be, and so on has produced a mountain of literature and mathematical calculations in both political science and economics.

Underlying the prevalent political paradigm in the last half of the twentieth century was a worldview rooted in the scientific revolution of the sixteenth and seventeenth centuries, particularly in Newtonian physics. The image of billiard balls colliding, exchanging energy with each collision, and moving away from each other according to Newton's laws of motion has been used to convey the essence of Newtonian physics as applied to the social and political world. "The balls are discrete, bounded objects; they have no permanent relationships; theirs is an individualistic universe," writes biologist Mary Clark.

> What happened in the West was that this same understanding of events as interactions between independent objects—so appropriate for a game of billiards—was extrapolated to all events, everywhere in the universe. . . .

. . . It is relatively easy to frame an event in mathematical models if only one or two objects (or conditions) are varying. . . .

It is so convenient, it has even become *de rigueur* for those who study human societies and human nature . . . [in] disciplines that attempt to explain human behavior . . . now lumped together as the "social sciences." And in the standard tradition of the billiard-ball universe (also known as the "atomistic" or "individualistic" universe) human beings are imagined very much like independent, isolated, bounded objects having a variety of cause-and-effect "collisions" with each other.[18]

States and governmental and nongovernmental institutions have been the manageable units for study within the rules and methods of such a worldview.

Increasingly toward the end of the twentieth century, however, we recognized that governments alone cannot solve all problems, and the political upheavals of 1989–1991 demonstrated that active citizenries as critical parts of bodies politic can produce decisive change. Citizens outside government with no raw power toppled governments despite governments' material power.

In the early years of the twenty-first century, many in and out of academe are formulating new assumptions. I must be open in stating my own view: *A paradigm that limits thinking about politics to the actions of governments and institutions is incomplete. A paradigm that builds thinking about politics around the struggle for power defined as control cannot capture the complexity of human efforts to act together peacefully and constructively. A paradigm that leaves out most of the world's people can only be of limited use. Most important, such a paradigm ignores human resources critical to meeting the countless challenges to our survival.*

Politics Is about Relationship: Citizens' Capacity to Concert

Toward the other end of the range of approaches to the study of politics is another point of entry—and a different definition of power. This starts with the citizen—not the state, its leaders, and its institutions. Here we find numberless citizens outside formal structures of power with varying capacities to concert—to act together or in complementary ways that reinforce each other and can produce change.[19]

At this end of the spectrum, *politics is what happens when citizens outside government come together and build relationships to solve collective problems. Power—their capacity to influence the course of events—is generated by their capacity to concert.* This seems quite different from governments' power to control, to coerce, or to impose punishment or sanctions. The capacity to influence the course of events through an open-ended political process seems sharply different from "producing intended results."

In the words of one of the political scientists—Adrian Leftwich—who has argued for a broader approach: "Politics is *not* a separate realm of public life and activity. On the contrary, politics involves all the activities of co-operation and conflict, within and between societies, whereby the human species goes about organizing the use, production and distribution of human, natural and other *resources* in the course of the production and reproduction of its biological and social life."[20] Or, as David Mathews, president of the Kettering Foundation, puts the point succinctly: "Politics is not a separate area of life. It is not doing something different. It is doing what we do every day differently."[21]

Five ideas are basic to this view of politics: First is the concept of the citizen as a political actor. Second is the concept of civil society as the complex of associations that active citizens form and through which they interact with other groups to do their work and to extend their reach. Third is the view that politics is a cumulative, multilevel, open-ended process of continuous interaction—not just action and reaction—involving these citizens and associations. Fourth, the interactions of citizens around a particular problem seem to unfold and deepen through a progression of stages outlined below that I call the "Citizens' Political Process."[22] Fifth, as I will discuss in more detail in chapter four, since citizens do not normally exercise power in the form of coercion, power in their context must be defined as the capacity through the relationships they form to influence the course of events.

Through the Citizens' Political Process, a disparate collection of citizens taking responsibility to deal with problems can form itself into an engaged public with capacity to change the course of events. The process, in effect, provides the public space in which citizens can come together to make the choices and form the relationships and associations within the civil society that they need to solve their problems in the larger body politic. That public space is the physical and psychological space where each citizen can feel he or she belongs, which is not the territory of any single faction. It is psychological in that participants experience the views and feelings of other citizens in a way that creates a new context for personal thought and a different way of relating. By working within that process, citizens can generate their form of power, which lies partly in their effective conduct of the process.

Lest I be charged with idealizing this process or ignoring that many citizens choose not to engage, let me say that this is a conceptualization of the experience through which citizens seem to progress when they tackle a problem together over time. In transforming their relationships, they develop the capacity to talk, plan, and work together to accomplish goals on which they agree. This conceptualization is rooted in participation with and observation of countless groups that have chosen to engage. Conceptualizing the process enables citizens to move it from one problem to another and to teach it. I make no claim that this experience is normal; the stories in chapters six through ten, however, suggest that it is not uncommon, that it can be analyzed, and that it can be taught and spread. I describe it here as a way of saying that a framework for research at this end of the spectrum exists.

The Citizens' Political Process

Following briefly are the stages through which the Citizens' Political Process seems to evolve. I present them as a vehicle for reflecting on the process that citizens with no formal structures to rely on use to accomplish their goals. To speak of a sequence of stages is not to present a rigid template for action. Citizens move back and forth through the stages to rethink, to absorb new events or insights, to reframe problems, and to judge progress. Defining a process simply opens the door to studying how citizens act together. Each stage reflects the broadening and deepening of a process of interaction—relationships—among citizens.

Stage One: Coming Together around a Problem

This process begins when a citizen concludes that a situation hurts her or his interests badly enough to require change. Seeing a connection between personal interests and this situation, the citizen reaches out to other citizens whose interests may also be hurt. Citizens with comparable concerns talk informally. This can take time. The problem may seem daunting; citizens may fear the reactions of those who oppose change; widening circles of talk may be needed to create a critical mass who are ready for systematic talk.

Beyond the internal interactions that define individual groups are the interactions among groups. Much new thinking about politics recognizes that many fundamental problems are problems of relationships. Some citizens' organizations have concluded that basic change can be made only by fundamentally changing working relationships—how people habitually deal with one another. The idea is to construct relationships that can solve problems whether the individuals involved like and fully trust each other or not.

The associations that citizens form are held together by the promises citizens make to each other—their covenants. "A covenant," writes David Mathews, "contains certain principles for structuring the way people work together. . . . the partnerships are voluntary; no one can be forced. Each party remains independent; no one is asked to merge her or his identity into some collective melting pot. People are not asked . . . to like one another. They just have to be willing to work together. The [association's purposes] have to be agreed upon mutually. . . . The partners 'own' the association; they are not employees or clients. Partners need not have equal resources. . . . [Yet] everyone has to treat everyone else as an equal . . . [b]ecause everyone is dependent on the agreement of others, and everyone has a say in what the association's purposes are."[23]

Stage Two: Mapping the Problem, Naming It, and Framing Choices

When the group meets, participants need to spend time talking about the situation to identify its important dimensions, the relationships that cause it, and the interests affected by it. I call this "mapping" the problem—laying out its main elements. As participants say how the problem affects them, they provide the ingredients for a definition—a naming—of the problem from the citizen's viewpoint, not the expert's or the government's.

An important task at this stage of their talk is to learn why and how the problem threatens what these citizens value. Unless they name the problem in a way that reflects their connection to it—why it hurts their interests—their efforts to deal with it will not be as effective as they might be. Naming the problem in a way that engages each participant is essential in building the common ground necessary to start tackling the problem.

When the group has named the problem in this way, they need to probe its dynamics in ways that help them frame the questions that enter their minds about possible approaches, opportunities, and consequences as they prepare themselves to weigh possible directions for dealing with it. Citizens do not frame questions as experts do in terms of technical approaches; they frame choices in terms of what they value. This stage ends when they have defined the problem they must deal with and identified the approaches they must take in tackling it.

Stage Three: Deliberating and Setting a Direction

Next, citizens meet to deliberate—to weigh possible approaches in light of what they value. To deliberate is not just to "talk about" problems; to deliberate is to agonize within oneself and with others over the advantages and disadvantages—the consequences—of each possible approach they have framed. Often more than one approach contains elements that a person values, so they must make difficult trade-offs. As they weigh the approaches with others, they deepen their understanding of the consequences of different approaches for themselves and for those whose cooperation is critical in dealing with the problem. Their deliberation gradually identifies common ground. This defines the starting point for setting the broad direction in which they want to move together to create a situation that all can live with. It does not signify total agreement—just enough agreement to undergird shared purpose in a particular situation.

As citizens grapple with their questions and possible approaches together, they begin to change the quality of their relationships. They emerge with a sense of what is tolerable and intolerable for each actor—and why. They consider their commitments to engage in the common task of dealing with the problem. The mutual promises they make will bind them in whatever associations they form to accomplish the task.

Deliberation involves choice. Citizens must choose before they can act. Taking responsibility for their future begins with citizens recognizing that *they* have choices. They remain subject to forces beyond their control, but choices come partly from the way they deal with those circumstances.

David Mathews says that choices are made in two different ways. In one case, politicians and government propose options that are often framed in complicated technical terms. Citizens are expected to choose among them. Alternatively, "[t]he most basic choices citizens make are about what kind of community and country they want. These choices aren't the same as preferences for one solution or another. People really can't select a particular solution until they have made more fundamental choices about purposes."[24] The alternative to making public choices is likely to be relatively uninformed, knee-jerk reactions. We call the outcome of deliberation "public judgment," not "public opinion," which one practitioner calls "what people think before they think."[25]

Deliberation leads to determining whether there is political will to pursue the course chosen. The final choice is: do the consequences of doing nothing outweigh the anticipated results of the chosen course, or not? If the consequences of maintaining the status quo are more serious than attempting the course chosen, there is presumably a tentative will to move ahead. The most important resource in a community is often political will: citizens' commitment to pursue a problem until they have it under control.

Stage Four: Planning a Course of Complementary Actions—Scenario-Building

When citizens have determined the direction in which they want to move, they must then decide how to get there. One way is to work through these five steps:

- List resources they can marshal for tackling the problem.[26]
- List obstacles to moving in this direction. Responses include not just physical obstacles but deep-rooted human resistance. Often cancerous relationships are more serious than practical obstacles.
- List steps for removing these obstacles. Again, these may include psychological moves to change relationships as well as concrete actions to remove material barriers.
- List actors who can take such steps. The aim is to engage multiple actors who can generate momentum through complementary actions.
- Try to connect actions so they become mutually reinforcing and encourage cooperation as one actor responds to a previous actor and stimulates another to join the process.

Unlike the discrete actions of institutions, complementary actions are not directed toward a single objective. Rather, they are more organic and repeating, like a jazz group in which each player supports the others within an overall theme but is free to improvise and express individual style without following a conductor.

I call this building a "scenario" of interactive steps because it unfolds much as a scene of a play might develop. Party A is asked whether it could take Step 1 and responds that it could do so but only if Party B would respond constructively by taking Step 2. Party B agrees in principle but wants Party C to take supportive Step 3. And so on, until more and more actors join and momentum for change builds and is consolidated.

Stage Five: Acting Together

Once a scenario of complementary actions has been designed, the group must decide whether and how it will put that scenario into action. The options include moving insights from this small group out into the community through the associations to which members relate in order to engage a complex of groups. If the group has not consulted with others along the way, it may need to spend time within its own associations sharing the experience in the deliberation with others and allowing time for them to digest insights from the deliberation. The group might even engage others in a wider series of deliberations before surfacing an action scenario.

An essential component of each stage, but particularly of Stage Five, is taking stock: What did we set out to accomplish? How are we doing?

I have found that a relationship is not fully formed until parties to it have asked and responded to these questions together. The process of learning together—the systems analysts write of feedback—strengthens a relationship.

These five stages are not intended to be rigid or linear. A group can at any point go back and reexamine initial assumptions or judgments in light of new developments, learning, or insights. The human mind is not always bound by a conclusion that has been reached; it often washes back and forth through thoughts that are in formation or relationships that are unfolding in unexpected ways.

Some have argued that thinking of this kind ignores a central concept of politics: power. They ask how citizens get things done if they don't accumulate power. This framework does not ignore power; it recognizes broader bases for power and defines power in terms less absolute than control—as the capacity to make things happen that are within the reach of the actors. Citizens' capacities to influence the course of events have a different quality from governments' ability to coerce. I am not sure the Czechs, Serbs, or South Africans *forced* their governments to back down; by acting together with no apparatus of raw power they created conditions in which government could not function adequately. That is power defined differently.

I do not suggest that any group will necessarily follow the stages of the Citizens' Political Process exactly as described here. Experience does suggest that these stages reflect a progression of interactions through which citizens seem to move in tackling a problem together. The process is a conceptualization of experience—not a theoretical construct. The purpose of thinking of such a political process is to state that citizens outside formal power structures can have their own systematic processes, practices, and political strategies with a sense of direction, destination, and potential accomplishment. Through such processes, they can generate the capacity or power they need.

Such a process is the citizens' instrument for change, *their* version of political instruments.

Focusing on citizens interacting in concert—human beings in relationship—enables us to integrate whole human beings in whole bodies politic into our view of politics. It includes the arena where political practitioners work, the arena where many conflicts are initiated and resolved, the arena where citizens build spaces for resolving differences peacefully, the arena where citizens improve the quality of their own lives. Above all, it includes the arena where most human beings live!

Citizens' Capacity to Concert as Social Capital

This view of politics as relationship—the citizens' capacity to concert—opens a door from politics to economics, particularly economic development. One exciting idea formulated in the 1990s was the concept named "social capital." This burst on the scene with Harvard professor Robert Putnam's 1993 book, *Making Democracy Work: Civic Traditions in Modern Italy*.[27]

As citizens interact through their associations, networks among these groups develop. These networks nourish continuous interaction that becomes the context for gradual development of what Putnam calls a "normal generalized reciprocity." As citizens observe the predictability and the reliability of how each interacts with others, trust grows, and the glue of potential cooperation is added to the social mix. This reservoir of predictable reciprocity becomes part of what Putnam calls "social capital." It is also essential to sound relationships.

More specifically, the economic premise underlying the concept of social capital is that the economy of a community with dense civic interactions is more likely to function effectively than one without. Citizens in a community with a rich civic culture have developed broadly accepted "rules" of interacting that provide the predictability of which Putnam wrote. One might call these accepted practices "unwritten covenants." The assurance that people will do what they promise reduces the costs of transactions. A consistent environment makes investors' calculation of risk more reliable than when economic behavior is unreliable or erratic. Habitual civic behavior in tune with understood "rules" makes an economic difference.

Economists at the World Bank, after analyzing this proposition in widespread communities, have generally accepted this analysis. The problem next is how to put the theory into practice. Michael Woolcock, then at the Bank, has distinguished between the "bonding" social capital of smaller, coherent communities or regions where inhabitants know each other and "bridging" social capital when strangers interact.[28] In smaller regions, people are likely to meet commitments because they believe that a favor for a known person will be reciprocated or that a promise broken will be "punished" in some way. The greater economic opportunity results when communities of strangers develop shared rules of relating—covenants.

Major funders have difficulty "operationalizing" this theory because only citizens outside government can grow or change political culture. Big lenders feel they need to work through established organizations. To use the graphic words of a young colleague, "the thick fingers of the World Bank" have trouble working with citizens. The Bank recognizes that lending at the wrong time or through the wrong channels can damage or destroy growing sinews in a community where citizens are developing their own capacity to concert. A project underwritten with development assistance before a community has consolidated its capacity to concert is likely not to be sustained when the external money runs out. In this frustrating situation, some analysts at the World Bank have given currency to medicine's historic warning: at least, "do no harm."

It is now clear that a long missing ingredient in economic development theory is the citizens' capacity to concert.[29] Placed in the context of the Citizens' Political Process, the common practice of international organizations providing development assistance has been to enter the picture when a community has a problem. They bring experts, design a solution for the problem as they define it, and offer money to implement that solution. They ignore or short circuit these stages in the Citizens' Political Process when people in the community name the problem themselves and decide what needs to be done, utilizing methods and materials consistent with their culture and skill level. International grant-makers began to recognize in the mid-1990s that loans for big projects had not produced the broadly based, sustainable development that funders had anticipated.

Dialogue: The Citizens' Instrument

Those who say that politics is about power defined as control or coercion focus on instruments that institutions of state and government use—force, economic sanctions, taxation, law enforcement, mediation, negotiation. Those whose point of entry into the study and practice of politics is the citizen as political actor focus on the instruments for change that citizens use—their instruments of power. If citizens generate the capacity to change through the relationships they form, the key to their generation of that capacity is the instrument they use to form these relationships.

At the heart of the Citizens' Political Process is dialogue in some form. Its exact form as a political instrument depends on the setting in which it is used.

In some communities with well formed relationships, citizens can talk together reasonably, even when they disagree sharply about how to approach a problem. Relationships and political practices are strong enough to enable citizens to resolve their differences collaboratively. I refer to an elaboration of dialogue in such settings as a *deliberative* or *collaborative process*. Citizens work their way through the Citizens' Political Process in a more or less orderly way.

Toward the other end of the spectrum are communities that are divided by deep-rooted human conflicts, ranging from violent intercommunal wars to subsurface tensions not yet violent that nevertheless block collaboration. For these situations, we have developed the *process of Sustained Dialogue* to transform relationships that block collaboration and must be changed if citizens are to work together. This process also develops through five stages, but with distinctive attention to a *dual* agenda—*both* the practical problems at hand *and* the relationships that may be the main cause of these problems. This process can extend over months or even years.

The five stages of Sustained Dialogue are essentially those of the Citizens' Political Process, but the process is anything but neat and orderly. When they sit down together, participants are often so angry that they can barely look at each other. Their language for mapping problems and relationships is accusation and vituperation. One stage does not fully end before the next begins. Participants move back and forth across the stages when they need to update a situation, rethink an earlier judgment, or tackle a new problem. Or their minds may be all over the place when they are groping for focus. Despite their rocky path, they continuously deepen their experience with their relationships through dialogue.

In short, Sustained Dialogue can create a microcosm of the relationships between whole groups and an experience in analyzing and changing these relationships. In the 1980s, the process was developed in dialogues among Americans and Soviets and Israelis and Palestinians. In the 1990s, it was tested and refined by Americans and Russians working together in conflicts that broke out in the territory of the former Soviet Union—Tajikistan beginning in 1993 and Armenia-Azerbaijan-Nagorno Karabakh beginning in 2001. It is now being used on university campuses and in community organizations in North America and South Africa to reduce ethnic and racial tensions and to deal with visceral issues such as sexual orientation and the extremes of the conservative–liberal divide.

Between these two well worked out and widely tested processes of dialogue are variations on both that citizens have devised to meet their needs. But the essence of their work is dialogue.

Citizens in Relationship as the Starting Point

At the heart of citizens' capacity to concert are nonviolent and constructive ways of relating. Human beings in relationship—acting in concert with one another—have too long been neglected in the study of politics.[30] It is time to highlight the human dimension of politics and the enormous potential of citizens working in concert to complement the work of governments in meeting the world's challenges.

As a practitioner, I am interested in what would happen to political thought if one started from citizens outside formal structures of traditionally defined power as a point of entry into the study and practice of politics.

Some conflicts seem beyond the reach of governments until citizens achieve understanding on living together in peace. Some problems such as drug addiction, alcoholism, and AIDS will not be dealt with until human beings change their behavior. Even corruption has roots in what citizens will tolerate in their daily interactions. It is unfair to expect governments to solve problems that can only be dealt with by citizens in and out of government collaborating as citizens of whole bodies politic.

As the twenty-first century dawns, many of us hold to an aspiration of whole bodies politic in which governments and citizens each take a strong place and, in the best of worlds, collaborate creatively. As this happens, political thinking must respond to the new reality. Not to change lenses to bring this emerging, troubled, and demanding world into focus seems unthinkable and possibly catastrophic.

As our political thinking makes room for multiple actors, the focus of our lenses widens. Whereas we used to focus on a few key institutions, we must now find a way to keep track of a complex of continuous human as well as institutional interactions. It probably never was adequate to think only about how institutions *acted on* each other. Even in the simplest of communities, human beings shaped *inter*actions. Now we must focus on politics as a multilevel process of continuous interaction among citizens in whole bodies politic. This is the subject of chapter three—the relational paradigm.

Before moving to that subject, I must address the second of our starting points—the thinking of the physical and life scientists through the twentieth century that shaped the principles of a post-Newtonian worldview. It is a worldview that underpins the broader approach to politics presented in this book.

CHAPTER TWO

"A Proper World View, Appropriate for Its Time"

Those working to articulate new assumptions for the study and practice of politics have found resonance in the insights of many physical and life scientists in the last century and a half. Their assumptions implicitly posed an alternative to the worldview that had dominated Western thinking since the eighteenth-century Enlightenment. They set the stage not only for a new political paradigm, but also for a dialogue between Eastern and Western worldviews. Their worldview sets the backdrop for the paradigm proposed in the next chapter.

"My suggestion is that a proper world view, appropriate for its time, is generally one of the basic factors that is essential for harmony in the individual and in society as a whole," writes David Bohm, a leading twentieth-century physicist and philosopher who devoted his last years to promoting dialogue. ". . . [M]an's general way of thinking of the totality, i.e. his general world view, is crucial for overall order of the human mind itself. If he thinks of the totality as constituted of independent fragments, then that is how his mind will tend to operate, but if he can include everything coherently and harmoniously in an overall whole that is undivided, unbroken, and without a border (for every border is a division or break) then his mind will tend to move in a similar way, and from this will flow an orderly action within the whole."[1]

Determining how we act are the assumptions we hold about how the world works—our worldview. "The beliefs and assumptions by which an individual makes sense of experience are hidden deep within the language and traditions of the surrounding society," writes biologist Mary Clark. "They are the gestalt—the pilings, the vision of reality—on which rest the customs, the norms, and the institutions of a given culture. They are tacitly communicated through origin myths, narrative stories, linguistic metaphors, and cautionary tales. They set the ground-rules for shared cultural meaning."[2]

Changing the assumptions that underlie a worldview begins with needing to address crisis, new problems, new opportunities, and change—with asking different questions. In May 2003, molecular biologist Shirley Tilghman, president of Princeton University, spotlighted such a transitional moment. Noting the fiftieth anniversary of the discovery of the structure of DNA and completion of the human genome's sequencing in which she played a prominent part, she wrote following the dedication of Princeton's new Institute for Integrative Genomics:

> . . . faculty and students are in a wonderful position to tackle entirely new questions about the fundamental nature of organisms that could not be asked in the past.
>
> For, looming on the near horizon is a fundamental paradigm shift in biology. In the past biologists approached the study of an organism by studying genes or proteins in isolation from one another. . . . we now have the possibility of knowing all the genes and proteins expressed in a cell, and we can begin to ask entirely new kinds of questions. Does the cell coordinate the activities of all these molecules? Is there a conductor orchestrating the music of the cell, or is it a cacophony with the loudest instrument winning the day? Using a different metaphor, this paradigm shift is the difference between taking the radio apart and putting it back together.[3]

This challenge, she continued, requires a "multidisciplinary approach. . . . For the future we will need to continue to ground our students in one of the fundamental disciplines, but to teach in such a way that they make the essential connections to underlying scientific principles and techniques that cut across the conventional disciplines." This is in sharp contrast to the narrowly bounded social science disciplines at the beginning of the twenty-first century.

The Prevailing Western Worldview

The worldview articulated during the eighteenth-century Enlightenment evolved from the revolutionary thinking of Sir Isaac Newton (1642–1727), French mathematician and philosopher René Descartes (1596–1650), and the philosophers of the latter half of that century called in France the "physiocrats." Early in the twenty-first century, some see this worldview spreading around the world as the companion of technological progress and globalization, thus setting the stage for intense interaction between worldviews of West and East. The emerging Western worldview crystallized below contains elements that open the door to dialogue between the two.[4]

Newton's was a universe within which actions and reactions between physical bodies were governed by universal laws mathematically defined. Central were the universal law of gravitation and the laws of motion through which physical bodies exchanged reciprocal attractions on each other.[5] These enabled Newton and others to plot precisely and predictably the orbits of celestial bodies. As Pierre Simon Laplace wrote in the early nineteenth century: "Mathematicians have, since [Newton's] epoch, succeeded in reducing to this great law of nature all the known phenomena of the system of the world, and have thus given to the theories of the heavenly bodies, and to astronomical tables, an unexpected degree of precision."[6] As Newton's third law of motion states: "When a body exerts a force on a second body, a second force, equal in magnitude and opposite in direction, is exerted by the second body on the first body. Action is equal to reaction."[7] This exchange of energy kept bodies in position relative to each other.

As Mary Clark puts it, "Force and mass explained everything."[8] In the summation of J. Bernard Cohen, former professor of the history of science at Harvard University: "The success of the theory and applications of universal gravitation, or of what—since Einstein—is called 'classical' mechanics (or Newtonian mechanics), caused this subject to become the model or ideal for all the sciences."[9] In Newton's way of thinking, "mathematics is applied to the external world as it is revealed by experiment and critical observation."[10] His achievement lay in "producing a mathematical theory of nature."[11]

Before Newton in France, René "Descartes' outstanding reform of science was the establishment of [a] mechanical philosophy, which sought to explain the properties and actions of bodies in terms of the parts of which they are composed. . . . Descartes' method . . . was intended to serve in the making of discoveries, through the resolution of a general and complex problem into its simpler elements or component parts."[12]

Enlightenment thinkers hoped that laws such as these laws of nature could be discovered as governing human societies. In the words of Bernard Cohen: "Men and women everywhere saw a promise that all of human knowledge and the regulation of human affairs would yield to a similar rational system of deduction and mathematical inference coupled with experiment and critical observation. The eighteenth century became 'preeminently the age of faith in science.' "[13] Or in the words of Isaiah Berlin:

> The impact of Newton's ideas was immense; whether they were correctly understood or not, the entire programme of the Enlightenment, especially in France, was consciously founded on Newton's principles and methods, and derived its confidence and its vast influence from his spectacular achievements. And this, in due course, transformed—indeed, largely created—some of the central concepts and directions of modern culture in the west, moral, political, technological, historical, social—no sphere of thought or life escaped the consequences of this cultural mutation.[14]

The West entered the twenty-first century with this worldview. This book questions that worldview.

The Voices of Twentieth-Century Scientists

Leaders in the physical and life sciences over the past century or more have arrived at different assumptions about how the world works—to the elements of a different worldview. They have not discarded Newtonian physics; as it relates to motion and to the dynamics of the universe, it is still remarkably accurate. As they delved into the subatomic realm, however, they needed new ways of thinking.

This chapter's principal purpose is to surface their assumptions as elements of an alternative worldview—in David Bohm's words, "a proper world view, appropriate for its time." This worldview lies behind the new political paradigm presented in chapter three. I have tried as much as possible in the following to let the scientists of this era speak to us under headings that contrast their thoughts to the principles of the prevailing worldview.

First. Reality is a cumulative, multilevel, open-ended continuous process of interaction and change—not a linear sequence of discrete actions and reactions. We must learn to focus, as much as possible, on the process of interaction itself rather than only on the actors, their actions, and their reactions. Some have spoken of this process as what happens in the "space between" actors.

The biologists. Charles Darwin's publication of *The Origin of Species* in 1859 and the complementary work of geologists and paleontologists established what has become the prevailing paradigm in one of the main fields of biological study. In the words of John Moore, emeritus professor of biology at the University of California, Riverside: "The new paradigm was that life has had a complex, ever-changing history. [The creationists'] belief that 'the Works created by God at the first, and conserv'd to this Day in the Same State and Condition in which they were first made' was replaced by the hypothesis of descent with change; that is, life had evolved."[15]

Darwin's central concept, natural selection—"the accumulative action of Selection"—is a continuous process operating pervasively over millennia. Variations in species that give some individuals an advantage in the ongoing struggle for existence are likely over long periods to be passed on to succeeding generations, thereby changing prevailing characteristics.

> It may be said that natural selection is daily and hourly scrutinising, throughout the world, every variation, even the slightest; rejecting that which is bad, preserving and adding up all that is good; silently and insensibly working, whenever and wherever opportunity offers, at the improvement of each organic being in relation to its organic and inorganic conditions of life.[16]

Darwin focused on a process at work among organic beings that demanded understanding in its own right—not instead of but in addition to close observation of individual beings.

To quote Ernst Mayr, former Alexander Agassiz Professor of Zoology at Harvard: "Organisms are the product of 3.8 billion years of evolution. . . . Historically there has been an unbroken stream from the origin of life and the simplest prokaryotes up to gigantic trees, elephants, whales, and humans."[17]

A key question has been: What is the mechanism for that "unbroken stream"—that continuous process in which living beings demonstrated the capacity to replicate themselves and in which variations in that replication produced countless species? The study of cells—cytology—over three centuries gradually produced the theory that, as John A. Moore states, "the bodies of animals and plants are composed solely of cells or cell products," and then the observation of "the origin of new cells by the division of old cells." The complex changes in the nucleus of a cell that take place when it divides came to be called *mitosis*—"a continuous process that, for descriptive purposes, was divided into discrete stages by cytologists."[18]

The evolutionary biologists further recognize the open-endedness of a process. Darwin's concept of *natural selection* assumes "a good deal of randomness." Whereas predictability ruling out chance had been seen as a requirement of precise science, Ernst Mayr writes: "The reason why so many biological theories are probabilistic is that the outcome is simultaneously influenced by several factors, many of them random, and this multiple causation prevents any one factor from being 100 percent responsible for the outcome."[19]

The physicists. Albert Einstein and one of his coworkers, Leopold Infeld, describe the importance in probing the physical world of understanding what happens in the "space between" actors. They began their book for the lay reader, *The Evolution of Physics*, by explaining: "Throughout two hundred years of scientific research [since Galileo] force and matter were the underlying concepts in all endeavors to understand nature. . . . The great results of classical mechanics suggest that . . . all phenomena can be explained by the action of forces representing either attraction or repulsion, depending only upon distance and acting between unchangeable particles."[20]

"During the second half of the nineteenth century new and revolutionary ideas were introduced into physics," they continued; "they opened the way to a new philosophical view, differing from the mechanical one." This was the concept of the electromagnetic *field*. "In the new field language it is the description of the field between the two [electric] charges, and not the charges themselves, which is essential for an understanding of their action. . . . It was realized that something of great importance had happened in physics. A new reality was created, a new concept for which there was no place in the mechanical description. . . . The electromagnetic field is, for the modern physicist, as real as the chair on which he sits." They describe this as "the most important invention since Newton's time." To emphasize for our purposes here: it is "the field in the *space between* the charges and the particles which is essential for the description of physical phenomena [emphasis added]."[21]

In the introduction to a 1980 collection of essays written over the previous 20 years, David Bohm underscores the importance of a continuous process from his perspective:

Whenever one *thinks* of anything, it seems to be apprehended either as static, or as a series of static images. Yet, in the actual experience of movement, one *senses* an unbroken, undivided process of flow, to which the series of static images in thought is related as a series of "still" photographs might be related to the actuality of a speeding car. . . . Does the content of thought merely give us abstract and simplified "snapshots" of reality, or can it go further, somehow to grasp the very essence of the living movement that we sense in actual experience?[22]

Bohm's response as a physicist:

What is needed in a relativistic theory is to give up altogether the notion that the world is constituted of basic objects or "building blocks." Rather, one has to view the world in terms of universal flux of events and processes. . . . The new form of insight can perhaps best be called *Undivided Wholeness in Flowing Movement*. . . .

The notion that reality is to be understood as process is an ancient one, going back at least to Heraclitus, who said that everything flows. . . .

I regard the essence of the notion of process as given by the statement: Not only is everything changing, but all *is* flux. That is to say, *what is* is the process of becoming itself, while all objects, events, entities, conditions, structures, etc., are forms that can be abstracted from this process.

The best image of process is perhaps that of the flowing stream, whose substance is never the same. On this stream, one may see an ever-changing pattern of vortices, ripples, waves, splashes, etc., which evidently have no independent existence as such. Rather, they are abstracted from the flowing movement, arising and vanishing in the total process of the flow.[23]

My purpose is not to enter the intricacies of physicists' debates. It is to point out that the worldview emerging from their work causes us to focus on the complex ongoing process of interaction itself. We may not yet have ways of doing that in the polity. The next best thing for the moment is to begin our analysis from a framework that assumes a multilevel process of continuous interaction—not from one act following another. We can at least change perspective—lenses—enough to broaden our base of action and perhaps to act differently.

Second. Continuous interactions are the essence of that process. What is important are the interplay and even interpenetration between entities—not just the action by one self-contained, bounded body on another.

The biologists. At the heart of Darwin's theory of evolution by natural selection is, in my words, a process of continuous interaction, which he calls a "struggle for existence" or refers to as "infinitely complex relations." He describes the interactions in these words:

. . . as more individuals are produced than can possibly survive, there must in every case be a struggle for existence, either one individual with another of the same species, or with individuals of distinct species, or with the physical conditions of life. . . .

Owing to this struggle for life, any variation, however slight and from whatever cause proceeding, if it be in any degree profitable to an individual of any species, in its infinitely complex relations to other organic beings and to external nature, will tend to the preservation of that individual and will generally be inherited by its offspring. . . . I have called this principle, by which each slight variation, if useful, is preserved, by the term Natural Selection.[24]

As we see in the next section, the biologists explained living organisms as whole systems that emerge from the intimate interaction of components and become more than one could predict from simply examining the parts. "What are wholes on one level become parts on a higher one . . . both parts and wholes are material entities, and integration results from the interaction of parts as a consequence of their properties," wrote Alex Novikoff in 1947. This view "does not regard living organisms as machines made of a multitude of discrete parts (physico-chemical units), removable like pistons of an engine and capable of description without regard to the system from which they are removed."[25]

Focusing on a multilevel process allows for multiple causes. "When one looks carefully at a biological problem, one can usually discover more than one causal explanation . . . the importance of multiple simultaneous causes," writes Ernst Mayr.[26]

The word *ecology* most nearly captures in popular biological parlance today an even vaster complex of interactions that I am speaking of. ". . . [I]n a word," Mayr writes, "ecology is the study of all those complex interrelations referred to by Darwin as the conditions for the struggle for existence." The idea of the ecosystem, however, also demonstrates the problems science encounters in complex systems. "Although the ecosystem concept was very popular in the 1950s and '60s, . . . it is no longer the dominant paradigm. . . . the number of interactions is so great that they are difficult to analyze, even with the help of large computers."[27]

The physicists. If reality is continuous flux, we cannot focus primarily on analyzing a sequence of discrete actions. We must learn to think in the context of a flowing process of interactions. Without going into the complexity of the physicists' theories, it is sufficient here to note the centrality of interaction to their thinking.

Nobel Laureate Richard Feynman put the point most succinctly in 1948: "All mass is interaction." During a meeting where some two dozen renowned physicists came together to "confront a crisis in their understanding of the atom," he scribbled the following verse in the back of a little black address book:

> Principles
> You can't say A is made of B
> or vice versa.
> All mass is interaction.[28]

What we might have called the "building blocks" of matter—the "particles" or the "photons" of which the physicists speak—the physicists describe as interactions in words such as these: "The best answer that physicists have so far is that 'particles' are actually interactions between fields."[29] Or: ". . . an elementary particle is not an independently existing, unanalyzable entity. It is, in essence, a set of relationships that reach outward to other things."[30] Or: "Photons do not exist by themselves. All that exists by itself is an unbroken wholeness that presents itself to us as webs (more patterns) of relations. Individual entities are idealizations which are correlations made by us."[31]

Going even further, author Gary Zukav, who put the essence of modern physics before a wider audience, describes one conclusion that flows from thinking in quantum mechanics: "Philosophically . . . the world consists not of things, but of interactions. Properties belong to interactions, not to independently existing things, like 'light'. . . . In short, what we experience is not external reality, but our *interaction* with it."[32]

Third. We must focus first on the whole—not the parts—recognizing that it still may be necessary for practical reasons to probe specific entities and areas of interaction in traditional ways. When we focus on the parts, we do so in the context of the whole, not starting from the parts to connect them to other parts. Action in the context of the whole is dramatically different from action in the interests of any of the particular parts.

The physicists. Bohm sees this as a point of agreement between two theories: ". . . approaching the question in different ways, relativity and quantum theory agree, in that they both imply the need to look on the world as an *undivided whole*, in which all parts of the universe, including the observer and his instruments, merge and unite in one totality. In this totality, the atomistic form of insight is a simplification and an abstraction, valid only in some limited context."[33]

Focusing on the whole rather than the parts is a reversal of the Newtonian and Cartesian worldviews. "Classical science starts with the assumption of separate parts which together constitute physical reality," explains Gary Zukav. "Since its inception, it has concerned itself with how these separate parts are related. . . . Newtonian science is the effort to find the relationships between pre-existing 'separate parts'. . . . Quantum mechanics is based upon the opposite epistemological assumption." Zukav then cites Bohm who "proposes that quantum physics is, in fact, based upon a perception of a new order. According to Bohm, 'We must turn physics around. Instead of starting with parts and showing how they work together (the Cartesian order) . . . we start with the whole.' "[34]

In a chapter titled, "Fragmentation and Wholeness," Bohm reflects on the social and political problems created by focusing on parts rather than the whole:

> Fragmentation is now very widespread, not only throughout society, but also in each individual; and this is leading to a kind of general confusion of the mind, which creates an endless series of problems and interferes with our clarity of perception so seriously as to prevent us from being able to solve most of them.
>
> . . . society as a whole has developed in such a way that it is broken up into separate nations and different religious, political, economic, racial groups, etc. Man's natural environment has correspondingly been seen as an aggregate of separately existent parts, to be exploited by different groups of people. Similarly, each individual human being has been fragmented into a large number of separate and conflicting compartments, according to his different desires, aims, ambitions, loyalties, psychological characteristics, etc., to such an extent that it is generally accepted that some degree of neurosis is inevitable.

Despite his proposal that we think of "undivided wholeness in flowing movement," Bohm acknowledges that it is necessary in dealing with some practical problems to break them into manageable units to avoid being "swamped" by having to deal with everything at once. Specialization has important practical advantages. Similarly, humans' much earlier recognition that they are different from nature was an important step "because it made possible a kind of autonomy in his thinking, which allowed him to go beyond the immediately given limits of nature, first in his imagination and ultimately in his practical work."

Necessary as these practical steps were, Bohm feels that "this sort of ability of man to separate himself from his environment and to divide and apportion things ultimately led to a wide range of negative and destructive results, because man lost awareness of what he was doing and thus extended the process of division beyond the limits within which it works properly. In essence, the process of division is a way of *thinking about things* that is convenient and useful mainly in the domain of practical, technical and functional activities." He sees this tendency to make "the widespread and pervasive distinctions between people (race, nation, family, profession, etc., etc.)" as "preventing mankind from working together for the common good, and indeed, even for survival."[35]

Humankind instinctively recognizes this problem. "Indeed," Bohm writes, "man has always been seeking wholeness—mental, physical, social, individual."[36]

The biologists. Darwin's picture of the struggle for existence repeatedly returns to the thought "that the structure of every organic being is related, in the most essential yet often hidden manner, to that of all other organic beings, with which it comes into competition for food or residence, or from which it has to escape, or on which it preys." Or: "Let it be borne in mind how infinitely complex and close-fitting are the mutual relations of all organic beings to each other and to their physical conditions of life." The whole he refers to as the "polity of nature."[37]

As Michael R. Rose says in *Darwin's Spectre*, "The starting point for Darwinism is ecology, the study of the interactions between species, within species, and between species and environment."[38] The natural system is seen as a whole, but Darwin's picture of the whole was one that included infinite capacity for variation.

> . . . it is really surprising to note the endless points in structure and constitution in which the varieties and subvarieties differ slightly from each other. The whole organization seems to have become plastic, and tends to depart in some small degree from that of the parental type. . . . the number and diversity of inheritable deviations of structure, both those of slight and those of considerable physiological importance, is endless.[39]

Rose points out how much of a departure from traditional academic thought Darwin's focus on variation was: " . . . the foundations of science were defined by physicists using mathematical representations of reality in which any type of variation or randomness was neglected. . . . Elegance, precision, and generality were brought together by Galileo, Newton, and Laplace to an extent that had never been seen before. And their highly abstract theories became the model, the paradigm, for the construction of science. . . . It is almost inherent to academic knowledge that it abstracts, neglecting distracting variation." Rose concludes: ". . . it turns out that these important tendencies of human thought, and the thought of moderns particularly, are highly counterproductive in biology. Variation is not merely characteristic of living things, it is also essential to their very evolution. Darwin was the first person to see this clearly."[40]

"The whole is greater than the sum of its parts." With these words Ernst Mayr captures the concept of emergence and a mode of thinking referred to as *organicism*. He defines *emergence* in this way: "In a structural system, new properties emerge at higher levels of integration which could not have been predicted from a knowledge of lower-level components." Organicism is "[t]he belief that the unique characteristics of living organisms are due not to their composition but rather to their organization."

"For reductionists, the problem of explanation is in principle resolved as soon as the reduction to the smallest components has been accomplished," writes Mayr. "They claim that as soon as one has completed the inventory of these components and has determined the function of each of them, it should be an easy task to explain also everything observed at the higher levels of organization." They are simply wrong, Mayr concludes. "Owing to the interaction of the parts, a description of the isolated parts fails to convey the properties of the system as a whole. It is the organization of these parts that controls the entire system."[41]

The work of *academics and policymakers* has been structured by the tendency to compartmentalize knowledge around the parts of learning that stemmed from the worldview that emerged from the Scientific Revolution of the Enlightenment. "Thus art, science, technology, and human work in general, are divided up into specialties, each considered to be separate in essence from the others," comments David Bohm. "Becoming dissatisfied with this state of affairs, men have set up further interdisciplinary subjects, which were intended to unite the specialties, but these new subjects have ultimately served mainly to add further separate fragments."[42]

Donald Stokes, dean of the Woodrow Wilson School of Public and International Affairs at Princeton University from 1974 to 1992, just before his death in 1997 finished a study of government science policy. He described the "postwar paradigm . . . for understanding science and its relation to technology" as based on a sharp distinction between basic and applied research. In this view, the aim of basic research is to contribute to "general understanding of nature and its laws"; its creativity would be constrained by "premature thought of its practical use." Following from this view is the "belief that if basic research is appropriately insulated from short-circuiting by premature considerations of use, it will prove to be a remote but powerful dynamo of technological progress as applied research and development convert the discoveries of basic science into technological innovations to meet the full range of society's economic, defense, health, and other needs." The image that captured this picture is a " 'linear model,' with basic research leading to applied research and development and on to production or operations."

Stokes concluded that this paradigm "has made it more difficult to think through a series of policy issues that require a clear vision of . . . the relationship of scientific discovery to technological improvement." Citing the career of Louis Pasteur, Stokes presses for recognition of the experience in "basic research that seeks to extend the frontiers of understanding but is also inspired by considerations of use." He calls for a clearer understanding of the intimate interactions of purpose and inspiration in research. "Although the linear model saw the advances of science as fully determining the development of technology, . . . the relationship between the two is far more interactive." Stokes summarizes:

> It is not the case that in a scientific field of demonstrated importance for social goals, the fundamental research that is influenced by societal need is one kind of science, while the fundamental research that is driven by curiosity alone is another. Both fall within a common scientific framework, however real the difference in goals. . . . Breakthroughs achieved by use-inspired basic research can lead to further *pure* research, just as breakthroughs in pure research can lead to further use-inspired research, all in accord with Pasteur's famous dictum that "there is not pure science and applied science but only science and the applications of science."

He concludes with the words of Harvard's president, James B. Conant: "A science, such as physics or chemistry or mathematics, is not the sum of two discrete parts, one pure and the other applied. It is an organic whole, with complex interrelationships throughout."[43]

Fourth. Human beings are participants—not detached observers—in this process; as such, we know reality through experience as we interpret it. There is no such thing as a detached observer; we cannot observe anything without changing it because all we can know is our interaction with it.

The physicists. Human beings are themselves part of the unfolding process. As Zukav makes the point: ". . . the philosophical implication of quantum mechanics is that all of the things in our universe (including us) that appear to exist independently are actually parts of one all-encompassing organic pattern, and that no parts of that pattern are ever really separate from it or from each other. . . . Access to the physical world is through experience. The common denominator of all experiences is the 'I' that does the experiencing. In short, what we experience is not external reality, but our *interaction* with it."[44] Or in Bohm's words: ". . . it is useful to emphasize that experience and knowledge are one process, rather than to think that our knowledge is *about* some sort of separate experience."[45] Our picture of reality is just that—*our* picture. It is not a picture of reality itself, but our experience of interacting with reality.

The new thinking in physics explicitly rejects the idea of the detached observer—separating the observer from the observed. For example: "Because it is in the nature of things that we can know either the momentum of a particle or its position, but not both, *we must choose* which of these two properties we want to determine," writes Zukav. "Metaphysically, this is very close to saying that we *create* certain properties because we choose to measure those properties." He continues: "The old physics assumes that there is an external world which exists apart from us. It further assumes that we can observe, measure, and speculate about the external world without changing it. According to the old physics, the external world is indifferent to us and to our needs."

This point is an articulation of what came to be called Werner Heisenberg's "uncertainty principle." As Zukav explains it: ". . . there are limits beyond which we cannot measure accurately, at the same time, the processes of nature. . . . there exists an ambiguity barrier beyond which we can never pass without venturing into the realm of uncertainty. . . . as we penetrate deeper and deeper into the subatomic realm, we reach a certain point at which one part or another of our picture of nature becomes blurred."[46]

"The concept of scientific objectivity rests upon the assumption of an external world which is 'out there' as opposed to an 'I' which is 'in here'. . .," Zukav explains. "The task of the scientist is to observe the 'out there' as objectively as possible. . . . The new physics, quantum mechanics, tells us clearly that it is not possible to observe reality without changing it."[47]

This thinking originates in probes of the subatomic world, but the physicists would extend the thought more broadly. Bohm reflects on the pervasiveness of the separation between observer and observed in our culture:

> The notion that the one who thinks (the Ego) is at least in principle completely separate from and independent of the reality that he thinks about is of course firmly embedded in our entire tradition. (This notion is clearly almost universally accepted in the West, but in the East there is a general tendency to deny it verbally and philosophically while at the same time such an approach pervades most of life and daily practice as much as it does in the West.)[48]

Most outspoken on this subject was physicist and Nobel Laureate the late Richard Feynman speaking in a public lecture in 1963: "All scientific knowledge is uncertain. . . . I believe that to solve any problem that has never been solved before, you have to leave the door to the unknown ajar. You have to permit the possibility that you do not have it exactly right." At another point in his lecture: "Another important characteristic of science is its objectivity. It is necessary to look at the results of observation objectively, because you, the experimenter, might like one result better than another." Further: "But there are some things left out, for which the method does not work. This does not mean that those things are unimportant. They are, in fact, in many ways the most important."[49]

That the human dimension is critical in formation of hypotheses pervades writing on the scientific method: "Why are physicists always having to change the laws?" asks Feynman rhetorically. "The answer is, first that the laws are not the observations and, second, that the experiments are always inaccurate. The laws are guessed laws, extrapolations, not something that the observations insist upon. They are just good guesses that have gone through the sieve so far. . . . Every scientific law, every scientific principle, every statement of the results of an observation is some kind of a summary which leaves out details, because nothing can be stated precisely."[50]

The biologists. They are particularly insistent on greater flexibility than is permitted by a strict interpretation of "objectivity." Referring to the "prevailing concept of science during the Scientific Revolution" of the sixteenth and seventeenth centuries, Ernst Mayr says, "The ideals of this new, rational science were objectivity, empiricism, inductivism, and an endeavor to eliminate all remnants of metaphysics." Biology, he argues, often requires a different method:

> When a biologist tries to answer a question about a unique occurrence . . . he cannot rely on universal laws. The biologist has to study all the known facts relating to the particular problem, infer all sorts of consequences from the reconstructed constellations of factors, and then attempt to construct a scenario that would explain the

observed facts of this particular case. In other words, he constructs a historical narrative. . . .

The more complex a system is with which a given science works, the more interactions there are within the system, and these interactions very often cannot be determined by observation but can only be inferred. The nature of such inference is likely to depend on the background and the previous experience of the interpreter.

Mayr saw a shift across the sciences in the twentieth century: ". . . in both the life sciences and the physical sciences there has been a change from a strictly deterministic notion of how the natural world works to a conception that is largely probabilistic. . . . In the days . . . when everything was believed to be determined by an identifiable cause, to permit an outcome of a process to be also affected by chance or accident was considered unscientific."[51]

The biologists also dwell on the role of human imagination, inventiveness, genius in formulating the hypotheses and concepts that advance scientific work. John Moore describes *hypothesis* as "a tentative explanation of some phenomenon. It is an 'educated guess' to be tested."[52] Ernst Mayr stresses the importance of concepts such as natural selection in biology: ". . . the strong empiricism of the Scientific Revolution led to the heavy emphasis on the discovery of new facts, while *curiously little reference was made to the important role that the development of new concepts plays in the advancement of science* [emphasis added]." He further notes: ". . . Darwin could not have been awarded a [Nobel] prize for the development of the concept of natural selection—surely the greatest scientific achievement of the nineteenth century—because it was not a discovery."[53]

Fifth. Human beings through experience and analysis are central to defining reality. After more than two centuries of attempting to describe an objective reality "out there"—apart from ourselves—important twentieth-century physicists concluded that the only reality we can know is what whole human beings—rational and intuitive at the same time—experience and how they interpret that experience.

In 1927, leading physicists met in Brussels to discuss their experience with quantum mechanics. They produced a statement known as The Copenhagen Interpretation of Quantum Theory. In the years that followed, debate continued. In 1971–1972, Henry Pierce Stapp, then at the Lawrence Berkeley Laboratory of the University of California, presented "[a]n attempt . . . to give a coherent account of the logical essence of the Copenhagen interpretation."[54] He revised his paper in correspondence with Werner Heisenberg and with a close associate of Niels Bohr. The debate, in Stapp's description, started from a fundamental difference with classical physicists:

Scientists of the late twenties, led by Bohr and Heisenberg, proposed a conception of nature radically different from that of their predecessors. The new conception, which grew out of efforts to comprehend the apparently irrational behavior of nature in the realm of quantum effects, was not simply a new catalog of the elementary space-time realities and their modes of operation. It was essentially a rejection of the presumption that nature could be understood in terms of elementary space-time realities. According to the new view, the complete description of nature at the atomic level was given by probability functions that referred not to underlying microscopic space-time realities but rather to the macroscopic objects of sense experience. The theoretical structure did not extend down and anchor itself on fundamental microscopic space-time realities. Instead it turned back and anchored itself in the concrete sense realities that form the basis of social life.

"To prepare the mind for the Copenhagen interpretation," Stapp turns to pragmatic nineteenth-century American philosopher William James, whose basic "conception was, in brief, that an idea is true if it works." Stapp notes James' acceptance "that the truth of an idea means its agreement with reality." But the question then arises: "What is the 'reality' with which a true idea agrees?" He recognizes the argument that while human ideas obviously lie within the realm of human experience, reality "is usually considered to have parts lying outside this realm." Stapp asserts that whether "ideas 'agree' with external essences is of no practical importance. What is important is precisely the success of the ideas—if ideas are successful in bringing order to our experience then they are useful even if they do not 'agree,' in some absolute sense, with the external essences. . . . it is only this agreement with aspects of our experience that can ever really be comprehended by man."

"The significance of this viewpoint for science is its negation of the idea that the aim of science is to construct a mental or mathematical image of the world itself. According to the pragmatic view, the proper goal of science is to augment and order our experience. A scientific theory should be judged," Stapp continues, "on how well it serves to extend the range of our experience and reduce it to order. It need not provide a mental or mathematical image of the world itself, for the structural form of the world itself may be such that it cannot be placed in simple correspondence with the types of structures that our mental processes can form."

Central to the purposes of this book, it describes some of the scientists as bringing the human dimension back into the study and experience of life. It rejects the criterion of absolute objectivity as the standard by which the study of political and social life is to be judged.

A Transitional Word

Until we explicitly recognize that the old worldview no longer works adequately in our rapidly changing world, our actions will be stunted. Until we recognize that an alternative rooted in a century of profound insight is at hand, we will not move to a new worldview and a new political paradigm. This seeming detour into the thinking of those responsible for dramatic changes in our understanding of the world has been essential in establishing "a proper world view, appropriate for its time" and in setting the stage for exploration of the relational paradigm.

The Paradigm and the Concept

CHAPTER THREE

The Relational Paradigm: A Multilevel Process of Continuous Interaction

Politics, as presented in this book, is about relationships among significant clusters of citizens to solve public problems in a cumulative, multilevel, and open-ended process of continuous interaction over time in whole bodies politic across permeable borders, either within or between communities or countries. The focus of this statement is the *process* of continuous *interaction* among citizens at all levels—not only governments, not just institutions, not a linear series of actions and reactions. It is different from the institution-centered paradigm described in chapter one. I call this approach the "relational paradigm."

In metaphor, I have often described the difference between the old and the new inelegantly as the contrast between a chess game and a game of squash or racquet ball with four players in a five-sided court with six balls in motion at the same time. More elegantly, one might reflect on the difference between the symphony orchestra and the jazz band. In the former, each player focuses on her or his own performance within the set framework of a musical score, and the conductor orders the complementarity among the musicians. In a jazz band, everyone knows the themes, the language, and the overall composition, but once the theme is stated, players improvise and begin their own "conversation." In this interaction, they share a familiar vocabulary; some have basic roles—the bass establishes the chords, and with the drummer sets the beat; direction can pass among the musicians; certain conventions govern the interaction—not interrupting, listening thoughtfully to each other, and responding in kind. Above all, they play in mutually reinforcing ways to weave their own statement of a familiar piece. Like a political process, it is open-ended.

Of course, no metaphor or analogy is exact. No one would compare traditional politics with the order and beauty of a symphony orchestra, but there is a sense in which politicians play their respective roles within the outlines of a generally established skeletal script. The rules tend toward hierarchy and adversarial action and reaction. In the jazz band, there is far more genuine collaboration, careful listening, individual creativity and expression, and true *interaction*.

What Happens When Paradigms Change?

What happens when a paradigm is no longer adequate to the demands upon it? The answers, of course, vary from one field to another, but it is a question worth pondering for a moment.

Thomas Kuhn, Emeritus Laurance S. Rockefeller Professor of Philosophy at the Massachusetts Institute of Technology until his death in 1996, reflected on what has caused physical scientists to shift to a different way of explaining the world at historic turning points. Having reviewed the roots of the Copernican, Galilean, Newtonian, and Einsteinian "revolutions," he concludes: "In each case, a novel theory emerged only after a pronounced failure in the normal problem-solving activity. . . . The novel theory seems a direct response to crisis. . . . Crises are a necessary precondition for the emergence of novel theories." In the physical sciences, Kuhn sees science advancing through a series of revolutions characterized by a dramatic shift in the prevailing paradigm followed by long periods of "normal science" in which scientists flesh out details of the new paradigm.

Some biologists object that Kuhn's analysis does not apply to the life sciences. They see changes in thinking as more evolutionary than revolutionary. In Ernst Mayr's words: ". . . the Darwinians favored an entirely different conceptualization for theory change in biology. . . . [S]cience advances very much as does the organic world—through the Darwinian process." Ideas compete, and those that explain more convincingly survive.

Mayr summarizes: "(1) There are indeed major and minor revolutions in the history of biology. Yet even the major revolutions do not necessarily represent sudden, drastic paradigm shifts. (2) An earlier and a subsequent paradigm may coexist for long periods. They are not necessarily incommensurable. (3) Active branches of biology seem to experience no periods of 'normal science.' There is always a series of minor revolutions between the major revolutions. . . . (4) Darwinian evolutionary epistemology seems to fit theory change in biology far better than Kuhn's description of scientific revolutions. . . . And (5) a prevailing paradigm is likely to be more strongly affected by a new concept than by a new discovery."[1]

In political life, the transition from one paradigm to another is messier—perhaps because of the infinite complexities of human minds and emotions in bodies politic—but some similar ingredients are present. In the early twenty-first century, our lenses are out of focus. Our way of conducting politics is not working effectively for the public good. The evidence pressing us toward a different way of thinking surrounds us. New lenses have been in the grinding at least since the early 1970s. Experience writes their prescription. But few are ready to try them on. Since we are in the early stages of changing our mind-sets, the old and the new are simultaneously in use—still the old more than the new.

Politicians do not change mind-sets consciously—partly because they do not think about mind-sets. Although many act by instinct in the new conceptual framework because it is human, when they describe what they are doing, their language goes back to traditional rational and linear talk about action and reaction among social units. "We have always done it this way."

As discussed in previous chapters, research on social and political life is also in crisis. It contributes inadequately to public life and ignores critical resources for meeting public challenges.

Those who tackle the world's problems, whether as officeholders or as citizens outside government, need a larger framework for getting their minds around the dilemmas they face. They need a paradigm large enough to bring their efforts together in complementary ways in common work.

To begin, they need to bring citizens outside government—the human dimension—into the fullest practice of politics. Next, they need to set aside the notion of the decision-maker as "rational actor" plotting actions and reactions in the strategic chess game and to focus their study of policymaking on a much more complex process of interaction. "Remember," a wise senior colleague told me when I joined the National Security Council Staff in the White House of President John F. Kennedy in 1961, "policy isn't made on paper; it's a continuously changing mix of people and ideas."[2] The official becomes one actor—an important but not always dominant one—in a multilevel political process of continuous interaction among significant elements of whole bodies politic across permeable borders.

We will act differently only when we see the world through different lenses. As Kuhn says, ". . . when paradigms change, the world itself changes with them. Led by a new paradigm, scientists adopt new instruments and look in new places. Even more important, during revolutions scientists see new and different things when looking with familiar instruments in places they have looked before. . . . paradigm changes do cause scientists to see the world of their research-engagement differently. Insofar as their only recourse to that world is through what they see and do, we may want to say that after a revolution scientists are responding to a different world."[3]

What would cause us to put on new conceptual lenses to meet the challenges of the new century? What would cause us to give up familiar for more effective ways of thinking?

First, in response to crisis, people have to say, "Enough! Enough killing, enough inequity, enough squalor, enough unnecessary disease, enough injustice, enough environmental degradation! What we're doing isn't working!" That the present lenses are out of focus is clear—but for many that does not seem compelling.

Second, they need an alternative way of looking at the world—new lenses, a new way of thinking, a new paradigm—to which they can relate. They need a way of thinking that helps them design more effective analysis and action. To repeat, Kuhn observes of scientific revolutions: "The decision to reject one paradigm is always simultaneously the decision to accept another, and the judgment leading to that decision involves the comparison of both paradigms with nature *and* with each other."[4]

The Relational Paradigm

In our complex and interdependent world, we must think of whole bodies politic in which governments plus citizens as political actors along with nongovernmental political and economic institutions all engage simultaneously. Their interactions create relationships of many kinds. The human dimension is as at least as important as the institutional or the material, and the relationships people form generate their own kinds of power. It is not realistic to focus exclusively on states, governments, and institutions or on power defined only in their terms.

To repeat, it is more accurate today to say that *politics is a cumulative, multilevel, and open-ended process of continuous interaction over time engaging significant clusters of citizens in and out of government and the relationships they form to solve public problems in whole bodies politic across permeable borders, either within or between communities or countries.* Behind this paradigm is a sequence of thoughts that flesh it out. Those thoughts can be captured in the six propositions that follow.

To begin, *we must first see in a body politic a political process of continuous interaction among continuously shifting complexes of citizens, in and out of government, across permeable boundaries—not just a collection of institutions.*

Instead of focusing on formal organizations, let us try to clear our minds and bring a different range and mode of activity into focus: imagine a continuously shifting kaleidoscope with groups of interacting citizens—not institutions—in the field. Or imagine a satellite sensor able to plot the simultaneous interactions of citizens in a community or a region through all possible modes of communication and configurations over an extended period of time.

Picture citizens interacting around common concerns. Each values a number of personal, professional, identity, religious, cultural, family, and other interests. Each brings these interests into different interactions with others sharing some of those interests. Each citizen's life involves a complex of clustered interactions—some overlapping, some not. These clusters interact with other clusters in numberless ways. Picture clusters, groups, associations of citizens in and out of government thinking, talking, exchanging ideas, acting together because they are concerned about a particular problem. Suspend your inclination to define these clusters in terms of their structures and instead see the permeable boundaries of each group defined only by the pattern created by *individuals'* interactions—not by constitutions, bylaws, or hierarchical chains of command. Think of the body politic as the kaleidoscope in which these continuously changing groups interact.

How different this approach would be from our customary focus on institutions rather than on citizens! Within countries, we have focused on government, political parties, lobbies, media. Citizens appear in the story as voters, consumers of goods and government services, and objects of public opinion polling. Between countries, we have built theories of international relations around the state.

A word about government in this setting. Anyone who has served in a big government knows that even it breaks down into groups reaching across bureau, agency, and departmental boundaries in focusing on particular problems. These often interact informally with groups outside government whose members share the same interests. To be sure, citizens in government and citizens in other walks of life differ in their specific work, but they are parts of the same body politic. Their functions may differ, but their work can be complementary. The distance between citizens in and out of government is not always—and need not necessarily be—so great as some assume.

As these clusters of citizens interact, they form *networks*. In this computer age, we see electronic networks operating without necessarily requiring a hub or command center. Likewise, citizens relate in countless patterns of interaction.

It is worth spending a moment on a view of "network" that places it in the context of the relational paradigm. It is the view of Dee Hock, the man who played a major role in creating the remarkable network that functions around the VISA credit card—remarkable as both a human and an electronic organization. He coined the word "chaord," combining the words "chaos" and "order." Just to give you a feel for his thinking, he defines a "chaord" in terms of these characteristics:

1. any self-organizing, self-governing, adaptive, nonlinear, complex organism, organization, community, or system, whether physical, biological, or social, the behavior of which harmoniously combines characteristics of both chaos and order;
2. an entity whose behavior exhibits observable patterns and probabilities not governed or explained by its constituent parts;
3. any chaotically ordered complex;
4. an entity characterized by the fundamental organizing principles of evolution and nature.[5]

VISA is an enterprise which was built to "self-organize and evolve. . . ." Its products were among the most universally used and recognized in the world, yet the organization was so transparent its ultimate customers, most of its affiliates, and some of its members did not know it existed or how it functioned. At the same time, the core of the enterprise had no knowledge of, information about, or authority over a vast number of the constituent parts. VISA had multiple boards of directors within a single legal entity, none of which could be considered superior or inferior, as each had irrevocable authority and autonomy over geographic or functional areas. No part knew the whole, the whole did not know all the parts, and none had any need to. The entirety, like millions of other chaordic organizations, including those we call body, brain, forest, ocean, and biosphere, was largely self-regulating.[6]

Turning to the broader social application, he presents the "Principles of a Chaordic Organization" in these terms: "It should be equitably owned by all participants. . . . Participants should have equitable rights and obligations. . . . It should be open to all qualified participants. . . . Power, function, and resources should be distributive to the maximum degree. . . . Authority should be equitable and distributive within each governing entity. . . . No existing participant should be left in a lesser position by any new concept of organizations. . . . To the maximum degree possible, everything should be voluntary. . . . It should be nonassessable. . . . It should induce, not compel, change. . . . It should be infinitely malleable yet extremely durable."[7]

In short, we think of problems and functions drawing people together in different, constantly changing interactions. We can recognize the principles and machinery of democratic governance as one ingenious way for people to order one set of interactions within the body politic, but we will be looking in a moment at different ways of ordering other sets of interactions— every bit as democratic, maybe even more so.

Second, *we must shift our focus from action and reaction to interaction. We are talking about the permeability of boundaries—both of groups and of human beings.*

*Inter*action restores the human dimension to the practice and analysis of politics. It refers to conditions in which one person both receives and internalizes another's words and actions. One person or group learns about another and internalizes who that other is, what the other needs, how the other conducts interactions, what sensitivities, strengths, or vulnerabilities the other shows, what resources the other draws on. A person or group may even change in light of that knowledge. On the basis of this experience, each develops assumptions about how each affects the other, even how each needs the other. The two parties to the interaction begin to act from some common knowledge that has become part of each.

Even in a distant relationship—as blacks and whites in an American city or as Americans and Soviets during the Cold War—both parties develop pictures in their minds about how the other will act. Some of those pictures are misperceptions that can be changed, but for a time they are internalized as the picture of reality from which each acts. As each conducts the process of interaction that becomes increasingly complex on many levels, a relationship changes.

As parties grow closer, they interact more directly. As they interact through various forms of dialogue, they develop clearer pictures of the other as human beings. They listen, interpret, empathize, understand, respect, agree, or disagree. They gain a fuller sense of what experience has brought the other to the present place and moment, what the other needs and why. As they respond to each other in fuller knowledge and feeling, they do not just act and react—they *inter*act. This interaction may not always produce collaborative relationships, but it does produce deeper relationships, whether constructive or distrustful.

Third, *we must focus on the process of interaction. A process is a progression of steps in which each one includes what has gone before, is seen as contributing to the next, and may draw into its orbit a broadening range of resources. It is cumulative because it grows from what has preceded. It is open-ended because each step may create new conditions and unforeseen opportunities that widen its scope. Though I speak of a "progression" of steps, I hasten to say that it is not only linear; as circumstances evolve, we may circle back to revisit the past and reshape the lessons we learn from it.*

In 1974, as four of us flew with Secretary of State Henry Kissinger on the diplomatic shuttles in the Middle East after the 1973 Arab–Israeli war, I gained respect for the operational quality of a political process. We began with the strategy of mediating one interim agreement after another in the hope that each would open the door to dealing tomorrow with issues that could not have been negotiated yesterday. We first called what we were doing "the negotiating process" because we foresaw a cumulative series of interim agreements, each broadening the base for the next.

Then we became aware that these agreements were changing the political climate, thus giving people a sense of the possibility of peace that had not existed before. While continuing to use mediation as the vehicle for our involvement, we coined the phrase "peace process" to name the larger political project in which we were engaged. Experience since has established that it is possible to design a multilevel political process that can lead, step-by-step, toward peace.

In the 1990s as I began working with those in Latin America and in the former Soviet empire who were attempting to build or rebuild democratic civil society in the wake of the political upheavals from 1989 to 1991, I saw that citizens in relationships can develop their own political processes for tackling problems systematically. I further observed that these political processes could generate the power to solve these problems. At their heart is the Citizens' Political Process described in chapter one. In this process, citizens generate power by building relationships. As they involve others, they broaden their base of power.

For some reason, in the United States the word *process* often evokes a sneer. "That's all process and no substance," critics say. I don't know why. We talk with pride about a manufacturing process that increases efficiency and reduces cost, or a healing process following injury, or a mourning process following grief. We respect citizens with imagination and perseverance to accomplish a difficult task through a carefully designed, multitrack strategy and action plan. For those of us on the Kissinger shuttles, the phrase *peace process* signified a grueling, diplomatically careful, politically powerful, intensely interactive flow of moves that, in six years, produced five Arab–Israeli agreements ratified by parliaments, that changed lines on maps, moved troops, and began to change relationships after decades of enmity. The peace process was continuous; it changed perceptions of what was possible; it engaged people at all levels of bodies politic, sometimes across increasingly permeable borders. It was the context for change. I hasten to say that it obviously did not engage *all* people and that change has not been quick or comprehensive, but change, however glacial, is undeniable.

Behind the practical experience that citizens interacting in a systematic political process can generate the power to change a course of events is the difficult question of *how we can focus on the process as well as on the units in the process*. That focusing on the process itself is important seems to me to be affirmed by insights of twentieth-century biologists and physicists discussed in chapter two.

"The unique characteristics of living organisms," Ernst Mayr observes, "are not due to their composition but rather to their organization. This mode of thinking is now usually referred to as *organicism*." Further, he writes: "Owing to the interaction of the parts, a description of the isolated parts fails to convey the properties of the system as a whole. It is the organization of these parts that controls the system."

I do not in any way suggest an analogy between living organisms and a political process, but a simple point seems worth making: it is valid not to limit ourselves to studying only the simplest units of social and political life. Or to take the point a step further: the processes of interaction—the implicit "organization" of social and political life—are worthy of focus in their own right. Mayr cites as one of the earlier missing "pillars in the explanatory framework of modern biology . . . the concept of emergence—that in a structured system, new properties emerge at higher levels of integration which could not have been predicted from a knowledge of the lower-level components."[8] From the physicists, we recall from chapter two Albert Einstein's comment in 1938 on "the most important invention since Newton's time: the field . . . it is not the [electric] charges nor the particles but the field in the space between the charges and the particles which is essential for the description of physical phenomena."[9] In a sense, the process of continuous interaction operates in the "space between" the citizens interacting. We discuss further the application of this thought to relationships in chapter four.

Since World War II, a few scholars of social and political life from different disciplines came to conclusions similar to those stated by Mayr. Operating under an umbrella they named "general system theory," they developed the study of whole systems. They founded the Society for General System Theory in 1954. Perhaps one of its advantages has been that, consistent with its underlying philosophy, it has not become an established academic discipline. One of the leading figures in the field, Ludwig von Bertalanffy, by 1968 called "systems" one of the "fashionable catchwords" of the decade. He cited a Canadian prime minister saying: "[A]n interrelationship exists between all elements and constituents of society. The essential factors in public problems, issues, policies, and programs must always be considered and evaluated as interdependent components of a total system."[10] Secretary of Defense Robert McNamara, in a widely talked-about move, brought "systems analysis" to the Defense Department in 1961 at the start of the Kennedy administration. Henry Kissinger brought it to the National Security Council Staff in the White House in 1969.

Writing much later, in 1997, social and political psychologist Robert Jervis provided a series of simple statements describing the systems approach:

> We are dealing with a system when (a) a set of units or elements is interconnected so that changes in some elements or their relations produce changes in other parts of the system, and (b) the entire system exhibits properties and behaviors that are different from those of the parts. . . . A systems approach shows how individual actors following simple and uncoordinated strategies can produce aggregate behavior that is complex and ordered, although not necessarily predictable and stable. . . . In a system, the chains of consequences extend over time and many areas: The effects of action are always multiple. . . . If we are dealing with a system, the whole is *different from*, not *greater than*, the sum of the parts. . . . societies cannot be reduced to the sum of the individuals who compose them. . . . actions often interact to produce results that cannot be comprehended by linear models. . . . When elements interact it is difficult to apportion the responsibility among them as the extent and even the direction of the impact of each depends on the status of the others.[11]

My point is not to delve into systems theory. Like any group of scholars, some of them have moved to a theoretical or mathematical level that is more the subject of debate among them and does not, for the most part, speak to everyday political life.[12] I cite this work because it focuses on political processes of continuous interaction. As we have seen in the Citizens' Political Process described in chapter one, it does relate to the possibility of designing a scenario—a process—of interactive steps to engage a broad range of citizens with different interests in changing a political, social, or economic situation. Since conducting such a political process effectively can generate power, we need the help of social scientists in analyzing these processes in creative human ways to enhance their use.

Fourth, *we need a concept to help us analyze and guide this process of continuous interaction within and among clusters or associations of citizens that make up a whole body politic. The concept of relationship—a human word—captures that dynamic process and provides a tool for analyzing it, conducting it, and influencing its course.*

On first hearing, *relationship* seems an inadequate word for this purpose. In American English, it is almost a throwaway in common talk. I asked an Israeli political psychologist working on reconciliation between Germans and Holocaust survivors why he did not think in terms of changing relationships. "I shy away from the word because it was so overused in the 1960s," he replied. Some professional diplomats and psychologists tell me I cannot use an interpersonal word to describe a political phenomenon. Other languages often have no single word that captures the rich meaning I intend; they say "total pattern of interactions." Nevertheless, I often ask audiences to think about the human relationships that sustain them— husband–wife, parent–child, brother–sister, friend, lover, partner, colleague, teammate, buddy, comrade in arms. These words capture the depth, complexity, and dynamism of human ties that both sustain us and enable us through the covenants we make with each other to accomplish what we cannot do alone. The effective conduct of relationships generates what we call *relational power*.

After some years of searching for the right word, I concluded that there is no right word for an idea that has yet to be articulated in a particular context. The only answer is to pick a word and define it to meet my needs. I picked the word *relationship* precisely because it is a human word. I am not spinning a grand theory; I am suggesting a conceptual framework for citizens to use in changing the elements in their lives that they believe need changing. *Relationship* is a concept they can easily understand and use.

This is not a vague concept; I define it rigorously for analytical and operational use. I see relationship as a complex of five components—five arenas of interaction in constantly changing combinations within and between the parties interacting: (1) *identity*, defined in human as well as in physical characteristics—the life experience that brought a person or group to the present point; (2) *interests*, both concrete and psychological—what people care about—that bring them into the same space and into a sense of their dependence on one another, *interdependence*, to achieve their goals; (3) *power*, defined not only as control over superior resources and the actions of others but as the capacity of citizens acting together to influence the course of events with or especially without great material resources; (4) *perceptions, misperceptions, and stereotypes*; and (5) the *patterns of interaction*—distant and close—among those involved, including respect for certain *limits on behavior* in dealing with others. In some ways, interaction is the essence of relationship. Each of these is discussed more fully in chapter four.[13]

Power is, of course, an important component of relationship, but much of the time other components are more likely to determine how a person or group acts or to shape the character of an interaction. But as we discuss in the next chapter, power must be defined much more broadly than it has been. This broader spectrum of factors shaping an interaction leads toward a much more complete understanding of what causes are at play in any situation.

The concept can be both a diagnostic and an operational tool. One can analyze observable interactions through this prism and can actually get inside any of these components to enhance understanding or to change an interaction. In dialogue, one's own sense of identity can grow. Another's identity can be understood and a person can be humanized as misperceptions and stereotypes give way to realistic pictures. Common interests can be discovered. Patterns of interaction can change from confrontational to cooperative. As respect for another's identity grows, individuals impose limits on themselves to reflect that respect; their understanding of their own identities may even grow. As one understands this dynamic process of continuous interaction, one learns that power in part may emerge from careful and sensitive conduct of the process, rather than only from wielding material resources. The experiences in many countries at the end of the 1980s indeed saw parties with no raw power succeeding authorities who controlled the tanks and guns, the security apparatus, and government structures.

Relationships can be good or bad, constructive or destructive, mature or regressive, argumentative or cooperative, close or distant. They pervade our lives; the question is how to conduct and change them. It is the central thesis of this book that thinking in terms of relationship changes how we act. It enriches our capacity to conduct interactions productively, to manage them more carefully when they are destructive, and to enlarge our resources for conducting and changing relationships without resort to violence. Indeed, the purpose of chapters five–eleven is to examine this proposition.

Fifth, *the principles citizens develop to govern their interactions* can determine the *effectiveness of political, social, and economic life.*

As one examines the principles that govern the interactions of citizens within their clusters of activity, one often discovers ways of relating that differ markedly from the confrontational exchanges of everyday adversarial politics. Citizens more often follow the principles that normally guide dialogue and deliberation and offer problem-solving ways for them to interact constructively around their challenges.

How they relate can undermine or strengthen citizens' political capacity. "Along with other observers of American life, I am troubled by the growing power of the forces dividing Americans from one another, fragmenting our culture, causing us to grow apart," writes my long-time friend and colleague Daniel Yankelovich, who is extraordinarily perceptive in identifying shifts in peoples' perceptions, values, and beliefs. In the initial manuscript of his book, *The Magic of Dialogue*, he wrote: ". . . to a surprising extent a certain kind of dialogue can counterbalance the worst effects of the isolation and fragmentation that threaten to overwhelm us. It can create better understanding among people with divergent views, help to overcome the mistrust that increasingly separates Americans from their institutions (e.g., government, business, the media, educators), connect cultural, professional, and business interests, bring leaders and their constituents closer together, and create new possibilities in personal relationships and community."[14]

Dialogue and deliberation are citizens' antidotes to adversarial politics. They require treating colleagues with respect, listening carefully to their concerns and perspectives, and trying to find common ground for ways of thinking, talking, and working together. Relationships become more constructive as people learn this different way of relating. Increasingly, citizens refer to "deliberative" as contrasted to "adversarial" democracy. The logo of the National Issues Forums states the thought succinctly: "A Different Kind of Talk, Another Way to Act."[15]

I have already noted in my discussion of citizens' capacity to concert as social capital in chapter one the importance of such different ways of relating to increased efficiency and reduction of the costs of transacting in economic life. The covenants people form to regulate their interactions are the essence of social capital—perhaps the long-missing ingredient in economic development theory.

Sixth, *we have come to call the arena in which citizens outside government do their work "civil society." Under the traditional paradigm, it has been common to define civil society more in terms of which structures are included in civil society and* *which are not. For instance, are corporations or political parties part of civil society since they are not part of government? If we work from the new paradigm, we would <u>define civil society not by its structures but by the way citizens conduct their relationships—the principles by which they interact.</u>*

It has been common to define civil society loosely as that area between personal relationships and government where citizens form the wide range of associations they need to do their work. But in the mid-1990s, we became aware that a civil society could have a vibrant complex of NGOs that are anything but democratic. These organizations can be authoritarian within and exclusivist without.[16]

As we work with the new paradigm and see a whole body politic as a complex of interacting groups, it may be useful to make a distinction between civil society and democratic civil society. Civil society may encompass the complex of interactions, associations, relationships that citizens generate to deal with the problems that concern them; but we will consider them part of *democratic civil society* according to the ways citizens relate within them and how those groups relate to others—deliberation, dialogue, collaboration rather than authoritarian or adversarial interactions. In keeping with the new paradigm, the emphasis is on *how people order their interactions*—not primarily on institutions. The emphasis is on the character of their covenants, the generation of power through that interaction rather than by dictat, the processes through which they change the patterns of their interaction.[17]

A Bridging Word

In the next chapter, we focus on the concept of relationship—the diagnostic and operational concept through which we put the new paradigm to work. The purpose of this chapter has been to present this paradigm and the thinking behind it to enhance awareness of a more complex way of looking at social, political, and economic life. It enlarges our capacity for organizing peaceful change or for managing destructive change.

This book is for both academics and practitioners. All of us need to work together to flesh out the new paradigm. We need to understand the process of continuous interaction more deeply and learn how to make it, more often, a reality.

In presenting a new perspective, I do not suggest throwing away the old. It is in the nature of process that the new, as much as possible, incorporates or builds from the old. Much that we have learned is still valid and valuable; it just does not go far enough to explain what we experience and now know. Albert Einstein captured the point:

> Creating a new theory is not like destroying an old barn and erecting a skyscraper in its place. It is rather like climbing a mountain, gaining new and wider views, discovering unexpected connections between

our starting point and its rich environment. But the point from which we started out still exists and can be seen, although it appears smaller and forms a tiny part of our broad view gained by the mastery of the obstacles on our adventurous way up.[18]

I do not throw away what we have learned from the study of politics as power. I do suggest that we need a larger view—a view from the new mountains that we are climbing as we work to solve problems in political life. Politics is also about relationship.

CHAPTER FOUR

The Concept of Relationship

The concept of relationship provides the analytical and operational framework through which the relational paradigm reveals itself, may be studied, and is put into practice. This concept gives hands and voice to the process of continuous interaction in political, social, and economic life. *It is both a framework for analysis and an instrument of change.* Like the relational paradigm, it is conceptualized from 40 years of experience with peoples in conflict, citizens building democratic societies, communities engaged in economic development, policymakers and negotiators at the highest levels of government.

Its value lies in its being seen as a whole—an overall relationship. While recognizing individuals and their associations as the basic settings of relationship, this concept broadens the focus beyond individual components to the *process of interaction* among them and their groups—to the relationship itself. It shifts focus from discrete actions and reactions among individuals and groups to their *inter*action. It does not disregard reasons for each person's or each group's actions, but it applies that knowledge to understanding their interaction.

Interaction acquires a character and value of its own. It is the essence of relationship. *Relationship is the cumulative experience of interacting.*

In interaction each individual internalizes as a whole human being—rather than just intellectualizing—the complexity of other whole persons and groups. Each enters the flow of a multilevel process of interaction, not just acting and reacting rationally. As the parties interact, they are developing a common body of experience with each other, an understanding of their interaction, a growing perception of the relationship, and certain practices that come to be mutually understood (implicit covenants). This process is too complex to be measured, but it can be analyzed to the best of human ability provided we *name* it as worthy of attention in its own right and have a systematic way of organizing the analysis. Naming often creates facts that compel attention. Its name is *relationship*.

The purpose of this chapter is to explore the concept of relationship in a way that makes it usable in understanding interactions *and changing them*. Interaction—both intentional and subconscious—pervades all components of relationship. In the end, *interaction is the essence of relationship*.

The Challenge of Focusing on
Relationship—The "Space Between"

In chapter three, I asked you to try to shift your focus from institutions to clusters of citizens interacting around common concerns. Now I ask you to take an even more difficult conceptual leap.

This leap requires us to focus not only on the actions and reactions of individuals or groups but also on how they *interact*. If we can make that shift in mental gears, we can actually get inside the dynamics of a relationship and change it.

To be sure, two or more individuals or groups of human beings are parties to a relationship, so we will naturally begin by analyzing their characteristics. Even at this stage, we begin to recognize that the characteristics of an individual or a group are partly the product of interactions. But it is not enough to stop with a description of each party to a relationship and why each party acts as it does. It is not even enough to stop with describing how and why each party reacts to the other. We must go further to focus on the process of interaction between them—what Albert Einstein and Martin Buber, each in his own way, refer to as the "space between."[1]

Interaction is a difficult idea to get our minds around. We each have our own struggles with it, but we can see glimmers of ways into the challenge.

Some feel methodological constraints. In the late 1980s, I used the concept of relationship as a framework for analyzing Soviet-U.S. interactions in the Third World, suggesting that probing these interactions would deepen understanding of the overall superpower relationship. One editor of the book for which I was writing—a prize-winning social and political psychologist—penned on my manuscript: "I have done you the ultimate compliment of assigning your chapter to my graduate students. But I am still not convinced." Having learned much from his work, I asked what was unconvincing. "Your focus on relationship is right on target," he replied, "but I can't fit it into a social science research design."

One problem for some social scientists, they say, is that they can only manage analysis of data on how two persons in a relationship process actions by the other and decide to react. The practitioner, on the other hand, must often deal with multiple groups in interaction and countless variables. As Ernst Mayr writes of the ecologists, a large complex system can overwhelm even the most powerful computers.[2]

On another occasion, I was talking about interaction as taking place in the "space between" individuals or groups with a group of psychiatrists and philosophers in an informal gathering. A philosopher said, "I have trouble imagining anything 'between'—anything but two individuals processing each other's actions and reacting."

Others have tried on different conceptual lenses—often in response to practical problems they face. In that same meeting, a psychiatrist reached into his own experience to respond to the philosopher: "If you worked in marriage counseling, you would feel the difference. When husband and wife stop saying, 'He/she always/never . . .' and one of them says, 'We . . .,' the atmosphere changes palpably." *We* is often the word for relationship. The family therapists, like the systems thinkers, see the family as a body, a system, a complex of relationships to be healed.

My experience in the Arab–Israeli peace process or, later, in bringing the same groups together in nonofficial dialogue sustained over long periods has taught me four lessons. First, through interaction a cumulative agenda is created—a shared frame of reference. Questions unanswered in one meeting are engaged between meetings and form an agenda for the next. Second, through interaction a common body of knowledge grows. Each party learns why the other's interests are important. Third, the parties learn to talk differently. Mutual respect grows. Confrontational exchanges become inappropriate. Talking *with* each other and analyzing problems together becomes possible and productive. Ultimately, they may fall into ways of communicating almost without speaking, predictable habits of work, acceptance of different personal styles and traits. Fourth, they can learn to work together with shared purpose, agreed division of labor, and understood rules of interacting. They develop capacities of collaboration that achieve more than either could alone. Most important, they begin to think how their next action will affect their relationship because they value it for what it can accomplish.

In short, through interaction people create *a shared context in which they interact*—a world of their own. They create it together—often without talking about it; neither could create it alone; one cannot see it; but it is valued in its own right, and it shapes action. It is the essence of relationship.

Do these thoughts exist outside the minds of each party to the relationship? Physically, probably not. But has each internalized what the other values and fears and the experience of a flow of interactions in which they act as in a shared context? Do they act from a growing shared body of guidelines that in some way they have agreed—often without words—is mutually acceptable? Is that shared "code" or "covenant" definable? Do they value it for what it enables them to do together? Yes. We say there is a "chemistry" between them that facilitates their productive—or at least nondestructive—interaction. Can we describe that relationship? Can we analyze that interaction and change it? Yes, often. If that is the case—and we know it is—we must learn more deeply how that interaction works, how to change it if it is destructive, and how to enlarge its capacity if it is constructive.

Somehow a relationship acquires characteristics and dynamics of its own that form a shared mind-set and habit from which each party acts, even though, to be sure, only the discrete parties are observable. Relationships— marriage, partnership, treaty, comrades in arms, friendship—come to be valued for their own sakes. Some are sanctified as legal entities; others have no formal status, but men and women die for them. We are dealing with a phenomenon that can be both observable and mystical—but very real and powerful to those who are party to it.

Susan Collin Marks, a South African deeply immersed in implementing the South African National Peace Accord adopted in 1991, pondered ". . . [h]ow to convey the essence of a process so powerful that it carried a whole country across the abyss of self-destruction to the realm of hope? How to put spirit into words?"

> I remember a high summer's day among the hills of the undulating game reserve Hluhluwe. . . . I had clambered into a cool hollow among the roots of a great wild fig tree . . . and looked out on the bush world spread below.
>
> That day, the wind was powerful, and I watched hawks wheeling without moving a feather, riding the updrafts, swooping into the angle of the wind that gives the most lift; the ebb and flow of an open field of sour grass; leaves skittering, dry and scratchy, in the pale shadows under the thorn bushes; clouds caught in a running tide.
>
> That day, I was watching the wind. The wind itself was invisible, but I saw its effect, its force and impact, its power and artistry.
>
> This is the essence of South Africa's peace process. . . . The National Peace Accord, invisible like the wind, swept powerfully through our land, blowing into troubled communities, turning upside down the established order of oppression and division, blowing the roof off structures rooted in centuries of separation and prejudice.
>
> The results were miraculous. . . . relationships built across formidable barriers; the discovery of the Other that legislation had denied.
>
> These were the wheeling hawks and the undulating grasses of the peace process. The peace process was invisible, but we could see its effects.[3]

And so it is with relationship—invisible, yet powerful, moving in the "space between."

I admit that focusing on the process of interaction—the "space between"—may seem an almost metaphysical step, but in political life these processes are real. Power can grow from conducting them thoughtfully and energetically. Violence can erupt when they run out of control. A peace treaty is a collection of negotiated points on a piece of paper; a peace process—a political process to change conflictual relationships—can transform decades of hostility and violence and build powerful coalitions. Governments can sign peace treaties; only people can build peaceful relationships.

All of us as political actors—be we citizens inside or outside government, scholars or practitioners—must find ways to analyze this process of interaction. The established ways of thinking about political life leave those who rely on them driving a political Model T in the age of space flight. My aim here is to make a dynamic picture of relationship real. My purpose is to suggest a framework that anyone can test in efforts to transform relationships.

The Concept of Relationship: Five Arenas of
Potential Change

When I presented the concept of relationship in a variety of writings in the late 1980s and early 1990s, culminating in *A Public Peace Process* in 1999, I focused more on the individual reflecting the experience of a group than on groups themselves.[4] I did so because I was concentrating on the process of Sustained Dialogue among individual citizens as a point of entry into the relationships among the groups with which they identified. I relied on participants in the dialogue's interaction to reflect the experience of their groups and to take their experiences and insights back to those groups.

In this book, I am going to focus more—though not exclusively—on relationships between groups. My colleague and friend, psychoanalyst Vamik Volkan, has focused on "large-group" identity and interactions.[5] I am not going to use that designation. I will, to be sure, consider relationships between large ethnic or national groups and whole countries, as he does, but I must also leave space in this framework at the other end of the spectrum for those loosely formed citizens' associations that weave the fabric of the Citizens' Political Process described in chapter one.

As noted briefly in chapter three, my concept of relationship embraces five arenas of interaction. Others may organize them differently or find additional arenas. However defined, the purposes of identifying them are to organize our observations and to focus our interventions.

Most of these arenas are reflected individually in the social science literature. The difference here is that, rather than examining each minutely, *the practitioner must see them together as parts of a whole relationship* and use them as points of entry for analyzing relationships thoughtfully enough to *change* them. The categorization presented here gives the practitioner a systematic analytical framework within which to collect her or his observations and experience and to develop hypotheses about the dynamics of a relationship before attempting to change them. Among those practitioners, of course, may be parties to a conflict themselves.

Within each party to a relationship—be it persons or groups—the relative importance and combinations of these components are different and may even be in flux as new experiences are absorbed. The bottom line is that thinking within this framework enables practitioners to get inside each of these arenas in practical ways to change the overall mix of components or the overall interaction and therefore to change relationships.

I must underscore the dynamism of this concept. It is impossible to make active relationships stand still. Each of these elements is itself complex; it is formed in continuous interaction with other persons or groups. These interactions shape and reshape the mix within each of the elements of relationship and the overall combination of the elements themselves. The changing mixes and combinations reveal how and perhaps why overall relationships improve or sour. Given the complexity of these changes within a continuously evolving process, it seems unlikely that they will be susceptible to measurement or prediction; but they are susceptible to thoughtful analysis and interpretation as a basis for action.

The outline below is placed here for two reasons: (1) to provide a quick checklist for the practitioner in working with a relationship; (2) to suggest to scholars the large bodies of literature in many fields that could amplify any of these components. It would be a useful project for a team of scholars inclined toward interdisciplinary work to marshal the insights from these respective fields to refine a working framework for analyzing relationships.[6] The brief description of each of the five components that follows the outline is written in a scope that practitioners can use. Just putting the five components with some understanding of each in the backs of our minds can help us organize our analyses. Practitioners cannot be expected to conduct the intricate analysis that the table below suggests.

ELEMENTS OF GROUP RELATIONSHIPS

- Identity
  —Observable characteristics
  —Experience: origins, "chosen traumas . . . chosen glories"[7]
  —Culture and social structure
  —Worldview, ideology, religion
  —Self-image in relation to the other
  —Points of entry for change

- Interests
  —How survival needs are defined
  —What are valued beyond survival needs
  —Interests defined as a function of relationship: interdependence
  —Points of entry for change

- Power
  —Authorities' ability to coerce or enforce
  —Citizens' capacity to influence events
  —One group's ability to coerce or influence another
  —Points of entry for change

- Perceptions, misperceptions, stereotypes
  —How one group sees the other
  —Why?
  —Points of entry for change

- Processes and patterns of interaction: ways of relating
  —Concept of relationship
  —Modes of communicating
  —Experiences: confrontation, competition, collaboration, cooperation
  —Shared consciousness of unwritten covenants, limits, predictable reciprocity
  —Points of entry for change

Identity

Many of today's conflicts are clashes of identity—not only contests over negotiable differences. People over the centuries have been killed because of identity—not necessarily because of what they possess or what they have done or threatened to do but because they are different.

Characteristics. Each partner to a relationship is described most simply in terms of observable characteristics. For an individual, these include sex, size, age, strength, intelligence, ethnic traits, place and circumstances of birth, language. For a group or country, they include size, geographic base, social and political structure, ethnic and demographic composition, resources, and functions. Just as a person's physical makeup affects, in part, that individual's behavior and sense of capacity, so the physical characteristics of a group or country partly affect its approach to the world around it.

Experience. No person, group, or country can be fully described in terms of a snapshot or measurement of physical characteristics at a particular time. It is essential to know where a person or group "is coming from." What developmental process or interactions with others have brought them to the present place and moment—shaped their worldviews and their approach to others? How individuals are taught to "remember" past interactions— traumatic experiences that produced a sense of grievance or victimhood or of great achievement—may be more important in shaping their present sense of identity than knowing objectively what happened. Each party to an experience depicts, mourns, or lauds it differently. People do not easily forgive. Some may let go of past pain; others will hug the pain close.

Culture and social structure. Our identity—as individuals and then as group members—is also shaped in interaction. We first learn in a *family setting*[8] to set ourselves off as not our mother or father. We learn a distinguishing language and other forms of communication. We learn the degree of authority and respect accorded to elders, obedience, acceptable behavior toward siblings and members of the extended family, tolerable ways of getting what we need. Gradually we absorb our broader *cultural heritage*— socially acceptable habits of interacting with others in our group, customs for organizing social interactions, ways of solving problems, broader patterns and rules for interacting with those outside our group.

As we reach out, we learn from the *experience* of interacting with those around us in ever widening circles. We emulate some. We define ourselves as not like others—those who are unfamiliar, those whom we learn to see as threatening, those whom we are told to dislike, fear, or hate. Ultimately, psychoanalysts tell us, we may project onto enemies those characteristics of ourselves that we do not like.[9] As we grow in judgment, we refine in dialogue with others our sense of what concerns us and what we value. We associate increasingly with those who share what we value.

Worldview, ideology, religion. With all of that, as discussed in chapter two, come assumptions that lie behind how people around us explain how the world works. These are often so deeply embedded in cultural inheritance that they are not articulated. That is just the way things are—or that is the way things are until something happens to cause questioning. This book itself suggests the need for change in the Western worldview. Since this point has been introduced in chapter two, I will not dwell further on it here.

Self-image in relation to the other. Each group will have its basic self-image, but it will also—like a person—define itself partly in terms of others in a relationship. We will define our group explicitly as not like the other. How each partner defines its own identity and how each feels about itself will affect how each perceives the other—as a source of threat or support. How a party perceives itself provides the lenses through which it sees external changes. For purposes of our work here it is important to recognize the core of a group's self-image, but it is obviously essential to understand what parts of that self-image may be functions of a relationship.

From the combination of physical circumstances and unfolding experience and growth, individuals and groups come to a sense of who they are—a sense of identity. For individuals, *self-image*—that sense of self—also reflects the fact that each individual embodies a *psychological makeup*—strengths, insecurities, vulnerabilities, fears. It is partly in these areas that interactions among people are played out. They include predispositions to play a dominant role in inter-actions with others or to hang back; some need to lead, others are more dependent. There is a different interplay—"chemistry," we often call it—between different personality types that produces different kinds of relation-ships. The same can be true of groups as one group that has historically seen itself as the victim of aggression will transfer to a present relationship that same self-characterization, even though the facts may not support it.

Sometimes these sources of identity become apparent to individuals and observers only as individuals and groups interact. A group that has long seen itself as victim may at the same time learn that it is seen as victimizing others. Blacks and whites in today's United States in Sustained Dialogue learn what part of their identities is owed to their interaction, past and pres-ent. For Serbians and other ethnic groups in the former Yugoslavia, identity differences sharpened as, for political purposes, leaders inflamed long-submerged tensions. Conversely, parties to the civil war in the former Soviet republic of Tajikistan came to understand in Sustained Dialogue that they shared more of a common identity—albeit still not fully formed—than their civil war suggested.

In the last half of the twentieth century and into the twenty-first—perhaps more than at any earlier time in history—group identities have been in the process of rediscovery, formation, or redefinition in remarkable numbers. Much like young people coming of age, peoples have emerged from colonial rule or become independent of empires and have had to take responsibility for their own futures while finding need for different kinds of interactions with former rulers and new neighbors. Through liberation movements, others gained consciousness of identities they wanted to develop, consolidate, and assert. While certain core elements of identity are precious and seemingly immutable, others will grow with experience. Peoples achieving independence following dissolution of the Soviet Union and years of Russian dominance struggled to find balance between Russian-trained minds and traditional cultures.

Possibilities for change. However deeply entrenched these self-images may be, they have been forged, in part, in interaction and can in many instances be changed, in part, through interaction in ways that can affect a relationship. Interactions form dependencies and rediscovered interdependence. To understand relationships, we need to focus not only on how one party changes but on how to change the mix in their interaction. In dialogue, participants are not asked to change their core identities, but they may change elements defined in terms of the adversary, or at a minimum, they may gain greater understanding and respect for the identity of the other(s). They may even deepen their understanding of who they themselves really are.

As a Soviet colleague in 1988 at the height of Chairman Mikhail Gorbachev's period of *glasnost* and *perestroika* said to a group of Americans: "We Soviets are going to do a terrible thing to you. We are going to deprive you of your enemy."[10] His insight became reality in the 1990s as the end of the Cold War threw Americans off stride in groping to redefine national purposes.

Coexistence of Needs and Interests—Developing Interdependence

A relationship begins when two or more parties are drawn into the same space by intersecting interests. Some scholars define the beginning of relationship as the point at which one party's actions affect another. Understanding a relationship requires probing those interests—what each needs or wants to achieve and avoid and, above all, why. Interests are defined on different levels. Some are essential to survival; some reflect what groups value for historic, political, ideological, or religious reasons; others are defined as a function of the relationship—what we need from others to achieve what we want or what we want to deny others. The important task is to understand how and why each party defines its interests because that is where possibilities for change emerge.

How survival needs are defined. The most fundamental needs and interests can be analytically and materially defined. They are what we refer to as survival needs. For individuals, these begin with the physical needs for survival—food, shelter, protection.[11] Groups have their own versions of these needs in the means to sustain their existence and in the resources, human and other, to accomplish their most essential objectives. Beyond needs for basic physical survival are interests defined in human terms. For individuals, these include psychological needs for identity, security, acceptance, dignity, and self-fulfillment. Groups again have their own version of such needs that may take the form of moral principles for which members might be willing to die rather than live without.

Already in this last statement, we are going beyond how interests have been traditionally defined. Most of us who have served in the professional ranks of government or in academic study of public policy or international affairs were taught to think in terms of analytically defined or "objective" interests— that is, those that are tangible and measurable. For instance, how much of a resource does a country need, or what geographic position is necessary for defense? These are important. But my experience in U.S. government poli- cymaking suggests that a purely analytical—or objective—statement of inter- ests is not always an adequate touchstone for making workable policy. Complex interests are often defined through human interaction.

Many interests—even those related to group survival—may be literally vital but still may be difficult to define. For instance, for two years before the United States entered World War II while Nazi Germany overran Europe, Americans debated whether their national interest required U.S. entry into the war. Only when Japan attacked Pearl Harbor was the issue resolved. Even these most basic of interests that turn out to be a matter of survival are defined in relationship within groups; they are anything but objective. In a closed political system, this interaction takes place only at the highest level; in an open system, it takes place more broadly. An important question is not only what these interests are but how and why they are defined as they are.

What are valued beyond survival needs? A variety of public issues beyond survival reflects group members' or citizens' judgments about priorities, moral commitments, or analysis of consequences of actions in relation to what they value. Such interests are defined in human terms and expressed politically through dialogue and deliberation among citizens.

Learning peoples' real interests requires probing the deep-rooted fears, hopes, wounds, perceptions, and values that form peoples' sense of what is threatening and of what is vital to protect their identity. What do they "care about" or value? Surprisingly, real interests—exactly what we fear or want and how much—are not easy to know precisely. Probing may reveal prem- ises more visceral than analytical—and perhaps more politically significant. As we learn the other's identity, we may uncover the roots of interests in history and culture, in human feelings, and in political processes.

As individuals struggle with complex problems, they often discover that the choice is not between good and bad but among options each of which offers something they value. The real choice is not a confrontation between right and wrong or a decision in an adversarial proceeding between the advocates of technically defined positions. The real choice often lies within human beings as they weigh one value against another. Interests are defined partly through this human process.

As bodies politic interact, people ask, "Do they care about the same things we care about?" This can become a central question as citizens begin to talk across group boundaries.

Even at the highest governmental level, besides receiving the bureau- cracy's analysis of interests, a U.S. president will go into the political arena to sense how American citizens see these interests, how intensely they feel, and why, especially when one set of interests competes for resources with another. He will try to learn not just what citizens' concrete interests are, but also what they really value. Citizens inject their own domestic needs and personal values into a definition of the national interest or the community interest as they engage in dialogue with each other. Probing that human dimension of interests reveals the deep-rooted fears, hopes, wounds, values, and perceptions that form peoples' sense of what is threatening and of what is vital to protect their identity, security, dignity, and well-being.

During an American–Soviet dialogue in the early 1980s, a senior Soviet colleague took me to task for saying that interests are politically as well as analytically defined. "That may be true in the United States," he said. "You have a Congress that has to respond to special interest groups. In the Soviet Union, we have objective interests. We know what our interests are." Over lunch, I responded: "You have a big government and a big country just as we do. Your leader has to respond to the different interests of the military, the farmers, the industrial managers, and senior colleagues with different ideological emphases. Don't tell me that your interests are so objective—that they're not politically defined."

Interests as a function of relationship—interdependence. A relationship starts when two parties are drawn into the same space by their interests. Some of those interests, of course, may be material. Both want equal access to the same land or water, the same market, the same resources, the same social spaces. But as we probe those interests—what each really wants to achieve and avoid and why—we begin to see deep-rooted interests that would rarely appear on a list of interests prepared for a negotiation. "Remember, Hal," a Jewish friend once said to me, "the fear of annihilation is seared on every Jewish soul." I never saw that as starkly stated on a list of Israel's interests, but its protection has to be defined in the context of relationships with neighbors. As interaction increases, parties may identify interests—at both the material and the psychological level—that neither could achieve without the other. This is the point at which *interdependence* in the common sense of the word begins. (Some social scientists describe interdependence as beginning earlier when each party's actions begin to affect the other.[12])

To begin, in a conflictual or competitive relationship such as turf battles among city gangs or the Cold War relationship between the Soviet Union and the United States, parties may start by using a zero–sum calculation whereby one defines what it wants at the other's expense or what it wants to deny the other. In a cooperative relationship such as a marriage or partnership, parties may use a positive-sum measure whereby pursuing one party's interests may produce a gain for both—for the relationship or partnership. Eventually, each party recognizes that its ability to realize its own interests depends in some way on the actions of the other. This is the essence of interdependence.

Possibilities for change. The stakes over which racial and ethnic conflicts are fought are often not objectively defined interests but interests defined in human and political terms in which identities are at stake and historical grievances drive groups to passionate crusades. When it is possible to bring one party to understand through dialogue others' deeply felt interests and hurts—imagined or real—then relationships begin to change. Governmental diplomacy will rarely surface interests so defined, yet in them lies a significant opportunity to change conflictual relationships.

Those kinds of changes are often achieved not in negotiation but in Sustained Dialogue—a form of interaction where each party listens carefully, internalizes what is said, and changes as a result. As participants' experience in dialogue deepens, they often find more common ground among their respective interests—stopping the killing, for instance—than they had imagined.

Power Broadly Defined

Power, as discussed in chapter one, has usually been defined as *control, coercion, or "power over."* It has been measured as the accumulation of tangible assets—physical, economic, military, geographic—that one party uses to get what it wants at another's expense. Power in a relationship has been measured for centuries as a balance or imbalance of these assets. It has been thought of as the means for producing a desired outcome, even against another's will, by taking what one wants or by forcing a negotiation in which what is wanted would be conceded.

As chapters one and three suggest, experience has caused us to question the validity of such a limited definition in many situations. Not that it is invalid in all circumstances, it is just not large enough to be useful in many situations. How does it, for instance, explain the endurance and ultimate success of nationalist movements against great empires? How does it explain the outcome of the U.S. intervention in Vietnam or the Soviet experience in Afghanistan in the 1980s? How does it explain the persistence of Palestinian nationalism against Israel, the nuclear superpower of the Middle East?

The questions now are: What insight into the nature of power results when power in its traditional forms does not produce predicted results? What insights would emerge if we started from analyzing relationships that have changed as one party generated an unpredicted capacity to influence the course of events?

For analytical purposes, it is important to place a group or a country on two spectra: (1) How is power organized within the group? Is decision-making highly centralized in authorities, or do those outside formal power structures play a role? (2) How are power and influence played out in a relationship with others?

Authorities' ability to coerce or enforce. To analyze interaction between groups or whole bodies politic, we need to learn how a group makes decisions about the relationship. At one extreme—for instance, Iraq before the U.S. military intervention and North Korea at the beginning of the twenty-first century—relations with a totalitarian regime may perhaps be more usefully analyzed in the context of the traditional realist paradigm. At the other, relationships among more open societies may require the relational paradigm. In many relationships, the mix of elements in the relationship is so complex that one party's capacity to influence the course of the relationship may be rooted in elements of the relationship that would not normally be seen as sources of power.

During the Cold War, participants in citizens' dialogues constantly confronted the difference between the highly centralized Soviet decision-making apparatus and the broad public base of U.S. policymaking. If one were to try to influence the overall relationship, it was essential for each side to know where changes might take place. This question is addressed in chapter ten on the China–U.S. relationship. The same question exists even among groups within civil society. Some may be authoritarian; others may be quite open in their decision-making.[13]

Citizens' capacity to influence events. The other side of this coin is what role citizens other than authorities play in setting the course for a group or a country. In the United States, there are many policy-influencing groups. In the case of U.S. policymaking toward China, for instance, the Taiwan lobby, U.S. corporations with strong interest in the potential Chinese market, and human rights organizations all exert heavy influence on the Congress. For all of that, public forums in the United States on what citizens think about the conduct of the relationship reveal that there are certain fundamental positions that policymakers may need to take into account in the long run. On the other side of the relationship, it is clear that a highly centralized government controls Chinese policymaking toward the United States, but research also suggests that Chinese citizens hold diverse views on the relationship in a number of instances. In addition, the diversification of the Chinese economy has reduced governmental control over many decisions in that area.[14]

One group's ability to coerce or influence another. Military power has been the classic instrument by which one country has coerced another. As the Cold War progressed, however, nuclear weapons raised questions about the limits on American or Soviet use of military power. Even the complex Soviet-U.S. nuclear relationship came to be regulated not by the balance of physical power but by the general doctrine of deterrence, which was essentially a doctrine based on assumptions about how minds would interact in a showdown—a function of relationship. In other circumstances, from Vietnam through Lebanon to Afghanistan, we have seen the limits of military power to accomplish political purposes.

This suggests that we need to think about power not only as the physical ability to control or to force a desired outcome but, in some circumstances, as the capacity to conduct an interactive process in such a way as to change the mix of elements in a relationship or to make things happen over time. The creative conduct of the process of continuous interaction between parties may in itself generate more effective power in this sense than economic or military resources.

Points of entry for change. We can explain why change takes place in the face of great disparities of military, social, and economic power only if we define power in *relational* terms. Mahatma Gandhi's campaign of principled nonviolence against the British Empire's control in India interacted with those in an exhausted Britain who argued against trying to continue to rule by force after an already costly war to preserve democracy. A decade and a half later, Martin Luther King, Jr., and a movement of largely anonymous blacks and whites challenged superior power in the conventional sense by interacting with custodians of a culture who felt that culture was wrong and needed to be changed. Egyptian President Sadat's trip to Israel in November 1977 may have done more to change the course of the Egyptian–Israeli relationship by his direct interaction with the Israeli people than either superpower could have.[15] Interactions between French and German citizens after World War II sowed the seeds of the reconciliation that became the sinews of the European Union.[16]

Power often emerges from political relationships. Events in East-Central Europe in 1989 dramatized that the power to generate change sometimes lies with those who have no raw power. Power emerged from relationships among people who challenged government on grounds of legitimacy, and those in authority decided not to use force in the circumstances that citizens, in part, created.

The discussion in chapter one of the Citizens' Political Process and of citizens' capacity to concert as the essence of social capital are first steps in suggesting that sources of power other than the ability to coerce do exist. My interest in this book is not so much in scholarly research into the nature of that power as it is in learning more about how to generate it. A further interest is in encouraging citizens in and out of government to recognize this as an essential resource available to them in whole bodies politic to meet our challenges.

In short, the power to change relationships may emerge as people interact in different ways. It may emerge from careful conduct of the political process of continuous interaction, as in the Citizens' Political Process. Citizens outside government can create this kind of power. Military power will not cease to be important, but in many circumstances, it may not be the vehicle for changing relationships and forging a peaceful future.

Evolving Perceptions, Misperceptions, Stereotypes

Perhaps the easiest element of relationship to change is this one. As people interact, misperceptions and stereotypes give way to pictures of others as human beings with legitimate interests, fears, and reasons for suspicion and hatred. Learning how one's own acts have appeared to others can cause one to rethink attitudes and actions.

How one group sees others. Part of a child's learning about who she is not includes stereotypes of others that are passed to her through interactions with those around her. These pictures are varyingly accurate or inaccurate. But they determine in part how we identify ourselves and how we act toward others—until we interact directly with them and can test those pictures. An early step in understanding relationships is learning how each party pictures others. These can emerge in the early stages of Sustained Dialogue, or they can be gleaned through public forums, focus groups, or opinion surveys.

Why? Learning what shapes the perceptions of one body politic toward another can be critical. Each party will start with preconceived ideas of how a person or a group of the other's background, role, race, religion, ideology, or nationality could be expected to behave. Often these stereotypes are based on myths of past interactions and on little current contact. As interactions multiply, each party's behavior may reshape others' perceptions by not matching preconceived pictures—or they may partially affirm or refine a negative stereotype.

Possibilities for change. Often in Sustained Dialogue, parties' pictures will change profoundly. This is the most direct way for individual citizens and small groups to develop more accurate pictures of the other. The more difficult question, however, is how perceptions may change on a larger scale.

A relationship may change and solutions to shared problems may become possible for a few groups, but until people *perceive* the relationship as changing, they may act no differently. Technical solutions for sharing sovereignty over Jerusalem, for instance, existed long before the Israeli–Palestinian relationship was such as to allow authorities to negotiate on that subject. On the other hand, working in what we perceive as a sustainable problem-solving relationship may encourage people to tackle problems that seem to have no immediate solution. An effective problem-solving relationship can prove so useful over time that it is eventually perceived as a valuable interest that must be protected for its own sake.

Even in a constrained relationship, cooperation on issues of vital importance to both is possible, but broader perceptions of hostility may limit cooperation past the time when fuller practical cooperation would otherwise become feasible. Two hostile parties can be locked into an ongoing interaction by a shared problem such as managing nuclear weapons or by common geography (e.g., Israelis and Palestinians living in the same homeland or urban gangs in the same part of a city) that requires them to work together to some extent. But they may fear, hate, mistrust, even "demonize" each other. Until these human feelings are dealt with and individuals perceive that the relationship might become constructive, it will remain constrained.

Even when hostility fades and some cooperation becomes possible, the perception of a durable relationship does not develop quickly, is often tenuous when it does, can rarely be complete, and can continue to grow or go sour again. Political leaders, such as Slobodan Milosevic, can reverse long-term positive development by fanning the flames of historic animosity for present political purposes.

As a problem-solving relationship evolves, changing perceptions may emerge from a sense that people are acting from at least some comparable human values. These growing perceptions are tested through talking, thinking, and working together—that is, in interaction—rather than only observing each other from a distance. When partners diagnose situations together, envision alternatives, analyze obstacles, and design courses of action, they test others' intent and their perception of it.

In a deepening relationship, thinking together about acting deliberately to change perceptions across group borders becomes possible. Groups have experienced developing together a scenario of interactive steps designed to change perceptions of a relationship and thereby enlarge their capacity to cooperate. This requires a different kind of conversation from the conversations of officials focusing on government-to-government issues. People need to talk together explicitly about the perceptions that constrain their capacity to act together and about how to change those perceptions that block evolution of a more constructive relationship.

Attempting to change a relationship in this way requires, above all, focusing on the relationship itself. It requires working from a full picture of what affects interaction, ranging from deep human fears and hopes, through cultures that shape behavior and worldviews, to hard calculations of security and decision-making. It requires thinking in a larger political context and using a broader array of instruments—presumably peaceful—to change perceptions of the relationship and its potential for positive accomplishments.

Processes and Patterns of Interaction

At the heart of any relationship is a complex of interactions—a continuous and reciprocal multilevel process among whole human beings. In that process, two or more parties act in ways that affect the others on multiple levels, taking into account what they have internalized from previous exchanges, what they hope for in future exchanges, and perhaps even immediate feedback from present actions. Gradually a shared body of experience on multiple levels and perhaps unwritten norms of behavior evolve as a context for acting. My hope is to find ways to focus on the process and patterns of interaction as the medium for analyzing a relationship. To repeat, my emphasis on whole human beings and multiple levels is intended to move beyond the concept of the rational actor.

How does *inter*action as presented here differ from discrete actions and reactions? Both include learning from the experience of acting in the same space over time in ways that affect each other's interests. The concept of *inter*action as presented here, however, goes beyond the notion of the rational actor assessing an action and devising a reaction; it focuses on the engagement of whole persons—the emotional as well as the rational. It introduces simultaneous interplay of stimuli on multiple levels—interplay that is complex and continuous rather than sequential.

Interaction, as noted earlier, starts when two or more parties are drawn into the same space—physical or mental—by similar interests and begin acting in ways that affect each other's interests, thoughts, and behavior. It may begin as simple action and reaction, but a relationship grows as these interactions develop over time, gradually engaging each party more broadly, more deeply, and more frequently on multiple levels.

Parties come to an interaction with their individual identities, interests, sources of power, and perceptions. As we have seen in the four preceding sections, each of these elements will itself have evolved in some degree through interaction with others. They also come with ideas about conducting a relationship.

Concept of relationship. Each group comes to an interaction with its own picture of what a relationship should be. As chapter ten on the China-U.S. relationship explains, Americans and Chinese have discovered that each brings quite a different concept of how relationship is formed. It may not be possible to change concepts that are deeply rooted in culture, but we must understand them.

Modes of communicating. The quality of interaction depends importantly on the nature of communication. At one end of a spectrum, parties may communicate by actions and reactions supplemented by signals of one sort or another to convey intent. Through repetition and experience, behavior patterns are discerned. Even through indirect communication, perceptions can begin to change. At the other end of the spectrum, the interaction may involve deepening person-to-person and group-to-group communication together with a growing understanding of the interdependence of interests and needs. When deepening communication develops over time and deals with a cumulative agenda, dialogue can partly replace adversarial interaction and contests of force as a means for resolving differences. Sustained Dialogue—an interactive relationship-changing process—can precede formal negotiation as a way of changing the political environment or redefining problems in moving toward solutions. Subjects may range from the most practical and essential to the depths of each party's interests.

Historically, governments have conducted formal communications between peoples. We have now learned that there can be a depth of communication among citizens outside government that reveals identity, interests, perceptions and misperceptions, priorities, purpose, and political dynamics. Indeed, governments often stand back to see what communication in nongovernmental channels produces before committing themselves. Systematic, Sustained Dialogues among citizens outside government broaden interaction, sharpen understanding, deepen communication, and partly replace adversarial interaction and contests of force as means of pursuing interests. Citizens outside government often communicate more meaningfully than officials. Beyond face-to-face communications are the proliferating opportunities to "talk" electronically.

Experiences. Interaction may be hostile, confrontational, cooperative within stated limits, collaborative, intimate. Two parties may have had long-standing habitual ways of relating that can affect new interaction.

The parties to an interaction in political life have choices about how to conduct an interaction—the rules of engaging. These choices range across a spectrum: avoidance, indifference, defensiveness, confrontation, cooperation, collaboration, conciliation, intimacy. They will in part reflect who they are (identity), what they really need and care about (interests), the resources (power) they can bring to bear, and their analysis of the character and real needs and intentions of the other (perceptions/misperceptions).

These choices, for the most part, are not made in isolation. They are made in light of what the parties have learned tacitly or explicitly in other processes of interaction. Nor are those choices made only rationally; they also reflect basic feelings and instincts. As a new interaction begins, each party tests approaches, adapts, changes behavior, and gradually learns what produces desired and undesired results. What each party learns can adjust the pattern of the interaction and become part of a cumulative pattern. As Harold Kelley writes of a two-person pair: ". . . the activity pattern is the product of their interaction (e.g., a particular mutual understanding or shared expectation that the two have evolved)."[17]

Shared consciousness of unwritten covenants, limits, predictable reciprocity. The parties learn, test, and introduce practices that seem to ease or enhance conduct of the relationship. As Kelley says, interaction will increasingly reflect a cumulative and shared body of experience. It may ultimately be governed by long-standing, unwritten "covenants" or "rules" of reciprocal behavior.

To begin, these may take the form of informal limits on behavior to assure, first, basic mutual security and then to assure against offending or hurting the others' feelings or interests. At a minimum, the imperative of avoiding fatal confrontation introduces a shared interest in a minimal level of regulating conflict. As groups interact over time, implicit "rules of the game" develop—a sort of tacit regulation of behavior. As a relationship develops further, parties can begin actually to write a "code of conduct" or "principles" for an explicit regulation of interaction. Each of these efforts played a role in Soviet-U.S. attempts to avoid nuclear war.

In interstate relations, we have traditionally defined the limits of one state's behavior toward another in terms of such principles as noninterference in others' internal affairs or nonintervention in another's territory. These principles were crafted to protect the sovereignty of the state.

Sometimes, in intrastate interactions, these are codified as laws, principles, or conventions. Actions have ranged in the United States, for instance, from civil rights and equal employment laws to prolonged social and educational campaigns to raise sensitivity to racial and gender issues. Many countries in their own ways work to curb the activities of hate groups. Often embedded in the common experience of a group is a body of understandings—I have called them "covenants"—on appropriate ways of relating. Often they are unspoken, embedded deeply in assumed norms.

Underlying tacit or explicit practices that regulate behavior are psychological limits sensitive to the human dimensions of interaction. These limits define when one is "stepping on another's toes" or "touching raw nerves." Limits must reflect what each party sees as threatening its sense of identity, integrity, and self-esteem, as well as its concrete interests. In the United States, African Americans, Native Americans, Hispanics, countless other minorities, whites, men, and women are increasingly—though still inadequately—aware of words that cause each other pain or slight another's dignity.

As interactions change, the question is whether there are new principles or practices that demonstrate respect and provide protection for the identity and integrity of each group or body politic in a relationship. As the world community in the twenty-first century increasingly asserts its right to express an interest in how governments treat their citizens, the emphasis has shifted from principles designed only to protect the rights of states to principles that also focus on the rights of human beings.

A body of shared experience develops that reflects mutually satisfactory outcomes. One key to assuring limits that protect the integrity of an evolving relationship may lie in the word *mutual*. Do the developing interactions reflect genuinely mutual interests or benefit? Do the interactions reflect efforts simply to transfer one side's way of doing things, or do they reflect parties sharing their respective values and experiences in order to work together in relationship to deal with problems that all want to deal with effectively for compatible individual or mutual purposes? Habits, practices, and "rules" of relating seem to grow out of the interaction in ways that neither party alone could create or predict. If parties eventually find themselves often working toward common goals, they may learn complementary ways of acting, perhaps without even talking about them.[18]

Possibilities for change. Change does not always result from a linear series of actions and reaction between groups. Change also evolves through a cumulative, generative process of continuous, multilevel interaction that can change perceptions and create opportunities that did not seem to exist before. Looking beyond specific issues and episodic transactions to the process of interaction over time may even enable us to design a process aimed at eroding underlying political obstacles to change.

As relationships are probed, it may be that new practices will emerge more appropriately from a dialogue about necessary limits in the interaction between participants' groups than from trying to redefine traditional principles of national or international law. Changing limits in practical and meaningful ways can change relationships.

Beyond discussion of limits, in Sustained Dialogue or the Citizens' Political Process as described in chapter one, participants can actually design a scenario of interactive steps that will gradually change patterns of interaction and make bodies politic aware of these changes. Participants identify actions that could cause the other side to believe that they can be more trusting of a constructive response to their actions. The scenario is a useful device when neither party will move without assurance of a response or when a progression of small reciprocal steps is needed. In contrast to an official action memo that concentrates on destinations and unilateral moves, a scenario starts with a sense of direction and then designs the dynamics of moving in that direction. A scenario developed cooperatively by partners becomes an instrument in strengthening their relationship. To stress the scenario as a framework for change is to add a political instrument usable both by governments and by citizens outside government. To think this way is to broaden thinking about the interaction between groups or whole bodies politic.

Finally, an exciting feature of interaction is that the confluence of actions may produce results that were not intended or foreseen even by the actors. Practitioners must be careful not to close the door on the exciting potential of an open-ended process of interaction to produce more than the actors could have hoped for. This can happen when funders insist on too precise a definition of outcomes or social scientists pursue a reductionist methodology that can promise only limited insights into very small parts of a much larger and more complex whole.

As a relationship evolves, a learning process occurs at the heart of the continuous interaction.[19] Definitions of each side's objectives in the relationship are sharpened and shared. Differences arise, and rules are established that allow the partners to coexist comfortably. But sometimes a core conflict emerges and the relationship deteriorates. If accommodation is found, the relationship can gain strength because the partners have discovered new elements of the relationship and have invested in sustaining it.

The Overall Relationship

Relationship then, to draw these elements together, comprises these five arenas of individual experience and interaction with others. Relationship reflects the whole that they create—what I have referred to as the overall relationship. While the components are important for organizing thinking, analysis, and intervention, the whole may well be more than or different from the sum of these parts—especially when seen in terms of what individual units can accomplish together in relationship. Despite the need to understand the components, the most important factor in political life is to consider the impact and conduct of the whole relationship.

To repeat, I do not expect a practitioner to keep track of every one of these elements. If a practitioner reflects on them and internalizes a full sense of the dynamic process of multilevel and continuous interaction that is relationship, keeping these elements in the back of the mind can become a useful analytical and operational instrument of change.

One reason for laying out in some detail the elements of relationship is to provide a wide-angled diagnostic instrument for identifying and examining carefully the points at which change may take place. It may permit us to see early the beginnings and causes of change. It could enable preemptive action to forestall deterioration or to consolidate constructive change.

Focusing on the Overall Relationship

Relationship can be analyzed by organizing experience in these five arenas and then by attempting to characterize the whole in terms of the capacities of the parties in the relationship together to accomplish what neither could accomplish alone. The concept of relationship provides a context for developing these capacities.

Relationship can be changed by enhancing the appreciation of one party for another's identity, and one's identity can change to the extent that one no longer defines oneself primarily as distinct from an enemy. Parties may not change their most basic interests, but they may come to understand that they share interests. They may come to see the balance of power between them differently as they understand that one party holds an important key to enabling the other to achieve an important goal. Surely, perceptions will change as interactions intensify. Patterns of interaction can be changed.

In that context, I see relationship as important in its own right. In many instances, relationships are highly valued for their own sake; they seem almost to have lives of their own. Social scientists also see them this way, even though their methodologies keep them from focusing on relationship itself defined in the complex way I have presented. The political practitioner needs her or his own methodology for dealing with the overall relationships among groups—the total pattern of interactions, as the Russians say.

The analyst of relationship in this sense may describe an overall relationship for working purposes by framing and responding to questions such as the following:

- What are the primary life experiences that have brought each party to a relationship to the present moment? In what ways, if any, has each party defined its *identity* in terms of the other?
- What does each party seem to feel are its greatest *needs*, or *interests*? Why are they *really* important? To what extent is a party defining these interests as a function of the relationship—that is, in terms of what it wants to take from or deny to the other? Why?
- What does each party see as the main elements of its own *power*—broadly defined—vis-à-vis the other? What means does it use to move the other? In what areas does either see that it needs the other's cooperation to achieve what it wants? What means does it use to gain that cooperation?
- How have each party's perceptions of the other evolved? What behaviors by the other reinforce old or new perceptions?
- How have the parties habitually interacted?
- In sum, what are the key points in this relationship that provide the potential for accomplishing what each party cares about?

In short, focusing on individual components can highlight causes of a conflict. Focusing on the whole combination of components and how it might be changed opens the door to a wide range of actions. In any case, focusing on the relationship itself differs significantly from focusing primarily on one group's decisions about how to behave toward other groups.

This provides the political practitioner with a conceptual framework within which to act. It provides her or him a way of thinking about the swirling interactions in the political arena and a guide for entering that process at any number of points along the way. The practitioner does not need a research design. The practitioner needs a way of thinking about conducting or transforming relationships.

A colleague[20] asked me in the late 1980s whether I saw relationship as a condition or an aspiration. I responded that, in political affairs, relationship is a condition more often than we recognize—a reality, not a hope, if only we will see it. The Soviet-U.S. relationship during the Cold War was a hostile, intense, and potentially devastating relationship. Failure to analyze it as a relationship between whole bodies politic may partly explain why the systematic effort to improve relations in the 1970s—*détente*—foundered. In other settings, working relationships have deteriorated unexpectedly, as between Serbs and neighbors in the former Yugoslavia or between racial and ethnic groups in U.S. cities. Analyzing them deeply as relationships might enable us to do better at preventing similar tragedies.

The concept of relationship is not a dream of utopia. Relationships are among the most pervasive phenomena in life. We are born because of them and into them. They sustain us through life. They can be good or bad; mature or immature; loving or angry; nurturing or vindictive; constructive or destructive; cooperative or confrontational. But they are part of life. Why should we ignore them in favor of an incomplete, reductionist, rationalistic view of political affairs?

The concept of relationship is my effort—drawn from experience—to understand more of how the political, social, and economic world works. It is my personal effort, but that—according to Albert Einstein in his famous metaphor of the "closed watch"—is what concepts are:

> Physical concepts are free creations of the human mind, and are not, however it may seem, uniquely determined by the external world. In our endeavor to understand reality we are somewhat like a man trying to understand the mechanism of a closed watch. He sees the face and the moving hands, even hears its ticking, but he has no way of opening the case. If he is ingenious he may form some picture of a mechanism which could be responsible for all the things he observes, but he may never be quite sure his picture is the only one which could explain his observations. . . . But he certainly believes that, as his knowledge increases, his picture of reality will become simpler and simpler and will explain a wider and wider range of his sensuous impressions.[21]

In that spirit I offer the concept of relationship.

Dialogue Makes It Happen

CHAPTER FIVE

A Different Way of Thinking—Another Way of Relating

Politics is about relationships among significant clusters of citizens in a cumulative, multilevel, and open-ended process of continuous interaction over time in whole bodies politic across permeable borders, either within or between countries or communities. In a whole body politic, citizens inside government must perform their tasks wisely, effectively, justly, and compassionately. In a whole body politic, citizens outside government must engage in the work of the body politic to do for themselves and for the greater good what governments cannot do. In a whole body politic, citizens inside and outside government together must relate in mutually respectful and productive ways. The political project of the twenty-first century—the citizens' century—is to build whole bodies politic.

This is the hypothesis to be tested. The old paradigm does not work. It does not address whole bodies politic. It excludes most of the world's people. It wastefully ignores the boundless resources that they could provide if engaged. Would the relational paradigm and its concept of relationship open the door to building whole bodies politic?

The inevitable question: "What difference will thinking this way make?" What if we go beyond focusing on elite power centers and engage whole bodies politic? What if we move from our argumentative, litigious, confrontational culture to one in which citizens in and out of government build relationships to work together effectively with mutual respect? These are the questions I invite you to explore in the following stories and in honest probing of your own experience. I do not ask: Can it happen? It is happening. I ask: What difference will it make if it happens more broadly? And how can that happen?

To begin, I invite you to consider the five stories that follow—stories of people in widely different places and conditions who are speaking the language of the relational paradigm instinctively from experience. They do so without thinking of paradigms. That they do so from diverse experiences may demonstrate the authenticity of a new way of thinking and relating.

Bodies politic are "whole" when all citizens are included in the polity's work. That is why we speak of a *multilevel* process of continuous interaction. From my own intensive involvement as a diplomat in the Arab–Israeli–Palestinian peace process in the 1970s, I have written in *The Other Walls: The Arab-Israeli Peace Process in a Global Perspective*[1] about a creative intergovernmental political process that produced five formal agreements in six years and changed the political environment. Out of government, I have developed the process of Sustained Dialogue for engaging the policy-influencing community and ultimately in Tajikistan enabling members of that community through their Public Committee for Democratic Processes to reach out to ever widening circles of citizens. Sustained Dialogue was the focus of *A Public Peace Process: Sustained Dialogue to Transform Racial and Ethnic Conflicts*.[2] The purpose of this book—the third in an unintended trilogy—is to nurture a political environment in which these ever widening circles can be extended to engage the world's greatest untapped resource—citizens outside government—to deal with the most daunting challenges of the citizens' century.

What will enable citizens to make that shift? Two steps: defining our task differently and relating differently.

First, in preceding chapters to refocus our task, I have presented a "proper world view, appropriate for its time," a paradigm for the study and practice of politics reflecting that worldview, and the concept of relationship as the real-world context in which that paradigm is revealed, studied, and put to work. Second, I have presented the Citizens' Political Process and its several instruments of dialogue as practical ways of transforming, building, and conducting the relationships that are the citizens' vehicle for generating the power to do their work.

The task, then, is not for significant clusters of citizens to design better actions but rather to see themselves as conducting the cumulative, multilevel, open-ended process of continuous interaction that builds the relationships essential to effective economies and bodies politic. These relationships can generate power—the capacity to influence the course of events. The citizens' instrument is not primarily adversarial politics, litigation, mediation, negotiation, legislation, or strategic planning. Their instrument is dialogue—a particular way of relating.

In short, "a different way of *thinking*, another way of *relating*." To repeat: The concepts we use to understand the world around us determine how we act; thinking in terms of relationship changes how we *inter*act. Politics is about relationship; dialogue is its instrument.

The Research Questions

My method of evaluation is to conceptualize experience as a framework for acting and then to ask whether the actors are interacting more productively. If the framework is "relationships among significant clusters of citizens in a cumulative, multilevel, and open-ended process of continuous interaction," what are the questions for judging what is being accomplished?

First, can citizens engage in public work—the work of improving the quality of their lives together? Two related questions: What causes citizens to engage? What enables citizens to engage in ways that make a difference?

Second, how can citizens extend their reach beyond their immediate spheres of contact to influence the larger political setting that enhances or constricts citizens' capacities to enlarge their opportunities?

Third, when and how is a catalyst useful or not useful in helping citizens to find an appropriate instrument or to extend their reach beyond their limited setting by connecting with others who share their goals? What characterizes the connectors?

Fourth, what enhances the capacities of citizens inside government and outside government to collaborate in the public interest—to bridge the disconnect that presently divides them?

Citizens outside government in the Citizens' Political Process ask themselves continuously: What did *we* set out to do? How are *we* doing? Answering these questions together are the essence of civic learning.

Fifth, beyond these questions that focus on citizens as political actors are conceptual questions of interest for those who analyze their work: Do citizens engaging their own problems in different settings instinctively voice a way of thinking about politics that differs from the traditional? Do the instruments they choose—for example, dialogue and deliberation rather than confrontational politics—reflect that different way of thinking and relating? Have they naturally resorted to dialogue in some form? Do they use vocabulary reflecting—in their own terms—that of the relational paradigm and the concept of relationship? Have they assumed the role of political actors even though they have little of what political scientists have defined as power?

In probing for answers to these conceptual questions, I have listened to citizens in each setting with the following questions in mind:

- What seems to be citizens' intuitive understanding of political life? Is it focused on the structures and machinery of power traditionally defined, or do they sense the potential wholeness—the multilevel range of interactions—of bodies politic?
- Do citizens think and talk in terms of relationship?
- What does using the five components of the concept of relationship as an analytical framework reveal about the relationships underlying the problems people face? Is it a usable analytical tool?
- What instruments do they see as most useful in bringing about change? How do these relate to traditional instruments for solving problems?
- What conclusions do we draw from the analysis?

The chapters that follow provide some initial material for responding to these questions. Do the relational paradigm and the concept of relationship provide more comprehensive analytical tools in understanding whole bodies politic than focusing on the acts of government and a political elite? Do they provide more useful instruments for organizing action? What do we hear that affirms, further refines, or dismisses the relational paradigm?

The Chapters Ahead

The worldview presented in chapter two, the paradigm in chapter three, the concept of relationship in chapter four, and the processes of dialogue in chapter one are conceptualizations of experience. They are not theoretical constructs. To use a word I much prefer, they are "frameworks"—ideas that frame our work. They are ideas to be internalized and made to work for us. They are not theoretically designed models to be applied slavishly. The purpose of the next chapters is to probe whether others facing great challenges have come to comparable conclusions and whether using this approach provides an alternative to present ways of acting.

Chapter six on the transformation in South Africa in its analysis of the identities of the parties to the conflict virtually attributes the nature of the change in significant measure to the African philosophy of *ubuntu*, which holds that "I am a person only through another person." The task, as participants saw it, was to transform a relationship. The structural change has been completed; the next challenge, as many South Africans now define it, is to transform human relationships—reconciliation—across many remaining lines of division. What is exciting in our context is to hear key actors use the language of the new paradigm before being exposed to it.

Chapter seven recounts the experience of three towns in Tajikistan, the poorest of the former Soviet republics in Central Asia on the border with Afghanistan. Deeply riven during the post-independence civil war in the early 1990s, citizens in three towns, after the transition to peace, formed Economic Development Committees to stitch their communities back together by improving their economic possibilities. Using a hybrid version of the Citizens' Political Process, they designed projects that would enlarge the number of engaged citizens. Citizen leaders in two of these towns then began working with other towns to see whether their experience could be more broadly useful. Their aspiration is to build a network impressive enough in its results ultimately to have nationwide impact.

Chapter eight turns to citizens in West Virginia, one of the poorer states in the United States, who in the early 1990s began using a deliberative process to bring citizens together in steadily widening circles until they had created state-wide networks. They have begun experimenting with ways of drawing the legislature and the governor into their network. Their deliberations have led to actions in a broad range of fields.

Chapters nine and ten in successive steps shift the focus from citizens as political actors to relationships between countries—between whole bodies politic. I make that shift in two steps—first focusing on how citizens of two bodies politic view the relationship between them and second, focusing on how governments might conduct the relationship more productively if they were to think in terms of an overall relationship. These chapters focus on two of the most important and potentially dangerous international relationships of the United States in the twenty-first century. Both are written within the framework of the concept of relationship, each with a different point of entry.

Chapter nine on the Russian-U.S. relationship reflects for the first time the insights of citizens of the two countries expressed in more than a hundred mirror-image public forums on how the relationship between the two countries should be conducted. This analysis has been accomplished in the context of what we at the Kettering Foundation and our Russian colleagues are calling the "New Dartmouth Conference." It has also been tested in two dialogues with Russian colleagues in the Dartmouth Conference Regional Conflicts Task Force. Working from this analysis, the next step in the project is to determine how the thinking of citizens about the relationship can be conveyed in effective and compelling ways to those making government policies.

In chapter ten, I have shifted focus from citizens outside government to citizens inside government. From more than 15 years of dialogue with Chinese colleagues and from my own experience of 25 years in the U.S. government, I have analyzed the overall relationship between China and the United States. I have checked my approach in yearly dialogues, in numerous interviews with Chinese scholars and diplomats, and in seminars at leading Chinese universities. I have used my concept of relationship to suggest how in a small dialogue group one could identify approaches to changing the overall relationship. As a former diplomat, I have also suggested that the two governments could conduct the relationship more effectively if they focused on the overall relationship.

The examples could go on, but I want to keep this book to manageable size. My hope is that practitioners will begin applying this way of thinking to their own challenges and that scholars will be intrigued by the possibilities of a new paradigm for the study as well as the practice of politics.

Each story is different. Each is told in its own complexity and in its own voice. Variables are numberless. These stories are offered in hopes that others may find inspiration and insight in them. As you read, please listen for the notes of the relational paradigm in the voices of the actors; please look through the lenses of the relational paradigm and the concept of relationship to see whether these enhance your understanding. Please look to see how thinking this way affected the actors. Please ponder how this way of thinking and relating may reflect your experience.

CHAPTER SIX

Transformation in South Africa: A People Engaged

At the end of a two-hour conversation in his Johannesburg home over tea in September 1999, my wife and I moved to take our leave of Allister Sparks, prize-winning South African journalist and one-time editor of the *Rand Daily Mail*, the country's leading opposition newspaper. He concluded our conversation with this peroration after citing a statement by the U.S. ambassador at a dinner the previous evening that "all countries have a stake in South Africa":

> Right at the end of a century which has arguably been the most terrible in all history—millions have died because of ideology and racial nationalism all the way through to Bosnia, Rwanda, Chechnya—we, who have been the polecat of the world because of our ideology and our racism, are actually pointing the way to the next century. And we've got to get it right!
>
> This place is the world in microcosm. One quarter of the world's population is developed, rich, and white. Three quarters are dark-skinned, poor, and underdeveloped. These are exactly our proportions and our circumstances. So this is the world in microcosm.
>
> I don't believe the world can continue to function with its own kind of segregation. You Americans have armies of people along the Rio Grande River to keep out the poor, the unwashed; others are trying to stop them from crossing the Mediterranean. It's all apartheid really. Not in my backyard. Let my country remain prosperous.
>
> Can we all remain islands of prosperity in an ocean of poverty? We can't. And it's not only South Africa. Look at our continent—our backyard. We can't survive unless we can pioneer some kind of African recovery. I don't believe the world can survive with a continent of a billion people that sinks into an abyss of poverty, misery, environmental decay, and God knows what else.
>
> So this place matters. If we fail, Africa fails. If Africa fails, it will be an enormous global problem.[1]

And so we begin with South Africa in addressing what difference the relational paradigm makes. Violence pervades the story—the violence of conquest; the violence of institutions that exclude, discriminate, and repress; and the violence of an angry resistance. It is also a story of men and women understanding the wholeness of a body politic, sensing the power in mutually reinforcing interactions, learning to talk with the enemy, building new relationships through dialogue, and historically believing that people are people only in relationship.

Despite pervasive violence, the "miracle" in South Africa, as it has been called, is that there was no bloodbath, no massive revenge by blacks against whites for three centuries of oppression, but rather the establishment of a "nonracial" society. As Sparks said: "We were all going to die in a bloodbath. Armageddon was coming. When you've escaped Armageddon, it's no time to become a pessimist!" What was in South African souls and worldview that made creation of a nonracial society top priority?

Answers have come from numerous perspectives, many with compelling elements of truth. My purpose is not to write a detailed analysis. This chapter reviews the South African transformation through the minds, eyes, and words of key actors in that transformation. Although they might not always use the words I use, their accounts demonstrate that the relational paradigm and the concept of relationship played out in dialogue pulls together a more comprehensive picture than the traditional political paradigm would offer. It is a richly human story.

Relationships among Whole Human Beings in a Whole Body Politic

My first answer came from Pravin Gordhan, head of the revenue service when I interviewed him in September 1999. He described how his way of thinking developed from the mid-1970s to the early 1990s:

> *There was a picture of change made up of more than just who sits in power.* There was a complex understanding about what the nature of change would be. If you see your objective as dismantling one system and replacing it with another, *change is of a holistic order.* In the first instance, yes, you have to have access to political power; in the second instance, that access would allow you to have the resources, the authority, and the legislative means to introduce other changes; third, that would have to be underpinned by changes in the economy; fourthly, there would be a social element to this change which involved *a change in relationships—the development of a nonracial culture, reconciliation of sorts between black and white, introducing a new set of values* which would enable people to respect each other, to accept each other as equals, etc. [emphasis added].[2]

As South Africans look back on the decade from the early 1980s to the mid-1990s, they reflect on the cumulative impact of citizen engagement, armed struggle, and international economic and political pressure coupled with readiness to negotiate—a multilevel political process always in motion. As Leon Wessels, a National Party negotiator, former cabinet member, member of the Truth and Reconciliation Commission, and then member of parliament said: "We never arrive. We're always on the move."[3] A whole body politic in motion.

A critical part of this picture of a multilevel political process is, in the words of Charles Villa-Vicencio, then a theologian at the University of Cape Town and a minister of the Anglican Church, that "we had a strong civil society. The apartheid government didn't like that. They were never able to attack the churches. The churches and NGOs were creating a space in the early 1980s where people began saying, 'It can't go on like this.' "[4]

Voice after voice sounded the emptiness of the conventional concept of power. "Power was the dominant philosophy among white politicians," said Villa-Vicencio. "This was the philosophy backed by the West, supported by Calvinist theology. We had God on our side. *Political theory was a theory of force*" (emphasis added).[5] Nelson Mandela put the counterview succinctly to a leading general: "We have concluded that we can't overthrow you militarily, but I hope you know you can't kill all of us." Again to quote Villa-Vicencio: "What began to crack this philosophy of power was that the top military people began to tell the top politicians, 'This is a war we cannot win.' "[6]

Scholars of negotiation and conflict resolution echoed these thoughts. As Laurie Nathan, then director of the Centre for Conflict Resolution in Cape Town, said: "*We are intensely critical of power-based negotiation in a civil war. . . .* such efforts are ineffectual and counterproductive. They heighten insecurity and intransigence. When people are fighting over freedom, justice, security, identity, they will not be easily bullied. They will die for their cause. *The application of coercive force won't last* (emphasis added)."[7]

Nathan also emphasized the multilevel talks that became an integral part of the peace process. In that context, he underscored the importance of both governmental and community structures. "You need both." While "states provide framework and legitimacy, *community talks address relationships*— our personal hatreds and grievances (emphasis added)."

Finally, many emphasized the importance of a complete change of lenses. As Paul Graham, executive director of the Institute for Democracy in South Africa (IDASA), one of the first NGOs to promote dialogue across the lines of apartheid, put it: "The negotiations were not about inclusion. They were not about adjusting the system within a narrowly defined rectangle. They were rather about defining a new field to play on."[8] Others described the story of the 1980s in terms of initial efforts and ultimate inadequacy of incremental reforms.

Having noted the themes of the relational paradigm in the comments above, I continue with sketches of the two main protagonists in the relationships that were changed. My framework is the five components of relationship described in chapters three and four. The fifth—patterns of interaction—leads naturally into how their interactions set the stage for the transformation. I repeat: I do not present a complete history. My point is that looking at this remarkable story through the lenses of the relational paradigm and the concept of relationship makes more sense than trying to explain what happened by focusing on the structures of traditionally defined power.

Parties to the Critical Relationships

Throughout much of this history, to quote Allister Sparks: ". . . what is deeper than any [physical division] is the division that runs through the psyche of the nation. . . . Two minds, two worlds, one country. . . . where people occupy the same space but live in different time frames so that they do not see each other and perceive different realities."[9] Of those two minds were four main peoples—the indigenous blacks and the mix of peoples called "colored," on the one side, and the white Afrikaner and English, on the other. For brevity's sake, I focus only on the indigenous black Africans and the Afrikaners. My focus is first the perpetrators and objects of apartheid and then to probe how they transformed their relationships without a full-scale bloodbath.

Sparks describes life in southern Africa before the coming of the white man:

> Traditional African societies were sophisticated organisms. . . . In their communal relationships and elaborate links of mutual responsibility, with their generic love of children and respect for the aged, they cultivated a respect for human values and human worth far in advance of the materialistic West.
>
> Political systems were interwoven with the social order, with chieftancies based on extensions of family and lineage relationships. Whites, given their own history of autocratic monarchies, mistook the tribal chiefs for dictators and dealt with them accordingly. In fact, the chiefs' powers were heavily circumscribed and the systems they presided over incorporated a considerable degree of grass-roots democracy. At the time that the first Portuguese navigators made their voyages of discovery around the Cape of Good Hope, it is arguable that Darkest Africa was a more democratic place than the medieval Europe from which they had sailed.[10]

When Jan van Riebeeck landed in 1652 at what is now Cape Town with a small Dutch group to plant a victualing station for Dutch trading ships, that area was inhabited by a yellow-skinned Stone Age people called the Khoikhoi. A migration of black Africans from the north was underway, bringing with it agricultural cultivation and "the Iron Age culture—the hoe and the spear." They eventually absorbed the indigenous people but had not quite reached the tip of the continent, though the white settlers were aware of them—the Xhosa—a little farther east. The story of the next century and a half is that of the two very different peoples who were joined in this drama at its outset.

The indigenous Africans. At the beginning, there were several indigenous peoples. What follows depicts the strains who became the dominant people.

Identity

Sparks roots the identity of the indigenous African peoples in their experience with the harsh extremes of life in this part of Africa—the sharp swings between plenty and dire want.

> African societies cushioned themselves against these capricious changes of fortune by building elaborate systems of mutual support. If disaster struck one person he could turn to another for help, and the same went for whole communities. The social systems were based on units of the extended family, in which ties of kinship, age group, and other associations were woven together into a web of relationships that extended over a wide area. . . . Thus was created a social security system of reciprocal obligations.[11]

Then Sparks introduces a key concept that may lie at the heart of responses to the question: Why did the indigenous African leaders commit themselves to a nonracial society rather than a segregated one? The concept is called *ubuntu.* Archbishop Desmond Tutu frequently joined it with the Christian heritage of black and colored Africans.

> . . . these traditional African societies placed a high value on human worth, but it was a humanism that found its expression in a communal context rather than in the individualism of the West. There is a word for it in the Nguni languages, *ubuntu.* . . . It is a subtle and not easily translatable concept which means broadly that each individual's humanity is ideally expressed through his relationship with others and theirs in turn through a recognition of his humanity. . . . [As] goes the Xhosa proverb—"People are people through other people." It is a saying that Archbishop Desmond Tutu likes to quote, and it never fails to bring sighs and nods of understanding from his black audiences.[12]

Although history heard different voices emerge in response to the desperation of the black and colored people, it may be that this cultural heritage in the souls of leaders—more than any other single factor—accounted for the character of the transformation. In any case, it was the foundation of this African culture and identity.

Interests

One of the basic interests of the black Africans is a strong commitment to the land. As Sparks puts it:

> One thing the subsistence economy does produce is an intense, life-long passion for the land. For land means security—not only those patches that are actually under cultivation or providing pasturage for livestock but also the surrounding bushveld, which in the worst of times, when all the crops have failed and all the cattle have died, will still yield a few edible leaves and roots and grubs and so sustain the life of the tribe. Land and community became inseparable, woven together in the matrix of tribal society. The land was revered in ritual, it held the bodies of the tribal ancestors, it was the concretion of the tribe itself, the thing that gave it life and substance and security and identity. It could not be owned individually. It was held by the tribe collectively and vested in the chief, who could allocate its use but not its title.[13]

Power

In addition to writing of the black African concept of *ubuntu*—the "remarkable strength of affection" and "general spirit of sharing"—Sparks cites other observations of whites who spent time among the blacks in those early days:

> These early visitors were impressed, too, with the amount of dem-ocratic debate that took place within tribal systems, with the high degree of freedom to criticize the chiefs that was permitted, and with the application of the rule of law through a sophisticated court system presided over by the chiefs but in which the chiefs themselves were beneath the law and could be tried and fined by their own councillors.
> . . . "The king is absolute sovereign," Lichtenstein wrote. "Yet there is a power to balance his in the people; he governs only as long as they choose to obey."[14] . . . Families would simply pack up and leave, emigrating to another chiefdom where they would be assured of a welcome since they would add to its wealth and prestige. This was the public's ultimate sanction.[15]

Perceptions, Misperceptions, and Stereotypes

Strangely, the perceptions of black Africans seemed to be not so much perceptions of the whites alone as a response to all the elements of a harsh environment. They were a combination of the insecurity, oppression, and hourly uncertainties they faced and some inner resilience. It seemed impossible to feel hope or self-esteem in light of the obstacles to self-realization and self-fulfillment. "And yet," as Sparks writes, "when one has considered all this adversity, all the violence and oppression and psychological damage, one comes back again and again to the wondrous truth that the black townships . . . are not places of despair. . . . [but] full of vitality, life, and laughter, still exuding an enduring sense of survivability."[16]

For all of that, the blacks, as any servant or oppressed group, had to spend time and energy analyzing their white masters so as to seem to please them, to understand their limits, to strike back at them in ways subtle enough to avoid punishment. As Sparks writes: "Servitude produces habits of everyday resistance on the part of people who feel they are victims of an exploitative system they cannot fight or change, and who try therefore to work it to their minimum disadvantage. Foot dragging, evasiveness, negligence, desertion, false compliance, pilfering, feigned ignorance, carelessness, sabotage—these have been the weapons of the weak in the class struggle throughout history and their use in South Africa reinforces the stereotype."[17] That quiet resistance requires insight into the minds they are wrestling with.

Patterns of Interaction

As Charles Villa-Vicencio told me concisely: "The history of black politics in this country is a history of negotiation. The African National Congress has always been a very moderate political party with the elite as products of mission schools."[18]

Sparks again put the point in terms of the overriding need to preserve community in the face of hardship and potential disaster: "Although the expression of dissent was permitted and even encouraged, the object was to reach agreement and avoid division. In this compromise and consensus one again sees the pervasive influence of the subsistence economy and the need to avoid divisiveness in order to survive its uncertainties." He continued:

> The concept of a majority vote prevailing over a dissenting minority was totally alien to traditional African societies and remains so in some measure to this day. With time never a consideration in these unhurried communities, they were prepared to continue the discussion for as long as it took to iron out the last point of disagreement and bring the last dissenter into a consensus agreement.
>
> The court systems, too, were aimed more at reconciling disputes than enforcing a penal code.[19]

The Afrikaner. The unfolding experience of the Dutch settlers and the evolution of a new identity is a more complex story. Sparks reflects on the irony that the Dutch, in establishing this reprovisioning station, explicitly sought to avoid establishing a colony. "Yet these people who came without intending to settle stayed to become the most permanent and ineradicable settlers in all of Africa. They cut their ties with Europe, called themselves Afrikaners, and evolved a new language called Afrikaans, yet they continued to set themselves apart from Africa and its people."[20]

Identity

The Europe that the Dutch settlers left was a Europe in revolution on several fronts at the same time—intellectual, artistic, scientific, political, and theological. As Sparks recalls, Guttenberg had just invented the printing press; the primacy of the Roman Catholic Church was being challenged; new ideas about humans' relationship to God and to each other in polities were abroad.

> Holland was in the forefront of these events. Fired by Calvinist republicanism . . . the Dutch had just emerged from eighty years of bitter struggle to win their political and religious independence from the tyrannous domination of Hapsburg Spain. . . . As Jan van Riebeeck readied himself to sail for the Cape in the spring of 1652 . . . , Amsterdam was the greatest commercial centre in the world and the Vereenigde Oostindische Compagnie (VOC)—the United East India Company—for which he worked was the world's biggest commercial enterprise. . . . This was the Golden Age of Dutch civilization.[21]

To understand the identity of those Dutch who went to the southern tip of Africa, writers describe the Dutch as emerging from their long war with Spain and their struggles with the sea with "a national myth of a reenacted Exodus" in "a war for religious as well as national independence." Their leader, William of Orange, was portrayed as leading his people from bondage into their promised land. As Sparks develops the Biblical roots of this identity:

> The Dutch church . . . in 1618 . . . laid down as official dogma a sternly conservative interpretation of the predestination doctrine [of John Calvin], which holds that God has foreordained some of mankind for grace and salvation and others for eternal damnation.
>   As Erich Fromm and other psychologists have suggested, this doctrine can form the basis of a "chosen people" outlook. Implicit in it is the principle of the basic inequality of men.[22]

Sparks acknowledges that the first Dutch settlers—largely social and economic failures needing work—probably had little sense of themselves as a "chosen people" or indeed as a people at all. By the early nineteenth century, however, when it became politically necessary in their contest with the British to create a sense of peoplehood, the elite that had by then emerged was quite capable of articulating such a nationalist philosophy. The evolution of this thinking had a number of roots, and it is not my purpose to go into it in detail. It is enough here to point to these sources of the later doctrine of apartheid, which was thoroughly sanctioned by the mainline church. Those who want to read further should turn to Sparks' brilliant analysis in chapter two of *The Mind of South Africa*.

The real saga of the birth of a people began as some of the settlers broke away from the Company and began to trek inland. "They lived on their own," Sparks writes, "out of touch with the world, four months' sailing time from Europe and another one or two by ox wagon from where the ships called in, without . . . even a postal service. . . . There were no books and no schools . . . only the great States Bible . . . which each family carried with it and which was read with solemn ceremony and increasing difficulty as literacy dwindled. . . . This was the God of Abraham talking directly to his people of their circumstances."[23]

As Sparks concludes, citing an historian of South Africa, C. W. de Kiewiet: ". . . it was in the long quietude of the eighteenth century that the Boer race was formed. Their isolation froze them in time. . . . The early Afrikaners developed, in their way, perhaps the most boundless individualism that has existed anywhere. They built few villages and felt cramped if they lived within sight of a neighbour's chimney smoke. They had almost no institutions. Each man was absolute master of his own affairs, self-reliant, unencumbered, free. Here was the very opposite of *ubuntu*."[24]

Sparks broadens his picture by cautioning against "skimming too easily over the major role that Cape Afrikaners played in the forging of Afrikaner nationalism and its ideology of apartheid. . . . Strike the average between [those who trekked and those who did not] and you will have the core around which the mind of the Afrikaner was shaped during the six generations they were lost in Africa, a people who missed the momentous developments of eighteenth-century Europe, the Age of Reason in which liberalism and democracy were born and which had its climax in the great revolution of the French bourgeoisie; a people who spent that time instead in a deep solitude which, if anything, took them back to an even more elementary existence than the seventeenth-century Europe their forebears had left; a people who became, surely, the simplest and most backward fragment of Western civilization in modern times."[25]

Interests

Flowing from their identity, the foundational interest of the Afrikaner seems obvious: to create, protect, and preserve space where he could be his own master. This often meant trekking to new space when life in the old became too irksome. It meant developing the abilities needed to produce in that space what he needed for survival or what he needed to trade for what he could not produce.

Over time, interests came to include establishing a political position vis-à-vis the English that permitted him to defend that space and that identity. In the end, it meant developing and enforcing the political and social system called apartheid that, he hoped, would make permanent for himself and his posterity a nation that embodied the Afrikaner identity.

As many analysts have noted, the South African experience differed from other experiences in decolonization in one major respect. The primary white colonizers had no place to go home to. Whereas the English would feel culturally at home in many British Commonwealth countries, the Afrikaner had cut himself off from his country of origin. Yet he had also isolated himself from Africa and the black Africans. So his primary interest has been protecting a place to survive.

Power

Early experience led to a distinct understanding of the roots of power as force. Van Riebeeck was under constant pressure from his company to reduce his staff. To maintain the cohort he felt essential, he removed a number from the employment rolls and set them up on their own farms to grow produce and sell it to the company. The land taken for this purpose had belonged for time uncountable to the indigenous people. When they resisted, the settlers forced them back and declared the land theirs by right of conquest. "Thus was established . . . a tradition that the land was the white South Africans' for the taking," writes Sparks. "It was the first act in a long process of land dispossession that combined with slavery and cheap labour to create the institutions and the habits of the apartheid society." Sparks called what followed, "one of the most remarkable settlements in the history of colonialism. A small and scattered community of white men drifted beyond the effective reach of any law or administrative arm and lost themselves like so many Robinson Crusoes in the vastness of Africa for a century and a half"[26]—each one exercising without the restraint of any law such power as he could generate.

Only two centuries later did this sense of absolute power crack. To repeat Villa-Vicencio's reflection: "The change ultimately came when Afrikaner military leaders told political leaders, 'This is a war we cannot win.' "[27]

Perceptions and Stereotypes

The Afrikaners' stereotype of the blacks was the product of their interaction: the ethnocentric Afrikaners protected a master–servant relationship, rarely getting close enough to the blacks to know what was really in their minds; the blacks developed certain defense mechanisms and presented an image of themselves designed to keep the whites "off their backs" to the extent possible. The Afrikaner stereotype of the black African reflected the image of blacks as "stupid and feckless, mildly dishonest, but generally good-natured, a child dependent on whites for guidance and who, given it, is basically content with his lot provided he can be shielded from the influence of 'agitators' and the outside world."[28]

Referring to the blacks' passion for the land, Sparks writes: "This, too, the Europeans failed to understand as they advanced in their settlement, pressing the tribes back and dispossessing them of their land with little idea of the social disruption and psychological trauma they were causing." He continued:

> From the beginning, whites saw only those surface manifestations of African culture and the African mind that conflicted with their own concepts of approved social behaviour. What they failed to see, because they were not disposed to get close enough to do so, was the complexity and subtle texture of traditional African social organization, the restraints on the exercise of chiefly power, the elements of grass-roots democracy, the balance between communal, family, and individual rights, and the pervasive spirit of mutual obligation and respect, the spirit of *ubuntu*.
>
> Subsistence thinking was not an energizing influence. It inclined to a fatalistic outlook, which Europeans mistook for fecklessness and laziness. . . . There is no spirit of acquisitiveness in a subsistence economy, no deep-seated sense of work being intrinsically good apart from what it can produce, or idleness being shameful; nor any great pressure to plan and save for the future when there is no snowbound winter. Time is of little consequence when it is related only to the rising and the setting of the sun and the slow-changing seasons, when there is nowhere to go and there are no deadlines to keep.[29]

On the other hand, the Afrikaners came to despise the British missionaries, whose championing of racial equality assaulted their righteous sense of superiority over the blacks. The missionaries epitomized the interference to the way of life that the British administration represented.

Patterns of Interaction

The historic experience of many Afrikaners led them to develop their own way of dealing with others. "Always it was the most intransigent and disputatious spirits who trekked farthest, drawing ever deeper into isolation as they went. The isolation sank into their soul, feeding their pride and intensifying their obduracy," writes Sparks. "Each man became king on his own estate, unwilling to tolerate any challenge to his authority or questioning of his judgment. It made them a schismatic people who never acquired the habit of settling disputes through negotiation and compromise."[30]

As Villa-Vicencio commented: "Power was the dominant philosophy among white politicians. 'Make the black people understand that we will kill you.' . . . Political theory was a theory of force."[31]

Many have reflected on the fact that the master–slave relationship debases both and locks both in a mutually destructive relationship. In churchman Allan Boesak's words: "Whites will never be free as long as they have to kill our children in order to safeguard their own privileged position."[32]

The British presence grew out of the need to protect the Empire's "lifeline to India" during the struggle with Napoleonic France, first at the request of the Dutch in 1803 and then in earnest with their first group of settlers in 1820. It would be impossible to capture the powerful impact and the ambiguous role of the "English-speaking South Africans" as eloquently as does Allister Sparks, speaking of his own people. Without doing justice to his characterization, I must record his main points, written before 1990 and the transformation:

> The impact on the Afrikaners of the British arrival was enormous. Having missed the eighteenth century, they had the nineteenth burst in on them. . . .
>
> The impact on the blacks was no less profound. By the time the black tribes encountered the Trekboers on the eastern frontier, the latter had adopted a lifestyle not much different from their own. Only with the arrival of the British did they feel the destabilizing force of the modern world on their ancient institutions. Though the Afrikaners acquired the notoriety, it was the British who first broke black power, crushing the tribes in war, annexing their territory, and eroding their institutions with Christianization, education, and finally industrialization and urbanization.
>
> In truth the British created modern South Africa. Whereas the Afrikaners left Europe behind them, the English brought it with them. . . .
>
> The British dominated the Afrikaners economically and defeated them militarily, but they lost out to them politically, and the English-speaking South Africans are now a curiously helpless and rather pathetic community who do not identify with either side in the conflict of nationalisms they helped to create and cannot define a role for themselves in between.[33]

In the interest of focus on the ultimate conflict between the blacks and the Afrikaner policy of apartheid, I forego a detailed analysis of the English settlers' mind-set. I present only a minimal summary of the interactions between the English and the Afrikaners necessary to set the stage for that conflict.

With the coming of the British, as Sparks captures the setting in the early nineteenth century: "The age of separate freedom was at an end." Until now, the land had been big enough, for the most part, for the Afrikaners and the indigenous Africans each to find his own place. Now the Afrikaners felt the need to get beyond the reach of the intrusive British administration, and the indigenous Africans felt the pressure of the British in front of them and the buildup of the black migration behind them. "The age of interaction had begun, an age that commenced with the drama of attempted escape and a blood-spattered dispersal before the players came together again into an ongoing relationship of rejection and attraction, of mutual antipathy and dependency."[34]

In 1835, a mass exodus of Boers from the Cape Colony began as some fourteen thousand "Voortrekkers" became part of what came to be called the "Great Trek" toward the northern and eastern parts of the country. As they proceeded, they became enmeshed in warfare among black tribes kindled as they coped with their own increasingly overcrowded lands. My purpose is not to get into these clashes, but only to say that this Afrikaner experience would become an epic in the Afrikaner drama as Afrikaner nationalism took shape in the face of growing British domination. In 1852 and 1854, the British recognized the independence of two Boer republics, the Orange Free State in the east and the Transvaal in the north.

The discovery of diamonds and the beginning of mining in 1870 and the discovery of gold in Witwatersrand in 1886 led to massive industrialization, urbanization, and transformation of the economy—and with it over-whelming British control of these new enterprises. Political control, however, came only at the expense of three years of war. The Boer War, 1899–1902, was a military victory for the British, but in the end it was not a political defeat for the Afrikaners. The British expected to subdue the Boer rebellion quickly but did so only after marshalling forces from around the globe. As Sparks summarizes the outcome:

> The Boers lost the war, but in a wave of reparative sentiment for the perceived injustice done to a small nation by a powerful one they won the peace. And in that victory their exclusionist credo—the notion that the land was theirs by divine right and that the indigenous blacks were aliens in it, whose role was to serve not participate—was extended from the two Boer republics over the whole of South Africa. It triumphed over the more inclusionist liberalism that had been established in the two British colonies and became national policy in a new independent country created out of the union of all four territories.[35]

The outcome of the war was one thing; meanwhile the industrial and urban revolutions gained momentum dramatically:

> Neither the Afrikaner nor the black tribesman was equipped to cope with life in the city—the alien city where the Englishman was *baas*—and as they surged there in their economic plight they came into explosive contact and competition.
>
>   The impact on both was immense. It hardened and changed the whole focus of Afrikaner nationalism, switching its reference point from conflict with the English to conflict with the blacks. And it ripped apart the fabric of black tribal life, turning a landless peasantry

into an urban proletariat, and awakening a political consciousness that eventually demanded its own national liberation from white mastery just as Afrikaners had demanded theirs from the British.[36]

The First Half of the Twentieth Century

I mention just four events in the next half-century so as to move quickly to the transformation.

First, it is important to recall the early influence of the colored community on black politics through the work of Mohandas Gandhi in their midst between 1893 and 1914. He had come to South Africa from India as a British-trained barrister to represent an Indian trading firm in a case to be tried before the Pretoria Supreme Court.[37] He spent the next twenty-one years leading the Indian community in passive resistance against a series of discriminatory laws and practices. Here he developed and demonstrated the power of peaceful protest. While he confined his work to the Indian community, in Sparks' words, ". . . for black South Africans, Gandhi was an inspiration." In 1912, when the African National Congress was formed, "he was in a sense its progenitor."

Second, in 1905, the new parliament passed a Land Act that prohibited blacks from owning land outside the "reserves." Through the previous quarter-century, black peasants had become significant producers in their own right and had even become substantial landowners. The whites saw them as threats. The Land Act in one step threw more than a million blacks into the pool of "captive labor." In reaction, three young black lawyers in Johannesburg called a national conference of black leaders. What became the African National Congress (ANC) was formed in January 1912. This movement spawned protests and organizations over the following years. Most vital for the later transformation was its character, which is captured by Sparks in these words:

> Their experience has produced a black nationalism, just as the Afrikaner sense of grievance produced Afrikaner nationalism. But it is not a narrow, narcissistic, exclusivist nationalism intent on preserving its own little *volk* and isolating itself in its self-centered anxiety from the rest of mankind. Black nationalism embraces mankind. It does not shrink from humanity, it wants to be part of humanity. "People are people through other people. . . ." It is an open, inclusivist, integrationist nationalism. "South Africa belongs to all who live in it, black and white," says the Freedom Charter adopted by an ANC-sponsored Congress of the People in 1955.[38]

Third was the formation of the Afrikaners' National Party in 1914 by James Barry Munnik Herzog. Its first purpose was to support the Afrikaners in finding their moorings in the newly urbanizing and industrializing society and in gaining the self-respect to deal with the British on an equal footing. After nine years as prime minister in the 1920s, he felt the time for reconciliation had come and, in 1933, he proposed the formation of a coalition government with Jan Smuts and the creation of a new United Party. But hardliners in the National Party broke away and formed the Purified National Party with Daniel Malan as its leader. The coalition broke up over the issue of neutrality in World War II with Smuts opting for association with Britain and the opportunity to take South Africa into the larger community of nations.

Fourth, through those years, the hardliners shaped the philosophy that became apartheid—a philosophy drawing together conservative thought in the Dutch Reformed Church, in the National Socialism of Nazi Germany, in the fashioning of an Afrikaner history with a reenactment in 1938 of the Great Trek, and in efforts to place Afrikaners in the British-dominated economy. All these strands were drawn together in the Broederbond, a secret society that began in 1918 in a small meeting devoted to improving Afrikaners' lot in urban society, which blossomed into a nationwide organization of some 12,000 members organized into 800 cells. In 1945, one of its leading members published a book, the translated title of which is *A Home for Posterity*. A follow-up was published in 1947.[39] The platform for apartheid was ready.

Apartheid Becomes Policy and
Resistance Deepens

In May 1948, Daniel Malan's National Party assumed leadership in the narrowest of election victories over Jan Smuts, a figure of international stature. The Afrikaners were in control and set about consolidating their program.

As minister of Native Affairs, the later prime minister, Hendrik Verwoerd was responsible for the Native Laws Amendment Act in 1952, which limited the right of blacks to live permanently in urban areas and required everyone else to return to his assigned tribal Bantustan where he would need to get a migrant labor contract to work in the city. He turned political authority back into traditional tribal channels, cutting out the new black intelligentsia. In the Bantu Education Act of 1953, the government took over all mission schools and prohibited blacks from attending the major English universities.[40]

In its first decade, the program was to legislate the practices of segregation that had become common. These practices lost their flexibility and became enforced national policy.

In the second decade, under Prime Minister Verwoerd, beginning in September 1958, apartheid took hold ideologically. "[F]rom 1958 to 1966 . . . Verwoerd made his indelible mark on South Africa," writes Sparks, "imposing an ideological cast of mind on Afrikaner nationalism that still [1990] keeps it in thrall, holding his successors captive long after the ideology itself has been revealed as manifestly unworkable."[41]

In a global atmosphere of decolonization, he proclaimed that the black tribal reserves could move toward self-government and independence. The government attempted to establish the Bantustans as working political entities.

"It was another of those great South African ironies that Verwoerd's determined effort to bring about a total separation of the races came at a time when this was least capable of achievement," Sparks writes. "For it coincided with the take-off phase of South Africa's industrial revolution, the transition from its primary stage of agriculture and mining, both extractive industries that needed large quantities of cheap, unskilled labour, to a more sophisticated manufacturing phase in which skills, and therefore training and permanency, became increasingly important."[42]

In June 1955, a Congress of the People had been called by an alliance of the ANC, the Indian Congress, the Coloured People's Congress, a white organization called the Congress of Democrats, including members of the outlawed Communist party, and the nonracial South African Congress of Trade Unions. Despite police intrusion, the group adopted its Freedom Charter: "We, the People of South Africa, declare for all our country and the world to know: that South Africa belongs to all who live in it, black and white, and that no government can justly claim authority unless it is based on the will of all the people."

In what Sparks calls "a monument to the remarkable spirit of reconciliation that somehow manages to survive under apartheid and that has acquired a kind of canonical status in the resistance movement," the Charter then states its goals: "the people shall govern; all national groups shall have equal rights; the people shall share in the country's wealth; the land shall be shared among those who work it; all shall be equal before the law; all shall enjoy equal human rights; there shall be work and security; the doors of learning and culture shall be opened; there shall be houses, security, and comfort; and there shall be peace and friendship." It continues with more concrete provisions. A year later, the authors of the Charter and the organizers of the Defiance Campaign were arrested. The government's case collapsed in March 1961.[43]

By that time another corner had been turned. The Sharpeville massacre of March 21, 1960, left 69 dead and 180 wounded and drew worldwide condemnation. In response to countrywide protests, the government declared the ANC and the Pan-African Congress (PAC), which had broken away from the ANC a year before, to be "unlawful organizations." The ANC reorganized itself to work underground with Nelson Mandela as leader of the National Action Council and Oliver Tambo sent abroad to marshal international support. When the government responded to its first actions with a massive show of force, the ANC decided that, if every nonviolent act was to be met with violence, it had no choice but to form a guerrilla unit called *Umkhonto we Sizwe*, Spear of the Nation, to sabotage key installations and economic targets, trying to avoid taking human life. Their first action took place on December 16, 1961, with the blowing up of electricity installations and government offices in Johannesburg and Port Elizabeth.[44] As a result, the government, in July 1963, arrested virtually the entire ANC leadership. Mandela and others were convicted and sentenced to life imprisonment.

Black politics went silent for more than a decade. It was left to white liberals to speak for the black cause until the Black Consciousness movement sparked by Steve Biko, a medical student at the University of Natal, formed the South African Students Organization in 1969. It emphasized building black self-reliance. The movement was overwhelmed by the 1976 uprising in Soweto.

What began on June 16, 1976, as a student protest against the requirement that half of all classes in black schools be taught in Afrikaans turned into another massacre. Before the violence ended, it "had spread to 160 different communities. Within a week 176 people were dead, within a year more than 600. The uprising lasted seventeen months before it was finally quelled in another wave of repressive action."[45]

Black protest gained powerful support from a growing movement of black theologians. With its roots in the period after Sharpeville, it gathered momentum after Soweto. In 1981, Allan Boesak, one of its leading figures, "took the lead in forming an Alliance of Black Reformed Christians under a charter that denounced apartheid as a sin and declared that 'the moral and theological justification of it is a travesty of the Gospel, a betrayal of the Reformed tradition, and a heresy.' "[46] A year later, Boesak took the case to the World Alliance of Reformed Churches in Ottawa, which supported that position. It is impossible to recount these developments here except to add that, of course, Desmond Tutu became a leading figure in the challenge to the Afrikaner church.

The Seeds of Transition:
"It Can't Go on Like This"

As Pravin Gordhan described his political maturing: "My generation grew up politically in the '70s. We had to make a choice about which path to follow—the Black Consciousness path or the Congress path, captured in the Freedom Charter in terms of its nonracialism, its particular concept of democracy—'South Africa belongs to all who live in it, black and white.' What was interesting about that way of thinking was a thorough commitment to nonracialism—an understanding that you're fighting a system and not individuals in it."[47]

Many South Africans feel that the first cracks in apartheid appeared in the economy after 1969 as blacks began to move into skilled jobs in industry. People of different races began working in the same spaces. A worker class emerged. As Roelf Meyer, later minister of Constitutional Development and the principal government negotiator of the new constitution, said: "The business community saw the handwriting on the wall. By the mid-'70s, I had started asking myself how we can proceed with this sort of thing. My generation was engaged in soul-searching. I went to parliament in '79 with a mission to contribute to reform." As Sparks writes, ". . . it had become obvious to even the most faithful believers that the policy's central objective, the reversal of black urbanization in order to achieve at least enough racial separation to legitimize the separate political structures, was simply unattainable. . . . Accepting the permanence of the urban blacks was simply coming to terms with a reality that could no longer be denied."[48]

The first half of the 1980s for the Afrikaner regime was a time of experiment with incremental reforms. It coupled new emphasis on blacks running their own affairs through their own municipal councils in black areas with creation of a third house of Parliament for the Indian and colored population. This left the blacks as the one group excluded from the political system; further, the specifics of measures affecting them revealed that the autonomy of their councils was specious.

> . . . they had to implement government policy rather than be responsive to their own electorates. . . . The black councils had to do apartheid's dirty work, policing its oppressive regulations, and if they did not do it satisfactorily they would be replaced by others who would for the pay and the perks that came with the job. . . .
>
> Worse still, a conjunct government policy held that the townships should become financially self-supporting now that they had their own councils. . . . Given the low level of commercial development on which taxes could be levied, that could only be done by big rent increases.[49]

While the white referendum in November 1983 supported the new constitution and the third house of parliament with a two-thirds vote, more than four-fifths of the colored and Indian population rejected it in a major election boycott. Sparks writes: "It should have come as no surprise in 1984 when only five days after the last votes were cast for the 'coloured' and Indian houses in the tricameral system, the great black revolt began."[50]

Gordhan reflected on these efforts to make incremental changes in the system:

> . . . commission after commission, constitution after constitution which resulted in the tricameral system by 1984, consolidation of the homelands system. If one did not have this world view [described above], it's very easy to see some of those incremental changes as being viable steps toward the ultimate goal of a proper democracy in South Africa. But *we had learned to think holistically—to understand the multidimensional components that constitute any picture you are looking at. That enabled us to constantly evaluate the interaction among those components of the*

situation and to distinguish between qualitative and quantitative changes—
between reform and fundamental change, for example [emphasis added].[51]

"And so it was," writes Sparks, "that while the whites applauded the reforms, the blacks mobilized opposition to them. In August 1983, more than five hundred community, church, professional, sports, workers', students', women's, and youth organizations formed an alliance called the United Democratic Front (UDF) to campaign against the new constitution and the 'Koornhof Bills.'. . . . Within a few months seven hundred more organizations joined the UDF, representing more than two million people. Rallies were held everywhere. . . . For a year the UDF ran its campaign against the reform package, . . . the most vigourous, sustained political campaign that black South Africans had ever been able to run. . . . The boycott [of the referendum] was a dramatic success, robbing the new system of legitimacy. . . . Five days later the great revolt began." Sparks summarized its results this way:

> The 1984 insurrection was more intense and lasted longer than any previous one. For three years it raged, resulting in more than three thousand deaths, thirty thousand detentions, and untold damage to property and the national economy. The government had to mobilize the army and declare two states of emergency to bring it under control and even then it was only partially repressed.
>
> It also had more strategic shape and revolutionary thrust than any previous uprising. The participation of politically experienced adults and of a national organization with affiliates deeply rooted in the communities meant that militant young "comrades," the shock troops of the uprising, were subject to some measure of direction and discipline. Although events developed a momentum of their own, impromptu actions taken in one area could be evaluated and, if successful, repeated elsewhere. The result was that a variety of strategies were employed. . . .
>
> To the extent that there was a central strategic thrust, it was to drive out the township administrations . . . and replace them with the UDF's own organizational structures. . . . Things occurred spontaneously, and in the hurricane of events the black leaders did what they could to devise strategies around what was happening.[52]

By the Mid-1980s: "Four pillars"—A Multilevel Political Process

Now to pick up Pravin Gordhan's story of how his generation's thinking emerged. He had been intimately involved in the evolution of the ANC's strategy through the 1980s. In a 1999 interview, he described himself as of late 1991: "I was a hardline activist. I'd just come out of detention. . . . I had been in the underground for four and a half years until I was detained.

So I wasn't one of those nice chaps as far as the other side was concerned. I'm just a representative of a culture that was developing at that time—of a maturing among ANC activists from armed struggle to actual talking while struggling to get the balance right."

Looking back in 1999, Gordhan reflected on the maturing of the ANC's strategy. First was a form of politics that engaged people:

> *It wasn't power politics or the politics of maneuver that was going to give us fundamental change; it was mobilizing people and giving them organizational form and political direction that would have the necessary impact on apartheid institutions and give us the momentum we needed for fundamental change.* We learned to create forms for resistance organizations that were compatible with survival during that period—civic, women's, youth organizations, and ultimately the United Democratic Front (UDF). All of them were premised on building relationships with the masses around their needs. They could take the form of rejecting a particular apartheid institution on a local level or addressing macro-institutions on a national level [emphasis added].[53]

"The next issue was how to reconcile mass organizations with armed struggle," Gordhan recalled:

> Again, the holistic understanding enabled one to understand that there was no one way of doing it—that all of these mechanisms needed to be explored, that physical force would play a key role. What's interesting is, from the late '70s and early '80s, *a culture of struggle to the bitter end while at the same time leaving the door open for negotiations that were already beginning to emerge in local struggles.* When there were massive school boycotts around the country, for example, parents committees emerged and negotiated with the education authorities. We found ways of creating bridges between core political interests of different groups—sports, women, religious, commercial [emphasis added].[54]

Third, Gordhan recalls, "was a tradition that had developed in the '20s and the '30s in South Africa—one of working with the democratic whites. . . . An interesting trend developed from the early '80s onwards: young white activists working in their organizations would also engage with white democratic organizations to become members of the United Democratic Front."

"By the time we got to the mid-'80s," Gordhan summarized, "my generation would have the conceptual framework and strategic conception it needed. We spoke of 'the four pillars': armed struggle, economic sanctions, internal mobilization, and building the underground." He continued:

> Two trends emerged in the '80s: first, the four pillars; second, within internal mobilization, *a sub-trend that developed its own political culture*

within the country. That was the one that led to the mass democratic movement within the country. Those organizations ultimately engaged with the regime at various levels, though rarely then at the top level. *But implicit was the understanding that you could talk to your enemy—engage with your enemy.*

. . . Negotiation reflected possibility. Consumer boycotts led to local negotiation. The business community joined in promoting security.

. . . Both internally and externally, two trends: the sharp edge, and one that looked for a door [emphasis added].[55]

From another perspective came a similar response on what caused people to decide to engage. Judge Richard Goldstone was appointed by President F. W. De Klerk in 1990 to head a commission that investigated charges of police brutality and systematic clandestine anti-ANC activities. Looking back at earlier times, he reflected:

It's not a linear process. It's not a process of us and them. It's not a process between opponents. It's not that simple in this country. Some factors I have identified as crucial. *First, there must be for a successful rapprochement dialogue, readjustment, reconciliation, an appreciation that two people share more than divides them—a common destiny*; we'll sink together or we'll swim together; we're locked together. Second, in addition to mutual commitment is coming to terms with reality [emphasis added].[56]

Intensifying Dialogue, 1985–1989

Although local contacts had already begun, the milestone marking the beginning of tentative explorations into dialogue at higher levels was the visit by Hendrik Jacobus Coetsee, minister of Justice, Police, and Prisons, to Nelson Mandela in a Cape Town hospital room in November 1985. Four years of secret exchanges between Mandela, then in his twenty-third year in prison, and a small group of government officials followed.

Quite apart from these and local exchanges was the visit early in 1986 by the seven-member Eminent Persons Group (EPG) assigned by a British Commonwealth summit to visit South Africa to study prospects for change. The issue before the summit was whether to join the international community in sanctions against South Africa, which British Prime Minister Margaret Thatcher opposed. The mission was headed by former Australian Prime Minister Malcolm Fraser and the former military ruler of Nigeria, General Olusegun Obasanjo, who had voluntarily returned his country to civilian rule in 1979.

The group moved back and forth between Pretoria and Lusaka, Zambia, where the ANC's external branch under Oliver Tambo was based. The government permitted Obasanjo to meet alone with Mandela at first and then the whole group to meet with him twice. As Sparks describes the outcome of the EPG's talks: "Encouraged by what it had found on both sides of the political divide in South Africa, the EPG drew up a 'possible negotiating concept' for the release of political prisoners, the lifting of the ban on the ANC and other black organizations, the suspension both of the ANC's armed struggle and of government violence against blacks, and the start of all-party negotiations—almost exactly what De Klerk was to announce four years later."[57]

The government of President P. W. Botha was deeply divided, but the military's desire to crush the black resistance won out. On May 19, the military launched a series of raids on ANC camps in Zambia, Zimbabwe, and Botswana. The EPG cut off its work and left. It recommended imposition of broad sanctions by the Commonwealth. But Mandela, says Sparks, "remained optimistic because the Commonwealth group had ascertained that among ordinary South Africans there was a widespread desire for a negotiated settlement and enough potential common ground to get negotiations going."[58] He asked for a meeting with Botha. The response was the creation of a committee of five government officials, which in the end held some 47 meetings with him. Perhaps the most important outcome of the EPG mission was giving both sides a taste of what negotiations might look like by distilling from their experience the substance of a starting point.

As the secret dialogue with Mandela began, other channels opened. Pieter de Lange, chairman of the Broederbond since 1983, fortuitously met Thabo Mbecki, at a Ford Foundation conference on Long Island, New York, in 1986. Businessmen and white opposition figures began flying to Lusaka to meet with ANC leaders. In August 1987, Frederik van Zyl Slabbert, a founder of the Institute for Democratic Alternatives in South Africa (IDASA) in 1986, took 50 Afrikaner dissidents to Dakar, Senegal, for a week's talks with ANC leaders. In July 1989, the ANC hosted 115 representatives of 35 opposition organizations.

The premier dialogue was organized by a British businessman with corporate funding to bring together Afrikaners connected with top levels of the establishment and government and ANC leaders. At a meeting between Oliver Tambo and a small group of British business leaders, one asked what British business could do. He said he would like to "see whether we couldn't have a dialogue with the Afrikaners." The group that formed met a dozen times between November 1987 and May 1990 at a British estate—Mells Park House. After several meetings in which ANC participants posed fundamental questions about the moral and philosophical foundations of apartheid, a shift in the Afrikaners' approach took place, and they began talking about mechanisms for moving forward. The organizer, Michael Young, recalls as quoted by Sparks:

> The first few meetings were full of tensions and suspicion. There was fear among the Afrikaners, who didn't know what would happen if word of the meetings leaked out. It was my understanding that if that

happened the government would withdraw their passports to dissociate itself from the talks. But then the tensions eased and barriers between the two sides broke down quite dramatically. Indeed, the meetings remoulded long-held perceptions on both sides. On the Afrikaner side they dissolved the demonized image of the ANC that had been built up by years of propaganda, while on the ANC side they sensitized the black liberators to white anxieties, particularly Afrikaner fears about their survival prospects under black rule.[59]

Apart from the dialogue with Mandela, this seems to have been the one example of a systematic, sustained dialogue.

Out of these exchanges, the ANC in exile gained enough confidence in its positions to lay them out in what came to be known as the Harare Declaration adopted on August 21, 1989. "It set out five preconditions for negotiations," Sparks summarizes: "lifting the state of emergency, ending restrictions on political activity, legalizing all political organizations, releasing all political prisoners, and stopping all political executions. If these things were done, the document said, all armed violence could be suspended while the two sides agreed on constitutional principles and then on a mechanism for drafting a new, non-racial constitution."[60]

As Judge Johan Kriegler summarized the results of these contacts: "The main importance was that business, church, and political leaders found that black leaders were human. Their stereotype was that all black leaders were Communists who wanted to throw the whites into the sea."[61] In Pravin Gordhan's words: "By the late '80s, the big picture was clear on the ANC side. On the National Party side, they shied away from details."[62]

The Political Bombshell and a Multilevel
Peace Process

On February 2, 1990, President F. W. de Klerk delivered to parliament the speech announcing Mandela's release and the unbanning of banned parties. Beyond that, there was no clear objective. On February 11, Mandela was released. Judge Johan Kriegler reflected: "F. W. decided to abandon apartheid because it wouldn't work—not for moral reasons. Mandela and Tutu assumed F. W. had a moral component and then were disillusioned. That explains Mandela's treatment of him in Oslo and Tutu's weeping at F. W.'s 'apology' before the Truth Commission. F. W. was apologizing for a failed policy, not for a wrong policy."[63] It is not my purpose or in my capacity to analyze why De Klerk took this step. My interest is in its place in the multilevel peace process.

What followed over the next four years was the unfolding of a multilevel political process that involved at the top level a combination of formal negotiation and informal dialogue that bridged the impasses and, at the citizens' level, attempted nonviolent confrontation of apartheid institutions that also produced dialogue. As Pravin

Gordhan insists, *it was a way of acting, not a well defined or carefully master-minded strategy*.

Even before the De Klerk speech, South African intelligence operatives arranged four clandestine meetings in Switzerland with ANC leaders. The first took place in Lucerne on September 12, 1989, with Thabo Mbeki and Jacob Zuma from the ANC. It was described as "an investigation, not a negotiation." The report: the ANC was willing to negotiate. The second again took place in Lucerne four days after De Klerk's speech, and the meeting focused on the steps to be taken. Participants agreed that there would have to be "an initial phase of talks about talks." In the third and fourth meetings, they set up working groups to deal with practical problems and, finally, a joint steering committee to deal with return of exiles and to plan the first formal meeting between the government and the ANC in South Africa.[64]

The steering committee, including Roelf Meyer, met for the first time on March 21 in a country inn north of Johannesburg. Deep tensions pervaded the meeting. The government was sharply divided, so its delegation was on edge. ANC members feared a trap with the government allowing exiles to return in order to arrest them. They decided to keep their underground network poised in the role of "an insurance policy" by maintaining its mass mobilization. With all of that, their task was to organize the first formal meeting between the two sides. It took place on May 2–4 at Groote Schuur, "the gabled mansion at the foot of Table Mountain [in Cape Town] which Cecil John Rhodes bequeathed in 1902 as the official residence of South Africa's prime ministers." The result was an agreement called the Groote Schuur Minute, "facilitating the release of political prisoners, the return of exiles, and the amending of security legislation."

"Three months later, on August 7," continues Sparks, "the two sides met again in Pretoria, and after a day-long session Mandela announced the unilateral suspension of the ANC's armed struggle. It was a major concession," writes Sparks, "for which he got little in return, and it stirred the first ripples of concern among ANC radicals who thought he was giving away too much."[65] Because the ANC was essentially constituent based, a critical part of Mandela's task was to keep the people with him.

In the following months, each side—especially the government—was engaged in internal debate about how to move forward. It seemed clear that the next step was to embody a new regime in a new constitution, but each recognized that the way the negotiations would be organized would determine the nature of the new political formula. The details are not important for our purposes. With each side struggling for advantage, Mandela produced a breakthrough in January 1991 by proposing a three-stage process that responded to government demands and eventually got a negotiating process started; however, in reality, it simply pushed the impasse down the road.

In fact, the ANC "was arguably only ready to negotiate a new constitution after June 1991, when it held its first national conference in the country in decades. It was here, for the first time since its return from exile, that it elected a leadership with a mandate to negotiate," writes Steven Friedman and a team of analysts associated with the Centre for Policy Studies based in Johannesburg. "Mandela was, predictably, elected president. . . . Cyril Ramaphosa, general secretary of the National Union of Mineworkers, as secretary general. A seasoned negotiator and organiser, Ramaphosa seemed equipped to help steer the ANC into a new environment in which negotiating skill and strategy, as well as organisation, had replaced populist rhetoric and revolutionary activity as strategic priorities."[66]

Beyond those formalities, "the ANC's change of identity was a secondary obstacle" to negotiations.[67] For the ANC returnees and released prisoners, this was a difficult period of changing mind-sets and habits as they tried to become part of now well-established political movements. Even members of these movements had to shift gears from thinking as "underground" to thinking more as organizations moving toward engagement in more conventional politics. The debate continued through much of the year, but both sides had promised that negotiations would begin before the end of the year.

"By April–May 1991," recalled Roelf Meyer in an interview, "there was violence all over the place. The ANC increased pressure to get rid of the Minister of Defense and Police. The more violence, the more mistrust."[68] "Indeed," write Friedman and colleagues, "in May, negotiations broke off altogether when the ANC withdrew, charging the government with complicity in the violence and demanding measures to restore its confidence in negotiation."[69]

In November 1990, members of the South African Council of Churches (SACC) had begun planning a peace conference for spring 1991. Simultaneously, a group of business leaders was considering how to respond to the violence. When President De Klerk announced a summit on violence and the ANC rejected it, the church and business groups proposed a conference. Participants formed a committee that on June 22 produced an outline of what became the National Peace Accord.[70] As Meyer recalled, "From then on, we had the first elements of negotiations. . . . How important civil society can be! New people came into the picture. The process widened. The question became, how can we go further? Personal interactions became more important."[71]

Adopted on September 14, the National Peace Accord was a pact among 26 signatories including "the principal political parties and organizations, the government and security forces, the leadership of the independent and self-governing states (so-called homelands under apartheid), and business, trade union, traditional, and church leaders," writes Susan Collin Marks, a South African by birth, a journalist, and a worker in the Western Cape Regional Peace Committee. "They committed themselves to a multiparty democracy and promised to support and abide by the mechanisms laid out in the Peace Accord. . . . It . . . mandated a countrywide structure with peace committees operating at national, regional, and local levels. In the interests of defusing the violence, people from nearly every sector were willing to work together with adversaries on peace committees. Soon there were hundreds of peace workers from all sides, working with, rather than against, one another."[72]

Describing the process set in motion as "a peace process that would underpin the national negotiations, harness the energies of most South African peacemakers, and provide the framework for all South Africans to work together," Marks further summarizes the content of the Accord:

> All Peace Accord signatories bound themselves to a code of conduct for political parties and organizations, a code of conduct for every police officer in the country, guidelines for community reconstruction and development, and mechanisms for the implementation of peace committees. They affirmed fundamental rights and freedoms, and endorsed the establishment of a commission to investigate the causes of violence (which became known as the Goldstone Commission after its chair, Justice Richard Goldstone).
>
> The Peace Accord provided an organizational framework for reducing violence and solving problems collaboratively. Its guiding spirit was peacemaking in action. It was conceptualized as a living structure, a system of peace committees in which everyone—Afrikaner and African, policeman and community activist, business mogul and factory worker, liberal and conservative, from top to bottom, from shore to shore—could meet together often and regularly to find ways of trying to stop the violence that was erupting among them. . . .
>
> . . . Instead of seeing ourselves locked in a zero-sum, win-lose competition in which only one side could win, we started to see ourselves as partners in a problem-solving relationship.[73]

As Friedman and colleagues write: ". . . it was the first formal multi-party accord, and it built sufficient confidence among the parties to persuade them to proceed to constitutional talks."[74] On October 22, the ANC Executive Committee endorsed an all-party conference.

Back on the official track, the Convention for a Democratic South Africa (CODESA) met on December 21–22, 1991, at The World Trade Centre near Johannesburg Airport with "two hundred and twenty-eight delegates representing nineteen political parties—the broadest cross-section of the country's leaders ever to meet."[75] The assembly established five work groups that would report back to the plenary at a follow-up meeting in May 1992. In Work Group Two, the main issues on how to move toward a settlement came together. Confronted with an ungiving line from the government, the chief ANC negotiator announced its withdrawal from Working Group Two, and the follow-up plenary, CODESA 2, collapsed on May 15, never to reconvene.

"Even before the collapse of CODESA 2, groups within the liberation movement had started arguing the case for some kind of 'mass action,' "

Sparks recalls, "both to consolidate a support base that was becoming restless and to put pressure on the negotiators. . . . So the centre of political gravity within the ANC alliance shifted in mid–1992 towards its militant wing."[76]

Violence reached new heights that summer as a result of two courses of action: one, as later investigations made clear, was a series of violent attacks by Zulus supported by a "third force" within government security forces to weaken ANC groups; the other was the campaign of mass ANC action launched on June 16, the anniversary of the Soweto uprising. Unrelated, the following night, a group of Zulus entered "a township called Boipatong, south of Johannesburg, and in an orgy of slaughter hacked, stabbed, and shot thirty-eight people to death in their homes. Residents reported police presence supporting the attackers. . . . When De Klerk tried to make a conciliatory visit to Boipatong three days later, a crowd turned on him in a chilling display of hostility." Police opened fire on the crowd killing more. "Soon afterwards, Mandela announced the ANC's formal withdrawal from negotiations, listing fourteen demands the government would have to meet before talks could resume."[77]

Over the following months, the commission under Judge Richard Goldstone began to develop a partial picture of these covert operations. Evidence increasingly supported the allegations that these activities had increased after negotiations began and that there was a clandestine role being played by some elements of the security forces.[78]

The ANC's mass action campaign "was designed to climax on 3 August with the beginning of what was initially described as an indefinite general strike." At that point, talks intensified between the Congress of South African Trade Unions (COSATU) and the South African Employers' Consultative Committee on Labour Affairs, "the business community's national representative on labour issues, which were to bring the two within a hair's breadth of an embryonic social contract. . . . The result was a Charter for Peace, Democracy and Economic Reconstruction. . . . The economic clauses were the first evidence of something of which both sides had begun to talk but which until then had seemed a distant idea: a negotiated economic strategy—or 'social contract'—between business and labour. The political clauses endorsed labour's concern for quick movement towards a settlement."[79]

During this period of mounting violence after the collapse of CODESA 2, two key figures—Roelf Meyer, just appointed minister of Constitutional Development and head of the government's negotiating team, and Cyril Ramaphosa, secretary general and chief negotiator of the ANC—had continued their talks privately. Their talks took place against the background of serious rethinking in both camps.

In the cabinet, a division was developing between an Old Guard and younger members who recognized the need to build a new South Africa. Doubts grew about De Klerk's strategy of building a strong anti-ANC coalition.

In the ANC, "some of the moderates were exploring how they might bridge the vital gap between power sharing and majority rule." They arrived at three ideas: power sharing for a transitional period of three to five years and then majority rule; amnesty and an offer of security to the mainly white civil service, police, and military, which the ANC began to realize they would need to govern. In addition, they gave renewed attention to the principles and applications of federalism in a formula advocating "a new South Africa 'that is unified but not over-centralized,' and a distribution of powers at national, regional, and local levels."[80]

On August 22, Meyer and Ramaphosa "met officially for the first time since the suspension of negotiations. And on 3 September, the ANC published a draft Transition to Democracy Bill which spelt out in precise detail a proposed transition."[81] The "Cyril–Roelf" channel was enlarged to include others interested in the resumption of negotiations. They worked out a deal in which Mandela's original fourteen demands were reduced to three. The government and ANC met and signed the September 26, 1992 "Record of Understanding." The outcome was agreement to resume multiparty negotiations.

Meyer in a 1999 interview recalled this moment, perhaps reflecting an informal understanding that had emerged in these one-on-one talks:

> By September 1992, we started from the assumption that the government is the government. The ANC started from the assumption that the people are the people; they have to speak. The compromise was: OK, we will continue with a legitimate state all the time—that is, there will at all times be a government governing the state—but at the same time allowing the people to decide finally on the new constitution. They made the concession of constitutional continuity. That compromise allowed a large number of problems to be resolved.
>
> We developed joint ownership of the process. The three most important attributes were trust, credibility, and ownership. The last may distinguish the South African process because we never allowed outsiders to come in. That allowed us to become the drivers of the process ourselves. It was a passion. Any problem we will overcome. We knew we had to do it ourselves.
>
> We faced the complexity of how to manage constituencies. One credit I give De Klerk was that he kept the whites together in support of the referendum. The ANC used a rolling mass action to keep their constituency together. One must also give great credit to Mandela.[82]

"The Record of Understanding," Friedman and his colleagues reflected, "convinced the two 'main players' that *multiparty negotiations would succeed only if they reached understandings, if not agreements, in advance* (emphasis added)."[83] These understandings were reached in informal dialogue.

"The government and the ANC cemented their new understanding at two *bosberaad* meetings in December 1992 and January 1993," Sparks writes.

"For four days and nights they talked, lived, ate, and relaxed together in the seclusion of D'Nyala [the president's retreat in the bush]." Sparks records Meyer's memory of a night game-viewing trip when he and Ramaphosa rode together on the back of a Land Rover: "It was damn cold and we were sitting there—Cyril, his wife and I—and we were talking, not about the game we were seeing but about what lay ahead for us. We were reaching out to each other, sharing common values about what we wanted to achieve. It was one of those rare moments of Cyril and I finding each other."[84]

In March 1993, a new Negotiating Council met at the World Trade Centre. "The last clause of the new constitution was adopted just before dawn on November 18, 1993," Sparks records. Reflecting further, he writes:

> Its strange origins aside, the negotiating process itself had been a remarkable phenomenon. An authoritarian country with no history or experience of interracial dialogue had engaged in what David Welsh of Cape Town University called 'a gigantic and ongoing seminar' on South Africa's future. And it had reached concurrence. People as far apart as the Communist Party and the Old Guard of the National Party had agreed on the essential shape of that future. Moreover, it was all done without the help of outsiders.[85]

"April 27 [1994] was more than just the main election day," Sparks reflects. "On that day the new South Africa was born in spirit as well as constitutionally. . . . The nearest analogy was the mood of the great crowd at the Brandenburg Gate the day the Berlin Wall came down. . . . Two weeks later, on May 10, Nelson Mandela was inaugurated as President, with Thabo Mbecki as first deputy and F. W. De Klerk as second deputy president."[86]

Reflections on the Peace Process

Describing to Pravin Gordhan in 1999 my own experience in the Arab–Israeli peace process of the 1970s as a series of negotiated agreements embedded in a larger political process where relationships changed, I asked him whether he ever thought in terms of a peace process. After some reflection, he replied slowly:

> We did have a peace process. From 1990, there were many parallel processes. We had a National Peace Committee specifically focusing on ending the violence—conflict mediation to prevent and intervene.
> A second line from the early '80s: a plethora of negotiating, consensus-building forums—in education, health, housing. There was need for an institution at the national level across the political spectrum.
> By '92, the government began to run into trouble because the private sector in these areas were reaching agreements and drawing the government into these concessions.

Another tier of meeting places emerged: heads of government departments met with ANC policy units.

One of the choices that had to be made in conceiving the political process was how broad this process would be. One temptation was to make all these forums sub-components of CODESA; the other was to collapse all those issues and make them issues for negotiations. The decision was: no, CODESA will focus on the political transition.

So you had a multilevel process. And there was a study group looking at macro-economic options.[87]

"At the end of 1994," writes Susan Collin Marks, "the newly installed Government of National Unity closed down the Peace Accord nationwide. Members of the government saw it as competing for power and funds and, most of all, control." She acknowledges that "[e]ven during its short life, the Peace Accord had come in for a lot of criticism." In sum, she writes:

> Despite its flaws, the Peace Accord changed South Africa and South Africans. It provided a place where former enemies got to know one another and found the humanity behind the stereotypes that for decades, if not centuries, had kept South Africans apart. It provided a buffer against violence that allowed the 1994 elections to proceed and catapult us into democracy. It formed a bridge between the old world we were breaking down and the new world that had not yet been born. It introduced conflict resolution methodology into the fabric of South African society. For many of the thousands that it touched, it was the most transformative experience of our lives. It was a means by which thousands of South Africans found our voices as champions of community and political peacemaking, voices we did not even know we had.[88]

A Decade Later

South Africans with whom I talked at length in the fall of 2002 about their peace process reflected a concern about this process, which differed significantly from what I had heard three years earlier. All of them had played important roles in the political and social transformation in the decade that followed 1985. This time, I heard three compelling points.

First, the key instrument at all levels in the transformation was dialogue. Negotiation, of course, was critical in producing the necessary constitution, laws, and other binding agreements, but—as has been recounted earlier—nonofficial dialogue continuing over time was critical at every juncture and at every level.

"There is absolutely no doubt," said one person deeply involved in the National Peace Accord, "that dialogue is the key to further understanding and to unlocking energies which lead towards a momentum for peace."

Another who was critical in efforts to prevent the right-wing of the Afrikaner movement from moving toward armed resistance by establishing a dialogue between their chosen leaders and the leadership of the African National Congress (ANC) reflected: "The priority is that the rank and file of the people be involved—that the process not be regulated by politicians. . . . It was very much a public thing—it was not governmental." One of the two key figures in the dialogues that supplemented formal negotiations said: "Dialogue projected hope, positive expectation, and the fact that people could associate. . . . The dialogue itself created its own public impact."

Second, concern was emerging that advances in relationship across racial and ethnic lines made in the 1990s were regressing. One person even went so far as to say, "Relationships are breaking down."

Some spoke of the period from 1985 to 1998–1999 as the first phase of the peace process; they spoke in 2002 of an urgently needed second phase. The upheaval in Zimbabwe after a peaceful beginning was increasingly sobering.

"The vital dialogue of the public has disappeared," said a former professor of theology who played a critical role in the nonofficial dialogue in the transformation. "We have merged at the top level. But vital discussions going on within the divided society that we are have disappeared. We are still a divided society—culturally, economically, the haves and have-nots."

"We thought that by democratizing, our problems would be over," he continued. "It's not so. People distrust each other; people are frustrated; people are becoming really angry. . . . You see, the vital issue, also for public dialogue, is to develop a full culture of democracy. . . . The public thing is important because it will bring the citizens of Africa to understand what it means to be self-governing. . . . The problem is the whole development into a functioning, organic form of democracy—the creation of a public domain. The whole transition into this hope of genuine democracy at present in South Africa is being blocked by the same old conflicts that we had."

Third, many in 2002 saw a pressing need for renewed dialogue across the country at all levels. They saw this as even more difficult now, perhaps, because the need is not so dramatically visible as it was in that earlier period. Difficult as ending the injustice of apartheid was, today's problems— reflecting as many of them do the difficult economic divisions in the country—are perhaps even more deeply systemic.

"What we need is a systematic effort throughout the society to get more dialogue going in public," said one former activist. "For the present post-conflict South Africa," said another, "the most effective way of reassuring minority groups about the future is engaging them with others—call it 'dialogue' or 'engagement.' I have also called it 'interaction.' We are actually retreating from where we were in 1994–1996."

Meetings were held in 2002–2003 on this need. In 2003, the Institute for Democracy in South Africa established a full-time staff position to practice and to teach Sustained Dialogue.

Why Was the Transformation not a Bloodbath?

Charles Villa-Vicencio suggested a comprehensive confluence of theoretical, political, philosophical, and cultural factors:

> First, a stalemate captured in Mandela's statement to [an Afrikaner General]: "We have come to the conclusion that we cannot overthrow you militarily. But I hope you know that you cannot kill all of us." Both sides were forced into a situation where rationality prevailed, and they negotiated a settlement that both sides could live with. We needed each other.
>
> Second, the historical nature of our encounter in this country: white people and black people learned to live together to a greater and lesser extent for three hundred years—albeit in an unequal, a paternalistic relationship—especially in the rural areas. There was an interdependence between black workers and white landowners that has to be analyzed. We weren't negotiating with strangers.
>
> Third, there's African culture—the notion of *ubuntu*. This philosophy of a person being a person through another person leads to a fundamental belief that you just keep talking until you find one another. You talk around a problem until some consensus emerges. In African culture, one would be very reluctant to say, "You are a thief." By circling, the difference is narrowed to the point where the person will say, "I stole your stuff. Is there some way we can move on?"
>
> Fourth, it has to do with religion. I've spent my life studying missionary history. Yes, they undermined African culture. But the vast majority of Africans in this country are Christians: we're all brothers and sisters. . . . Black African people are remarkably tolerant people. I don't want to romanticize; there has been horrendous black-on-black violence. . . . But black people can have a fight and yet sit down together. There's the Zulu litany of "the washing of the spears."[89]

Susan Collin Marks cites a response by Roelf Meyer to a question at a conference in Johannesburg in 1995 about what the ANC and the National Party each won or lost during the negotiations: "We realized at a very early stage that we had to achieve a win–win solution." She reflects on his answer: "What we had done . . . was to shift the model, or paradigm, and begin building our brave new world from a completely fresh blueprint. . . . In the old South Africa, adversarial, win–lose systems prevailed. Mandela modeled nonadversarial, win–win approaches during his presidency, informing the emerging society, even though imperfectly."[90]

More broadly, like both Sparks and Villa-Vicencio, she focuses on the Africans' philosophy of *ubuntu*, but she also highlights the power that people discovered in themselves:

> At the reconciliation table, people rooted in the African ways of forgiveness were able to carry South Africa across the abyss. They were

black and white, but they were mostly black, because the black people had so much to forgive. The decades of oppression, humiliation, limitation, and loss hovered overhead as the first contacts were made, the first stories told—and listened to—and the first steps taken into the void that was the future. In the process, individuals discovered that they could make peace and that they had the power to change the world around them. They no longer needed to wait for the authorities of one sort or another to do it for them. . . . This, then, is the real spirit of Africa. In Xhosa and Zulu it is called *Ubuntu*. . . . "People are people through other people."[91]

People are people in relationship. Dialogue makes relationship happen, and dialogue is the place where people change relationships.

CHAPTER SEVEN

Public Peacemaking and Peacebuilding in Tajikistan

HAROLD H. SAUNDERS
PARVIZ MULLOJANOV[1]

"The government has neither the capacity nor the resources to put every town in our country on its feet economically," said a citizen of Tajikistan—the poorest of the former Soviet republics—in 2001. "If anyone is going to do that job, the citizens of the towns themselves will have to do it." Despite a decade of independence, this was still a revolutionary statement in the wake of 70 years of Soviet rule and centuries of rule by the Central Asian khanate that preceded.

"We expected for many years that the government would improve our sitution," said a former businessman. "Now people have gradually started to understand that in the new conditions the government is simply not able to cover all areas. We must do something ourselves—there is no other way."

"Paradoxically, the sense of dependency was higher in areas covered by the programs of international agencies and humanitarian organizations," observes another citizen. "In most cases, agency experts decide what kinds of projects are needed for a community. People were accustomed to getting assistance from outside without making efforts—almost as it was during the Soviet system."

The story of public engagement in peacemaking and peacebuilding in Tajikistan provides a glimpse into citizens taking initiatives and building relationships around making peace, tackling economic challenges, and, in the process, contributing to a new polity. In these relationships evolve the patterns and "rules" of interaction that increase the reliability and predictability of social and economic intercourse and therefore reduce the costs of economic transactions. These are the essence of what is now being called "social capital." This citizens' engagement has also been described as the missing ingredient in 50 years of economic development theory.[2]

Following dissolution of the Soviet Union and tight control from Moscow in December 1991, Tajikistanis slid into a vicious civil war over who should govern. When asked in March 1993 to reflect on the causes of that war, one participant in what became a Sustained Dialogue replied, "Independence was thrust upon us unexpectedly; we were unprepared for it."

A peace agreement ended the war in June 1997, but the governors and citizens of Tajikistan have struggled ever since to balance effective government and the spaces citizens need in contributing to democratic political and economic development. Horrible as the civil war was, governors learned—at least for a moment—that they could not govern alone, and citizens outside government claimed a role in shaping a country that had never before existed. Together in a contentious but nonviolent tug-of-war, they continue, in effect, to seek a balance between the power of government to do what only governments can do and the freedom and capacities of citizens outside government to do the work only they can do. In a country without significant natural resources, ranked by the World Bank to be among the poorest on earth, tapping the energies and capacities of citizens outside government is critical.

The unfolding story of Tajikistan in one aspect is the story of an uphill struggle by a few citizens to demonstrate that a strong society of citizens in partnership with an effective government constitutes the only equation that can make this poor country sustainable and profitable. Some will scoff at this picture as too optimistic. Fair enough. The roots of authoritarianism lie deep in Tajikistan's history.

That old mind-sets die hard but are being challenged is captured in an exchange during a training session for potential moderators of Sustained Dialogues in six regions of Tajikistan. They were discussing who should participate. A competent, dedicated local official felt it was important to exclude those with radical religious views, and to organize the dialogue to strengthen the state's authority. The chairman of the Public Committee for Democratic Processes, veteran of a seven-year dialogue, responded in paraphrase as follows:

> Democratic dialogue will not and cannot occur unless all voices in the community are represented. Democracy means that every view must be heard, even those with which we fundamentally disagree. Only when everyone feels that her or his views will have a full and fair hearing will dialogue be taken seriously by the community. Only when dialogue is taken seriously can a community begin to come to terms with its most serious and fundamental problems. If government is seen as manipulating or trying to manipulate the dialogue, it has already failed. As moderators, our job is first to make sure that all voices receive a fair and full hearing. To the degree that these conditions are sustained over time in public dialogue, Tajikistan will move forward in its democratic development.[3]

Despite the difficulty of changing deeply embedded mind-sets, I feel compelled to spotlight a struggling but persistent experiment in public engagement in the hope that others will recognize its importance—not only for Tajikistan but for all of Central Asia.

Even in the United States with its traditions of public engagement, scholars were arguing at the turn of the new century that public engagement was declining.[4] My response is not to engage in that argument nor to argue that a movement toward public engagement in Tajikistan is a prominent feature on the landscape. My response is to put the issue on the analytical agenda in the hope of persuading an increasing number of citizens that public engagement is critical to their future, wherever they live.

Dialogue in Conflict and in Peace

This story in Tajikistan must be traced back to 1959 and another experiment in public engagement that had nothing to do with Tajikistan at the time. In that year, Norman Cousins, then editor of *The Saturday Review*, talked with President Dwight Eisenhower about opening a dialogue between citizens of the two superpowers as a backup channel in case government relations soured. He sounded out potential Soviet counterparts in Moscow. After a series of tortuous exchanges, a group of prominent American and Soviet citizens outside government met at Dartmouth College in New Hampshire in October 1960. Only more than three decades later did we learn that Soviet Communist Party Chairman Nikita Khrushchev had also approved.[5]

By 1981, there had been 12 plenary meetings, held alternately in the Soviet Union and the United States. Always the focus was on issues of central importance to the Soviet-U.S. relationship. In November 1981, at Dartmouth XIII in Moscow, the question was: "What happened to détente?" The answers lay in the arenas of arms control and deployments and regional conflicts—those areas where the superpowers competed through proxies such as in the Middle East, Angola, Ethiopia, Nicaragua, Afghanistan. The Dartmouth Conference leaders created two task forces to to study superpower interactions in these arenas to learn more about the central Soviet-U.S. relationship. Evgeny Primakov, who became foreign minister and then prime minister of the new Russia in the 1990s, became the Soviet cochair of the Regional Conflicts Task Force, and I became the U.S. cochair.

Throughout the 1980s, we met on average every six months. We increasingly felt the challenge of getting more out of each successive meeting. At one point, Primakov said, "We will start the next meeting where the last one ended." We discovered that bringing the same participants back together repeatedly created four opportunities: (1) we developed a cumulative agenda, with unanswered questions from one meeting studied between meetings and reformulated as the agenda for the next; (2) we learned to talk analytically rather than vituperatively; (3) we created a common body of knowledge, including deeper understanding of why each side's interests were important; and (4) we ultimately learned to work together.

We exchanged analyses of our policies in the Middle East and in Afghanistan, which we shared with our governments. We also discussed Central America, southern Africa, and southeast and northeast Asia.

By 1991, looking back on our experience and my own experience in Arab–Israeli–Palestinian dialogues, I began to see a pattern in those dialogues where the same group returned regularly. I conceptualized this pattern as a five-stage process in 1991.[6] My Russian colleague—Gennady Chufrin, deputy director of the Institute of Oriental Studies in Moscow who had succeeded Primakov as Task Force cochair in 1989—and I first published that process in the spring of 1993. I developed that presentation and placed it in a larger context in 1999 in *A Public Peace Process: Sustained Dialogue to Transform Racial and Ethnic Conflicts*.[7]

Meanwhile, when the Soviet Union dissolved at the end of 1991, members of the Task Force had made three decisions: first, to conceptualize the process of dialogue we had learned; second, to focus on the new Russian-U.S. relationship; third, to apply the process to one of the conflicts that had erupted on the territory of the former Soviet Union. We chose Tajikistan (1) because its civil war potentially affected the strategic interests of Russia, the United States, China, Europe, Turkey, and Iran; (2) because our Russian colleagues had academic connections there and could explore interest in dialogue; and (3) because no other organizations, except a few humanitarian groups, were there.

Tajikistan had declared its independence from the Soviet Union in August 1991. When the Soviet Union dissolved in December 1991, it faced the challenge of governing itself. Through 1992, an attempted coalition government and a government by forces opposed to remnants of Communist-style rule failed to unite the country. A regional force seized control. Intensified fighting and widespread atrocities drove an estimated one-seventh of the people from their homes.

Many fault lines divided the factions. Regional rivalry in the fight to govern emerged as the most obvious. Power shifted from the Leninabad region in the northwest, which had supplied leadership during Soviet times, to the Hatlon region in the south. Ideological differences ranged from the Communists' preference for central control through moderate democrats and Tajik nationalists to moderate and militant Islamists. Ethnic Uzbeks were the main minority. Historically shaped subcultures defined inhabitants of other regions. Many were forcibly resettled to meet Soviet labor requirements, thus creating tensions in many communities.

In December 1992, the Dartmouth Conference Regional Conflicts Task Force deputized three American and three Russian members to explore beginning a dialogue among participants from the different factions.

In the past, Dartmouth Conference members had made proposals for collaboration between their governments, which had come to naught. Now for the first time, American and Russian citizens outside government actively engaged in a joint citizens' peacemaking venture.

Two Russians visited Tajikistan and talked with more than a hundred potential participants and to the head of state and foreign minister. They explained the work of the Dartmouth Regional Conflicts Task Force during the Cold War and invited interested Tajikistanis into the Task Force's space to engage in dialogue on their civil war. As the Russians said, "The Tajikistanis would not have come to an American nor a Russian meeting, but they accepted an invitation from an 'international movement'—namely, the Dartmouth Conference."

This project differed from most other conflict resolution efforts. In raising money for this venture, we Americans described our purpose as follows: We did not propose attempting to mediate an agreement among factions. "We want to see," we wrote, "whether a group can be formed in the middle of a civil war that can learn to shape a peace process for their own country."[8] We believed that only citizens living the dynamics of the conflict would be able to design a peace process sensitive to the multiple human interactions involved.

In that context, the "Inter-Tajik Dialogue within the Framework of the Dartmouth Conference," as participants eventually called themselves, first met in Moscow in March 1993. When they sat down together in a conference room of the Institute of Oriental Studies, they were barely able to look at each other as they exchanged accusations about responsibility for hostilities and atrocities. In March 2003, the group held its thirty-fifth meeting almost on its tenth anniversary. They worked through four periods.

First, from March 1993 through its sixth meeting in March 1994, the group played a significant role in opening the door to formal negotiations mediated by the United Nations. To our knowledge there was no other channel at that time between government and opposition. Through the first three meetings (March, June, August), participants continued to vent their grievances. Finally, in the third meeting, someone said: "Enough of this. We really need to work on starting negotiations between the government and the opposition on creating conditions so refugees can go home. We can't do anything until people return home."

In November, they discussed how to start such a negotiation. A major obstacle, they felt, was that opposition forces were geographically dispersed from Pakistan and Iran to Moscow and ideologically diffuse from moderate democrats to militant Islamists. "Who are you? Who would come to the table?" asked pro-government participants.

Shortly after, opposition groups met in Iran, wrote a common platform, and formed the United Tajik Opposition. Two members of the Dialogue signed that platform and explained it in depth in the fifth meeting of the Dialogue in January 1994. Pro-government participants left that meeting saying: "We think the basis for negotiation now exists. We will report to the government." A month later the government agreed to join negotiations mediated by a representative of the United Nations secretary general. Before negotiations began in April, Dialogue participants in March wrote their first joint memorandum, "A Negotiating Process for Tajikistan." Three of them became members of the negotiating teams when negotiations began.

Second, from April 1994 through the conclusion of a peace agreement in June 1997, the Inter-Tajik Dialogue continued to meet. We had informed the foreign minister that the Dialogue would continue but assured him that it would not interfere in the negotiations. The group decided to focus on a political process for reconciliation among the Tajikistanis. Since three members of the Dialogue were also members of the negotiating teams, ideas did flow back and forth.

One of those ideas reflected the Dialogue's concern for generating a public peace process. At one point, the negotiating teams had reached an impasse. The opposition had proposed creating either a coalition government or a supra-governmental commission with members divided equally between government and opposition. The government saw either proposal as a power grab. Dialogue participants wrote another joint memorandum that proposed creating a commission under the authority of the peace agreement to work alongside government to develop detailed implementation of the peace agreement through four subcommissions. These would bring together citizens and officials to implement decisions on refugee return, economic reconstruction, demilitarization of "illegal armed elements," and political reform.

One dramatic moment in the Dialogue crystallized a concept that captured participants' persistent interest in public involvement alongside government. An opposition member of the group had worked with a joint task force to mediate a ceasefire in a region where fighting had cut the main east–west road joining two parts of this mountainous country. The story was gripping because some of the task force members had been held hostage. In the end they succeeded in working out a protocol that involved the field commanders, local government officials, local notables, and representatives in the task force of both the national government and the opposition. When he concluded his account, another participant in the Dialogue said: "The reason ceasefires keep breaking down is that they are negotiated between the president and the opposition leader without reference to the people on the ground with the interests and the guns. What we need is *a multilevel peace process* which connects the top-level negotiators and the citizens through task forces."

Third, the National Reconciliation Commission—formed in July 1997—was mandated by the peace treaty. Five Dialogue participants were members. It was a unique mechanism for implementing a treaty. Half the members were from opposition organizations; half were appointed by the government. In effect, it was a nongovernmental but quasi-official space in which citizens in and out of government worked together through subcommissions on refugee return, disarmament, political reform, and constitutional drafting. For three years they worked through detailed solutions to problems that had not been resolved in the peace agreement.

The Dialogue itself also became a space where senior members of the civil society and citizens closely associated with officials could talk informally about critical issues. The normal pattern of a Dialogue meeting became spending the first morning of a three-day meeting talking about recent developments, identifying one problem, focusing on it, and then writing a joint memorandum to be shared with their organizations and the government. Perhaps even more important than the conclusions they reached were the relationships and perspectives they formed that often transcended partisan disagreements.

Fourth, by August 1999, the formal transition period for implementing the peace agreement neared its end. Dialogue participants decided to create a mechanism for bringing the ideas they had developed since 1993 to the citizens in their communities and organizations. They first formed a group to prepare citizens for the elections that would ratify the new constitution and elect a president and parliament. With the elections behind them and a new era ahead, they registered their own NGO in March 2000—the Public Committee for Democratic Processes (PC). The Board of Directors were mainly Dialogue participants, headed by Chairman Ashurboi Imomov, a constitutional law professor and a Dialogue participant since 1994. The executive director was Parviz Mullojanov, who had been an international fellow at the Kettering Foundation in the United States.

A senior member of the board described its purpose in these words: "Tajik society is passing through a complicated period of social, economic, political, and post-conflict transformation. There is a need to find common ground and reach a social and political compromise. Failure to do so may lead to new conflicts."[9]

"The experience of the Inter-Tajik Dialogue had proved to us that we could promote conflict resolution and prevention processes in Tajikistan by using the methods and approach of public deliberation and dialogue," said one of the senior figures. Avoiding duplication of efforts by other new NGOs, they decided to work on four tracks.

First, having long talked about forming "mini-dialogues" within Tajikistan, they began an experimental dialogue in Dushanbe, the capital. After having experienced forming and conducting a dialogue, they formed dialogue groups in six other regions of the country, focusing initially on "the state, religion, and society." With the only legitimate Islamic party in Central Asia and with the hotbeds of Islamic extremism in Afghanistan and Pakistan next door, the aim was to provide citizens spaces where they could develop new relationships peacefully. They saw these dialogues as possibly the foundation of a national dialogue.

Second, they developed a network of public issues forums, patterned on the National Issues Forums in the United States and a sister network in

Russia. The purpose was to give citizens experience in deliberation on major issues such as poverty, drugs, and education.

Third, they reached an agreement with the minister of Education to work with three professors from each of eight universities to develop a curriculum, a textbook, and teaching materials for courses in resolving conflict and peacebuilding. Their aim was to marry scholarship on local traditions and institutions of conflict resolution with Western scholarship and practice in the field.

Fourth, they decided to explore the possibilities for creating committees to tackle community economic development. I focus on this fourth track because it provides a laboratory for studying citizen engagement in economic development—the "missing ingredient" in 50 years of economic development theory. It touches citizens' most pressing needs. As one of the program directors said, "This project is one of the most important and most needed civic initiatives in today's Tajikistan. It enables us to deal with the most acute problems of our communities. I find deep personal satisfaction in being part of this effort by citizens to improve their lives." Said another: "Working with ordinary citizens at the community level is the only way we can improve our economy and solve the social and political problems of our society. Without the PC many of these citizens would not organize their work in the most effective way."

Public Engagement and Economic Development

In the summer of 2001, PC leaders began laying the groundwork for what came to be called Economic Development Committees (EDCs). Their move reflected a view of politics that they had developed in their dialogue over the previous eight years.

"They believed," writes Parviz Mullojanov, "that the really successful and definitive peace process goes on not on the top decision-making level but on the wider level of communities and ordinary citizens—the level on which most people live. Usually, the official peace process is restricted to a limited number of politicians; it can be violated at any time because of changed conditions or personal conflicts. The sustainability of the peace process can be ensured only if it is shifted to cover as many strata of people as possible." In effect, they returned to their thought of a multilevel peace process, which now included economic and peacebuilding as well as peacemaking purposes.

They further believed, in Mullojanov's words, that "the best mechanism to assure wide civic engagement in the peace process is the deliberative public dialogue approach as practiced in the Dartmouth Conference and the Inter-Tajik Dialogue. Its main idea is to create a public space in the form of a committee of 10–12 people representing different factions of society where citizens could deliberate on pressing problems. In dialogue, a sense of trust, cooperation, and cohesiveness grows among the participants. Dialogue changes conflicting relationships not only within the group but also the intercommunal and interethnic relationships beyond the group."

The EDCs embodied the experience of the Inter-Tajik Dialogue by bringing the same people together repeatedly over a long period. "This was a new phenomenon for Tajikistan where most initiatives involved one-time seminars around the country where participants were always different. In contrast, the EDC approach focuses more on quality than on quantity when a group meets repeatedly, gradually raising their knowledge and skills under the supervision of a third party."

In sum, "the EDC track includes a strong conflict resolution and conflict prevention component. Beyond that, the final goal is to create a network of community-based public committees that would be able to make an essential contribution to the improvement of inter-ethnic and inter-community relationships."

As PC members began to explore possible sites for their work, they learned a first lesson in adapting their processes to different situations. Their initial idea was to start Sustained Dialogues like the Inter-Tajik Dialogue in towns that had been torn apart both physically and ethnically during the civil war. The government strategy, however, was to state that the war was over and the country reunified, so there was no need for dialogues across lines dividing hostile groups. They feared reopening old wounds. On the other hand, local governments were more than eager to focus on difficult social and economic issues. The PC, therefore, began organizing committees with a dual agenda. "The idea was to engage people representing different strata and factions of local society in cooperation on economic problems. Working together, they would inevitably create connections and improve relationships both on the inter-personal and, later, on an inter-communal level."

"The approach used on the EDC track did not differ essentially from that of the Inter-Tajik Dialogue," Mullojanov felt. "Members of the EDCs discussed the most acute social and economic problems of their area. The final task was to design their community's economic development plan and to develop a set of quality proposals that could be submitted for funding by donor organizations."

The PC helped both to facilitate the overall process and to train local moderators in managing the process and in special skills such as grant-writing. The PC paid for the training and for the process leading to decision, planning, and grant-writing and promised a modest amount (no more than $5,000) to fund a start-up project. After that, the committees would raise their own funds and assure the sustainability of their work.

Choosing sites for their experiments was the PC's first challenge. In the spring of 2000, they made a series of fact-finding visits with the objective of selecting three communities, each in a different region of the country. As they gained experience from talking with local officials, local opinion leaders, ethnic groups, NGO leaders, traditional and religious authorities, five criteria for selection emerged: (1) The area must be one where, during the civil war, political, economic, social, and interethnic tensions led to violence and human rights violations and where new eruptions of violence seemed possible. (2) The area should be multiethnic with people from different regional backgrounds who seemed likely to profit from dialogue. (3) EDCs should be established at the community or at least at the local self-governance level. The *mahalla* is a community, an urban city block, or a rural village consisting of a few mahallas; the *jamoat* is a traditional Tajikistani administrative self-governance unit consisting of several mahallas or communities. "The community and grass roots level is the most conducive space for the best civic engagement results," writes Mullojanov. "Mahalla and village councils are parts of the traditional civic network that conventionally played an essential conflict resolution role." (4) The area had to be within reasonable driving distance from Dushanbe because the PC expected to have to play a regular monitoring role, at least at the outset. (5) Both local authorities and citizens had to be interested. Citizen participation was critical, but in former Soviet countries little could happen without at least the acquiescence of local officials.

Having defined these criteria, PC leaders had to decide on which level to focus their efforts: on the mahalla or jamoat level—the community level—or on the level of city or rayon—the level of what we in the United States would call municipal or county government bodies. Part of the PC working group preferred working at the community level on the grounds that this is where the largest quantity of human capacities and centuries-old civic institutions such as mahalla and elders' councils existed. Others in the PC group felt that it was necessary for future success to assure the approval of local authorities who could block any project they felt was not in their interest; they felt government could mobilize traditional institutions.

A misstep at this early stage, they feared, could doom the entire effort in the future. In the spirit of experiment, PC members decided to base two EDCs on the community/local jamoat level and the third on the level of city administration.

The PC selected three areas: (1) the Kafirnigan EDC was created in Yangi Bozor Jamoat of Kafirnigan rayon about 18 miles east of Dushanbe; (2) Kurgan-Tube, a city at the center of southern Khatlon province about 70 miles from Dushanbe; and (3) the Shartuz EDC was created in the Central Jamoat of Shartuz town in Khatlon province along the Tajik–Afghan border about 60 miles further beyond Kurgan-Tube City.

Finally, they had to decide on the composition of each EDC. They first decided that two moderators would run each EDC—one a person close to the official level in order to improve chances of a positive official attitude and the other a person representing the local NGO sector or the community to improve opportunities for broad civic engagement. Beyond the moderators, they determined that each participant should represent a certain ethnic group, political faction, vocational group, religious leaning. The idea, as in the Inter-Tajik Dialogue, was to create, as much as possible in a group of a dozen citizens, a microcosm of the whole community. The aim was to create a group of citizens with different needs and perspectives.

When experts were included, they were limited to only two or three who might sharpen thinking about specific problems. Participants had to be influential citizens whom others would respect and to whom they would listen—an attribute particularly important in oriental society. "Local non-official leaders such as heads of mahalla, village, and elders' councils, religious authorities, and highly respected community members conventionally play a key role in mobilizing society's human and material resources," says Mullojanov.

Once the PC members had set their course, they began a preparatory phase that lasted through numerous visits and conversations in order, first, to choose the best moderators. Then the moderators were asked to prepare a list of 30–40 potential participants. The final 12–15 members were selected through a wide range of consultations across community and government bodies. The PC team then conducted a training program first for the moderators and then for the participants themselves. Such training programs were repeated periodically with the aim of steadily raising the understanding of the process and the capacities of all involved.

When the groups were ready to begin work, they usually met once a month. Meetings were usually divided into three parts. Much as in the dialogue process, meetings began with a general discussion to collect all perspectives and gradually to define a problem and possible approaches to it. Then, participants delved deeply into the identified subject. "This approach," says Mullojanov, "is similar to traditional public meetings in Tajik society since ancient times, so it is accepted by ordinary citizens. The aim is to find common ground and to identify the best approaches. Of course, that goal is rarely achieved in only one meeting, so participants continue the discussion through a series of meetings." In that case, many private conversations in the community will take place between meetings. A meeting ends with a collective effort to summarize where the group is and what members need to do for the next meeting.

"The entire efforts of the EDC team would be useless if it is isolated from the community and if people are not informed and cannot influence EDC discussions," says Mullojanov. "Therefore, all along one of the main tasks of each EDC member is to keep durable relations with the part of local society he or she represents by getting public opinion on each of the issues discussed."

Over a period of two years, the progress of dialogue and planning in an EDC presented a pattern along the following lines.

The first several meetings were devoted to the definition of the most acute and serious economic and social problems their communities faced. "We called this procedure 'the problem naming and framing process,'" Mullojanov recalled. In the course of the dialogue, participants identified a substantial list of existing acute problems. They discussed this list with others in their communities. Then they began grouping related problems. After much further deliberation, they finally chose three or four top priority problems.

Next, they devoted a series of meetings to discussing ways of approaching these problems. Usually, each EDC divided itself into smaller working groups to concentrate on one problem cluster. They had to weigh the likely effectiveness, cost, and consequences of the approaches they identified. They also had to consider the resources that might be drawn from the community itself to accomplish their goal. Often, they found the human and material resources available within their communities.

At this point, the PC arranged for training first of moderators and then of all EDC members for designing a practical marshaling course of action that identified specific steps for implementing their proposals and for the resources they would need to take these steps. Part of this training focused on learning to write grant proposals to secure outside funding for resources they could not marshal within the community. Each group submitted its proposal for deliberation in the EDC plenary at the regular monthly meeting.

In the course of about a year and a half, an effective EDC could design a comprehensive strategy including both concrete steps for dealing with its most acute social and economic problems and intertwined steps for improving interethnic and intercommunal relationships. The PC left the latter implicit rather than explicit.

Three Economic Development Committees

Kafarnigan rayon is one of the biggest and most densely populated county-sized administrative units of Tajikistan. It is named for its center— Kafarnigan City, with a population of about 40,000. The rayon is divided into two parts by the Kafarnigan River—to the north, a mountainous region, and, in the valley, the mostly urban part. Located 18 miles from Dushanbe, the area is closely related to the capital economically. It is an ancient region that was often a center of resistance to external invasions or local despots.

The people of the region reflect a complicated mix of ethnic and regional backgrounds resulting from successive invasions of the sixteenth and seventeenth centuries, population movements in the eighteenth and nineteenth centuries, and in the 1930s, Soviet resettlement. In the 1950s during a second resettlement campaign, thousands of Tajiks were forcibly moved there from the eastern mountainous parts of the country. During the same period, many Russians and Ukrainians moved to Kafarnigan City from Dushanbe and other parts of the Soviet Union.

By the early 1990s when the civil war began, the main groups were Tajiks (70–80 percent) and then Uzbek and Russian speakers. Each major group included subgroups from very different regional backgrounds, separated by geography, history, and custom—mountain people, valley people, farmers, nomads. Although they lived in the same jurisdiction, each ethnic group kept pretty much to itself, and in religious, social, and business life, people preferred to deal with those of their own ethnic group. Instead of cooperation, there was ongoing competition between communities for land and water resources, jobs, and other benefits—competition that often led to tension and conflict.

The EDC was founded in one of the biggest Kafarnigan jamoats—Jamoat Yangi Bozor, an area of 57 square miles and 20,000 people living in 15 villages. Like the rest of the region, it is multiethnic with problems of unemployment (more than 3,000 jobless), discrimination, and poverty (about 1,500 refugees), social, and economic decay.

During the civil war, the area was considered an opposition stronghold; in 1996–1997, pro-opposition commanders seized control of most of the area, including some of the outskirts of Dushanbe. When the peace agreement was concluded in June 1997, one of the main problems was reintegrating former opposition fighters. For some time, they remained a potentially explosive and destabilizing element. The majority of local Uzbeks and Russians had remained neutral but leaning toward the government. Few escaped the robbing and looting, but the neutrality of the non-Tajiks somewhat reduced the potential for interethnic tension. In 1998, the region twice turned into an arena of fierce clashes between government and opposition troops, thereby threatening the peace agreement.

Economically, before the civil war the area was one of the main providers of agricultural products to the capital and of a network of transport routes connecting the capital with the southern and eastern rayons of the country. The civil war essentially destroyed the regional economy. As in many other places in the former Soviet Union, a land privatization program created a gap between a limited group of so-called new Tajiks—the local *nouveaux riches* consisting of pro-government and opposition leaders—and the rest of the population. High unemployment led some men in almost every family to emigrate to Russia to earn a living for their families.

From the beginning, the Kafarnigan EDC was the easiest group of people to work with. First, Jamoat Yangi Bozor during the civil war avoided the extreme atrocities experienced in other areas. While citizens had their sympathies, the majority were not involved in military clashes or political activities. The low level of tension between groups allowed the EDC team to move forward quickly without the need to spend time healing the wounds of the civil war and building confidence. Second, since the jamoat is densely populated and communities are close, people knew and respected each other, having gone to the same schools or worked together in Soviet times. Right from the start, there was a "peaceful working atmosphere in the EDC room." Third, the EDC was blessed with skilled, well-trained moderators. In training the EDC team, the two moderators often worked as cotrainers with the PC group.

After identifying 30 acute social and economic problems, they decided to give priority to three clusters of problems: (1) unemployment—both young people with no jobs and older people with only part-time or seasonal work—which was closely related to issues of poverty and labor migration; (2) decay of the local education system at all levels; (3) lack of communal infrastructure such as destroyed water and gas pipelines and roads.

The group began by assessing existing human and material resource; in order to ensure that any plans they developed would be achievable. For example, theirs is an agricultural area where many local farmers engage in livestock breeding. Since Soviet times, Kafarnigan was the main source of milk for the capital's milk-processing plants. As the EDC began its work, most milk-processing factories were in deep economic crisis and decay, and local farmers often could not sell their products. Their first project design focused on creating a milk-processing factory.

The EDC team also developed further proposals: a micro-credit project to provide local businessmen with startup capital to launch their own businesses; a business center where local people could gain the knowledge and skills necessary for developing a private business; and a series of proposals for developing the public services and utilities sector including rebuilding water and gas pipelines, the refurbishment of schools, repair of roads.

After lengthy deliberations, team members decided to focus mainly on proposals that would produce income to assure the EDC's sustainability and enable them to support one-time projects such as constructing a water supply system. By charging modest interest in the micro-credit program, they sustained it while attempting to attract funders to other projects.

The second EDC was established in *Shartuz Town—Central Jamoat*. Shartuz rayon is on the Tajikistan–Afghanistan border. It is mostly a desert area with most people living in a few isolated oases and engaging in agriculture. The rayon center, called Shartuz Town, is home to about 30,000 people. The Central Jamoat includes several city blocks with about 11,000, belonging to all ethnic communities in the rayon. The level of economic difficulty and unemployment was even higher than in the neighboring agricultural areas.

There are three main ethnic communities: Uzbeks, the so-called Tajik-Arabs (they speak Tajiki but trace their origin to Arab invaders who brought Islam 13 centuries ago), and Gharmis (Tajiks from the eastern mountainous areas) resettled, as in Kafarnigan. During the Civil War, Tajik-Arabs and Uzbeks supported the government; the Gharmis were forced to take refuge in Afghanistan. When they returned after the 1997 peace agreement, they found their homes looted or destroyed and faced economic difficulties and hostility. By the time the EDC was established, all three groups were suffering almost equally from unemployment and economic decay.

The EDC worked its way through essentially the same process as had the team in Kafarnigan, but there were two significant differences.

First, the process moved more slowly for several reasons: (1) Interethnic tensions and political divisions were much sharper. Lack of trust persisted. During our visit, participants repeatedly reaffirmed that "we are all one now" or "we are all brothers" with the strained intensity of those who hope repeating a mantra will make it so. Although they do not openly discuss them, past grievances inevitably affect interactions. (2) The team's composition included more community and NGO leaders, officials, and experts and fewer ordinary citizens. On the one hand, the group's intellectual capacity was higher. On the other, the involvement of so many different, experienced, and strong personalities required spending more time finding common ground and establishing an atmosphere of productive cooperation. (3) Unlike Kafarnigan, Shartuz since the late 1990s has been the focus of attention of international agencies. Their mode of work created an attitude of dependency. They even paid citizens to come to meetings. The PC took the position that the EDC would belong to the citizens with the PC only covering cost of meetings and between-meeting expenses while they would have to raise their own funds for projects. The Shartuz team seemed much more skeptical about the process.

Second, the composition of the EDC affected the team's decisions. Members were more dependent on local government. They paid much attention to problems of health, hygiene, and sanitary conditions, which are mostly the responsibility of the local government. Consequently, their first proposals had a one-time character; sustainability was not considered. "This situation demanded the direct involvement of the PC," Mullojanov recalls. "Its representatives asked the EDC to make a choice: either develop only one-time projects, after which the EDC would end, or develop a few projects that would provide income for their Committee. In the latter case, they could continue as a citizens' association or as an independent NGO. The choice was up to them; the PC would accept any decision."

After considerable thought, the EDC team asked the PC for permission to register as an independent branch of the PC with its own bank account and self-financing. The EDC explained that in Shartuz it is easier to work as a branch of a centrally based organization than as a local NGO. They revised most of their proposals to focus on sustainability.

Their first project was called "Garbage Collection Company in the Shartuz Region"—the first such private initiative in the country. EDC members had gone house to house asking whether householders would pay a monthly fee to have their garbage collected regularly. Usually, this service, when provided, is the responsibility of government. When they had established a potentially profitable base, they went into business, using the income to benefit the EDC.

In *Kurgan-Tube City*, as an experiment, the PC decided to base the EDC at the level of city administration. This was ultimately the one failure.

With a population of almost 90,000 people, Kurgan-Tube City is the center of Khatlon province in southern Tajikistan. During Soviet times, it was one of the country's most economically developed and Westernized cities. Many Russian speakers worked in industry and construction. There was even a small but influential and prosperous German community—individuals forcibly resettled by Stalin from Russia just before World War II.

As in the Kafarnigan rayon, people from different backgrounds lived together. Tajiks composed only about 60 percent of the population. Tens of thousands of Tajiks from Gharm were forcibly resettled there in the 1950s. Before the civil war, competition for land and water resources in the region was especially high between the Gharmis and the rest of the population.

At the beginning of the civil war in 1992, Kurgan–Tube province saw the fiercest clashes between opposition and government troops. The political division was defined along lines of ethnic and regional background: the majority of people resettled from eastern Tajikistan (Gharm and Badakhshan) supported opposition forces, while indigenous Uzbeks and Tajiks supported the government. When the opposition was defeated there at the end of 1992, a wave of brutal repressions forced thousands of Gharmis and Badakhshanis to take refuge in Afghanistan and countries of the former Soviet Union. Many were victims of atrocities by local groups supported by the government. Intergroup relations were much more complicated and tense than in Kafarnigan.

The PC group first described the project to the mayor. His reaction seemed positive. He wanted to involve his deputy, who was responsible for relations with the NGO sector, as the first moderator and government representative. He promised that the city leadership would support any projects the EDC developed but said it would be better if these programs paralleled the city's development plan.

Problems started from the very first months. They found it extremely difficult to arrange meetings, to gather at least a majority of members, and to preserve the core group of members. The PC found it difficult to get financial and other reports from both moderators. The PC persevered because of the sincere interest expressed by local communities and a few ordinary citizen members. After a few rather successful meetings, it could not sustain itself.

In the end, the team disintegrated. Its members failed to conduct meetings after June 2001 in spite of numerous promises by the two moderators. The first moderator excused herself because of the pressure of government work and repeatedly rescheduled meetings. The second moderator, a former official, said he could do nothing without the first moderator's permission. The first moderator then left her job without a word.

This situation left the PC with two options: (1) to reshape the EDC with new participants and moderators and to move to the base of a local community or (2) to disband the experiment. Finally, in November 2001, the PC working group decided to close down. It was a difficult decision because of the interest, hopes, and expectations of the ordinary citizens who had been faithful, but it was obvious that city leadership seemed unlikely to allow the effort to continue.

The PC working group in retrospect identified the following reasons for this failure.

The EDC tried to cover the entire city. The moderators made that decision under government pressure, despite initial agreements with the PC to focus first on one local jamoat as was done in the other two EDCs. They could not spread their attention across so large an area.

The mayor strictly controlled the EDC. He approved participant selection, and the moderators reported all decisions to him. Under his pressure, the moderators insisted on developing only large projects and on focusing on local state enterprises.

As a result, most participants were heads of local state enterprises or businessmen close to government. Always busy, they could not attend meetings. Later, the PC pressed moderators to include ordinary citizens, but they did not feel free to express their thoughts in the presence of the "big bosses."

Most EDC members were not sincerely interested in the process. Heads of state enterprises did not understand the reasons for public engagement and the deliberative approach. They wanted only final recommendations. Participants felt that the final benefits of their work would accrue to the city leadership and the communities would get nothing.

A Second Round of EDCs

At the beginning of 2003, the PC working group decided to explore other areas. They were not abandoning Kafirnigan and Shartuz, but they felt these two teams had enough knowledge, experience, and skills to take their first steps as independent citizen associations and to decide how they would continue. The Kafarnigan EDC registered as an independent NGO, while the Shartuz team registered as a separate branch of the PC.

In the autumn of 2003, the PC launched two new EDCs. They made the selection according to the criteria developed in the first round with modifications reflecting experience.

The new EDCs were established at the community or jamoat level. This allowed them to maintain independence as associations of citizens outside government.

The training program was made more effective by inclusion of the "old" moderators as cotrainers. They helped the new teams shape their ideas and develop proposals, as well as avoid their predecessors' mistakes. As a result, the two new EDCs moved through the process much more quickly than the first three. This demonstrates the feasibility of using experienced moderators as trainers and points toward the potential development of a network of EDCs staffed by experienced moderators and no longer entirely dependent on the PC.

The first of the new EDCs was established in Dahana Jamoat in the Kulyab region in southern Tajikistan next to Afghanistan, but well west of Shartuz. In the first few months, members developed three proposals. The first involved constructing a greenhouse to meet the need for fresh fruits and vegetables in the local market. Previously they were imported from other regions and were of poor quality and too expensive. A second proposal addressed a broader crisis in the agricultural sector. Although most of the common land from the Soviet period had been distributed among the citizens, much remained uncultivated because local farmers did not have money to buy fuel, fertilizer, seeds, and other essentials for producing a crop.

The EDC members developed a proposal for an Agricultural Fund to provide farmers with needed materials.

The second new EDC was established in Buston Jamoat in northern Sughd province along Tajikistan's border with Uzbekistan. Its members decided to focus first on a micro-credit program similar to the one started in Kafarnigan.

As of this writing, these four experiments are still unfolding, and new ones are in formation. Beyond their further development and increased funding is the potential of a nationwide network with long-term impact on development and on how citizens engage in development. A step in that direction was a decision by the United Nations Development Program (UNDP) to engage the PC team to train an additional group of local development committees.

What Has Been Accomplished?

The PC set out in the same spirit of citizen experimentation that had characterized our approach in launching the Inter-Tajik Dialogue. We wanted to "*see whether* a group could form from within the conflict that could design a peace process for their own country." The PC set out *to see whether* citizens could develop a mechanism and a process of economic development for their own communities instead of waiting for outside help. The answer is that they can.

In Mullojanov's words: "It was not an easy task because of the complicated social and political situation and because of the legacy of the totalitarian and then the post-communist system. However, in four regions of Tajikistan, such citizens' associations are established and are so far sustainable and skilled enough to run their first projects."

He continues: "The EDCs have a dual agenda. On the one hand, the task is to engage citizens in public life and to promote mobilization of community resources for the most acute issues of the society. On the other hand, the aim is to improve relationships first inside the EDC team and then in the wider society. These two tasks are strongly interrelated. People in tension cannot work together. People interacting and cooperating produce good relationships. The EDC process brings together representatives of different and often conflicting parts of society and raises a cluster of questions equally important to all of them. Working together, they steadily develop relationships—first among themselves and then among the communities they represent—that become the base for intercommunal cooperation for economic growth and social development."

EDC moderators and team members are all aware of the dual agenda from their first training sessions during which the entire process and its purposes are explained and explored. For most community members, on the other hand, the agenda's conflict resolution aspect remains in the shadows or is regarded as of minor importance. Officials dismiss it. "However," Mullojanov writes, "this aspect is at the heart of the approach. Therefore, the main question in assessing outcomes is: Economic conditions may have been changed, but are relationships among different ethnic, regional, political factions and social strata changed?"

In order to begin answering this question, the PC asked EDC teams and community members to respond to questionnaires, interviews, and focus groups. EDC members discussed this question in some depth during meetings. Mullojanov has clustered responses in the following way.

"First, most EDC members stressed that their skills, experience, and knowledge increased. One participant stated: 'We received much more than just information on civic education, public engagement, and community-based economy, proposal writing, and fund-raising. More important, we learned how to work with each other and with the people.' Another team member said: 'We learned to listen and accept different viewpoints and to take into account others' interests.' Many team members stated that they learned how to work with their communities and mobilize their resources. 'I started to understand that ordinary citizens may change the situation themselves without expecting something from the government. I learned what kind of means to use to solve our people's economic and social problems,' said a Dahana EDC member.

"Second, all EDC members mentioned improvement of interpersonal relationships within each team. During one meeting in Dahana, a team member stated: 'We are fifteen different people representing different parts of our society. Moving ahead towards the common goal, we became the closest of friends. Designing proposals, our working group members had to meet not once a month but a few times each week. Nowadays, we often visit each other's homes and offices to discuss different problems. As we become close to each other, it becomes easy to cooperate. Working together, we managed to identify our communities' most acute problems and ways of dealing with them. If at least some of our ideas were implemented, we would become the happiest group in the world.' A Kafarnigan participant stated, 'We learned more about each other that assisted us to design better proposals.'

"However," Mullojanov writes, "most team members and ordinary citizens are much more skeptical concerning changed relationships beyond the EDCs. As a Buston team member said: 'First, we have to prove the usefulness of our EDC for the rest of the community. To reach this goal, we have to implement successfully at least two or three of the designed projects. So far, the EDC's influence is limited because the community does not feel the practical outcome of our activities yet.' Another participant stated: 'When people work together, they become friends. We still don't have projects big enough to make wider groups of people cooperate with each other.' This is, of course, a central problem identified by students of social capital: when people who know each other well cooperate, they refer to 'bonding' social capital; when strangers learn to work together according to agreed rules of interaction, they refer to 'bridging social capital,' which is far more difficult but critical to develop.

"At the same time," Mullojanov reports, "almost all participants and community members stressed that they have faith in the future of their EDC. 'When I first came to the EDC meetings, I was so skeptical,' said a woman from Dahana. 'Now after I have participated in a series of meetings, I believe in the future—not because we have so many projects implemented but because I trust my colleagues.' Many community members expressed the same sense of trust. 'We trust the EDC people because we have known all of them over many years. We trust their decisions because when they identified problems and ways of dealing with them, they came to the community and asked our advice. Our voices were taken into account. EDC decisions are not taken out of the blue—we made them together,' said a community leader from Kafarnigan.

"On the other hand, many team members mentioned that they feel an increasing responsibility. Said one: 'Now the entire community knows about our committee. Their expectations are the heaviest burden for us. When people meet us on the street, they often ask: 'What happened with your programs? When will you implement them?' We have to justify people's expectations; otherwise we will lose prestige among the community.' Another participant added, 'We would lose our prestige not only as EDC members but even as community members as well.' "

What Has Been Learned?

Listen to four citizens reflecting on their experience in response to Mullojanov's questionnaires:

> Before I worked with the EDC, I thought that the sphere of politics is the preoccupation of politicians and that only professional politicians or officials are able to define politics. Now I think that citizens themselves finally define the destiny of their country.
>
> I used to think that if the country chose democracy and development of civil society and established an atmosphere of pluralism and political freedom, Tajikistan would change and prosper immediately. Unfortunately, I was wrong. Democratization is not a short-term process. We citizens have to prepare our society by making social, political, and economic changes.
>
> Each of us understands fully the importance of her and his participation in establishing a sustainable civil society.
>
> The Public Committee must be a means to unite people, to consolidate their efforts, to promote the civic engagement of ordinary citizens. By promoting civic engagement and citizens' active participation in public life, we would make a contribution to the democratization of politics in Tajikistan.

After four years of experience, Mullojanov crystallizes conclusions as follows.

The first part of the dual agenda for the EDCs has been tested and proved. EDCs are well established in four regions organizationally and structurally. Each has a well-trained facilitating team and a solid group of members regularly participating in its meetings. In all four jamoats, the EDCs are well known and respected by the rest of the community.

Each EDC has developed a detailed action plan and several concrete proposals aimed at changing the economic and social situation in the community. Two are already implementing their first projects, and the new EDCs will start soon.

While interpersonal relationships within the EDCs are significantly changed, the goal of changing intercommunal relationships is not fully reached. This will require larger projects with cooperation among a broader range of groups and strata to assure a major impact on society. So far, EDC projects are small.

The EDCs, therefore, are at a "decisive stage of their development. They have a solid base to continue and to make a real impact on their societies. However, in the next two years, they must assure their sustainability by successful fund-raising. Otherwise, they will have to limit their activities or close."

The EDCs have had difficulties obtaining funding inside Tajikistan. Local businesses are still in formation and, in any case, do not yet have a tradition of sponsoring civic or humanitarian programs. International organizations either do not have the capacity to operate at a community level or have chosen other priorities.

Beyond these factual judgments, Mullojanov sees a number of deeper lessons.

First, the EDC experience shows a strong correlation and interdependence between economic and democratic development. Moreover, in such post-communist countries as Tajikistan, economic development in most cases must come first. Indeed, the precondition for real democratic development is the existence of a stratum of small and medium owners or businessmen—the so-called middle class. This stratum must be influential and numerous enough to promote and support real economic, social, and democratic changes in the country. Even the most democratic legislation would remain on paper if such social strata were not available. In countries like Tajikistan, especially in rural areas, the only way to create such social strata is economic development at the community level. Therefore, civic initiatives such as those represented by the EDCs are critical for Tajikistan. Such initiatives stimulate wide-scale civic engagement and mobilization of both human and material community resources that are also an important precondition for democratic development.

Unfortunately, most programs implemented by the international agencies in Central Asia are oriented to education and training, usually excluding the economic component. Formation of real democratic and civil society is consequently slow and complicated.

Second, the Kurgan-Tube EDC's experience shows that economic and capacity growth must occur first on the community level—that is, on the level of ordinary citizens covering mostly the sphere of small and medium businesses. The large-scale projects that officials favor too often do not benefit communities and ordinary citizens. Therefore, most civic economic initiatives must be undertaken on a community level.

Third, the Kurgan-Tube experience also proves that civic initiatives taken over by officials are probably doomed to failure. The government contribution is important and useful—and often unavoidable. However, such involvement must be well balanced. The Kurgan-Tube EDC failed because it gradually lost its civic character and became an officially controlled action.

Fourth, the EDC approach has revealed its essential conflict resolution and prevention potential. That potential is based on public dialogue and deliberation, which is at the heart of the EDC approach. When people regularly meet and deliberate freely on problems that are acute for all of them regardless of ethnic or social background, they gradually create connections and habits of cooperation that are the main preconditions for improved relationships. The subject of discussion can range from economic to social to educational issues—it just should be equally important for all participants. In Tajikistan, discussion has focused mainly on economic and social issues because they are more acute in most communities. Whatever the subject, the result has been the same in all four jamoats—a base for successful further cooperation has been created."

As the Public Committee further expands its work to include new areas, the national impact of public bodies such as the Economic Development Committees—socially, economically, and politically—will depend heavily on whether funders will recognize their potential and will help move them to a national scale. Will they recognize that systematic public engagement is indeed the greatest untapped resource in meeting the challenges of the twenty-first century—the missing ingredient in 50 years of economic development theory?

CHAPTER EIGHT

Power and Public Work in West Virginia

"When people come together for the common good, power springs up there," said a board member of the West Virginia Center for Civic Life.[1] She is one of countless citizens in the United States working to engage citizens in public life and work. The experiences of Tajikistan and West Virginia are literally and culturally half a world apart. Both are mountainous states; West Virginia has one-third of the population and a little less than half the land area of Tajikistan. More significant, Tajikistanis' experience is rooted in a Central Asian khanate and 70 years of totalitarian Soviet rule while West Virginians have a tradition of democratic thought and practice. One people is Muslim, the other predominantly Christian. Despite their vivid differences, some citizens in each are deeply committed to developing an engaged public.

Five Revolutions in American Life

U.S. citizens from the mid-1950s through the mid-1970s generated profound change in five arenas of American life. At the same time, in the words of Carmen Sirianni and Lewis Friedland, two scholars of civic innovation: ". . . over the past several decades [Americans] have created forms of civic practice that are far more sophisticated in grappling with complex public problems and collaborating with highly diversified social actors than have ever existed in American history."[2]

First was the Civil Rights Movement, which legally redefined the rights of African Americans and reordered at least working relationships among people of different races. Much change was accomplished through nonviolent action with roots in the thought of Mohandas Gandhi, whose years in South Africa influenced the commitment of the ANC to a biracial country. As in South Africa after the structural transition, transforming underlying relationships is still a work in progress. Change was decisively influenced by citizens outside government. The citizenship schools of the rural South were vital in that they trained workers to help African Americans register to vote. As Harry Boyte, then a field secretary for the Southern Christian

Leadership Conference (SCLC), told me: "The schools were a place where *people reconceptualized themselves as citizens*. They learned the skills to claim responsibility for change."

Second was the "hippie revolution against the establishment." A new generation deeply questioned through dramatically different life styles, culture, dress, music, and literature the moral system and certitudes of the generation that had fought World War II and raised them. A corollary of this movement was the sudden springing up across America of citizens, in remarkable numbers, who were disillusioned with the political system, feeling they had no say in government actions. Through experiments in thousands of communes and collectives, they attempted to bring governance of daily affairs to community and neighborhood levels.[3] The spirit of this movement was captured in a book titled *The Greening of America*:

> There is a revolution coming. It will not be like revolutions of the past. It will originate with the individual and with culture, and it will change the political structure only as its final act. It will not require violence to succeed, and it cannot be successfully resisted by violence. It is now spreading with amazing rapidity, and already our laws, institutions and social structure are changing in consequence. It promises a higher reason, a more human community, and a new and liberated individual. Its ultimate creation will be a new and enduring wholeness and beauty—a renewed relationship of man to himself, to other men, to society, to nature, and to the land.[4]

Third was the feminist movement, launched to change the status of women in society and in the workplace. Sometimes militant and strident to dramatize a valid point and to change attitudes, it aimed, as had the Civil Rights Movement, at changing the rules through legislation and other mechanisms such as "equal opportunity" employment. In addition to redefining fairness, the movement upended the aspirations and standards for success of a generation of young women who felt they would lose respect if they did not choose career over family. As more and more committed themselves to careers—at least in the early years of professional life— community organizations that depended on women's volunteer work suffered. As social standards changed, the two-income family became a factor in the economy and in raising children. In the 1970s, major single-sex universities became co-ed.

Fourth, as the U.S. military involvement in Vietnam deepened, energies from each of these movements flowed into a broad and powerful antiwar movement. Engaging citizens at all levels, it built to a crescendo that caused President Lyndon Johnson to decide not to run for reelection in 1968 and pressed President Nixon to withdraw. This experience was the ultimate demonstration that no policy is sustainable in a democracy without the consent of the governed.

Fifth, perhaps reinforcing the new generation's challenge to the moral code, was the further change in sexual mores as the contraceptive pill reduced a major practical inhibition against sexual relationships outside marriage. Along with women's enhanced sense of professional freedom, this contributed to later marriage and to new patterns of relationship.[5]

In addition, World War II and the Cold War fundamentally changed the global role of the United States and American citizens. Our government became the "leader of the Free World"—defender against expansion of the godless, totalitarian Soviet Communist empire and its perceived goal of world domination. Citizens became Fulbright Scholars and Peace Corps volunteers, and government-supported language and foreign studies programs aimed to enhance national security by building a cadre of citizens capable of engaging in international life. By the early 1970s, scholars were writing about a "world without borders," "complex interdependence," and powerful corporations developing their transnational organizations, operations, and rules—perhaps a glimpse of what we later called "globalization."[6]

A Movement for Public Engagement and Civic Renewal

From this intense experience, two lines of thought and experience unfolded. One recognized what citizens in close working relationships could accomplish. The other focused on connecting citizens' capacities with governmental power by reducing citizens' alienation from government. Both caused rethinking about the nature of democracy.

In 1980, political scientist and sociologist Jane Mansbridge in *Beyond Adversary Democracy*,[7] sharpened the distinctive characteristics of what I call the two threads of Western democratic thought. She calls them "unitary" and "adversary" democracy. In my words, unitary democracy focuses on the citizen as political actor; adversary democracy focuses on the machinery of democracy connecting citizen to government.

The roots of unitary democracy, in her analysis, reach back to the hunting-gathering phase of human experience but, in recorded time, to ancient Athens. Unitary democracy, she writes, "makes formal and extends to the level of a polity the social relations of friendship"—I might say "relationship." "Friends are equals. . . . They share a common good, and are able, as a consequence, to make their decisions unanimously. The characteristics of unitary democracy—equal respect, face-to-face contact, common interest, and consensus—are from this perspective nothing but the natural conditions that prevail among friends."[8]

"On the adversary side," she writes, "the Athenians accepted as legitimate the separate interests of citizens. . . . The Athenian assembly allowed its decisions to be made by formal vote with majority rule, and a formal vote is the crucial mark of the legitimacy of conflict. . . . Yet amidst the competing interests of individuals . . . Athenian citizens could still believe that the goal of their deliberations, when they met regularly face to face in the assembly, should be the common good."[9]

"It was not until the advent of the large-scale nation-state and the market economy," she states, "that the foundations were laid for a full-fledged system of adversary democracy." Society was increasingly seen to be organized around the pursuit of individual self-interest. "Modern political scientists have taken this line of development to its logical conclusion. In current adversary theory, there is no common good or public interest."[10] In contrast, the burgeoning communes and collectives of the late 1960s and early 1970s "almost without exception . . . assumed that their members had common rather than conflicting interests."[11]

At the same time, citizens and governments in the United States in the 1980s and other nations in the 1990s in post-Communist and post-authoritarian systems increasingly recognized that government could not meet all the challenges of a society. They recognized the need in the common interest for a new equation bringing together the authority and resources of government and the energy and hands-on knowledge of citizens outside government.[12]

One leading organization focusing on the citizen as political actor has been the Kettering Foundation after 1981 when David Mathews became president. Mathews had been president of the University of Alabama and President Gerald Ford's secretary of Health, Education, and Welfare. During desegregation, he advocated the responsibility of institutions of higher learning to make central the preparation of tomorrow's citizens as political actors. He saw public deliberation as the essential act of an engaged public. He left government in January 1977, concerned at the public's absence from government policymaking. He became a trustee of the Kettering Foundation and a close associate of fellow trustee Daniel Yankelovich, cofounder with Cyrus Vance of the Public Agenda Foundation in New York and a leading scholar of how citizens reach "public judgment."[13] Mathews and his fellow trustees refocused the foundation on public engagement through deliberation. The vehicle for this work quickly became the deliberative public forum and ultimately a program named the National Issues Forums (NIF).

Two closely related activities were central to the rapid development of the NIF. One was a carefully worked out process for presenting issues to the public in a way most likely to elicit deliberation rather than debate. The other was the development by citizens of institutes for teaching moderators to use these materials in ways that would encourage deliberative exchanges in contrast to the confrontational debate of what Mathews called "politics as usual."

Five main thoughts underlay the production of "issue books" from which citizens could begin their deliberation of complex issues: (1) For citizens to act, they must first make choices. (2) To make choices together about complex issues, they need to "name" or define problems with other concerned citizens in a way that permits each citizen to see her or his concerns reflected in the problem statement. Those who name the problem often set the public agenda. Naming is a powerful political act. (3) Because public problems are complex, there are rarely clear-cut answers. Each possible approach must be "framed" in a way that captures something that citizens value. (4) As citizens weigh these approaches—that is, as they deliberate—they hear what others value and why, and they have to weigh conflicts within themselves. (5) From deliberation will emerge not a course of action but a sense of direction—enough common ground to enable them to talk further about specific actions or at least to act individually in ways that reflect others' interests.[14]

With this conceptual framework in place, Kettering and its associates began conducting the Summer Public Policy Institute to train those who would moderate—facilitate—forums. When the numbers went beyond Kettering's capacity, a group of regionally diverse local training sites grew rapidly in the 1990s until there were more than 30 in the first years of the new century. This explosion was paralleled by the dramatic increase in the numbers of community organizations across the country holding NIFs until no accurate count was possible. Forums were held by civic organizations, adult literacy programs, high schools and colleges, corrections facilities, extension services, 4-H clubs, environmental associations. Issues ran a wide gamut from alcoholism and drugs, through democratic governance, social security, the national debt, abortion, economic pressures on families, and race relations to the role of the United States in the world, China-U.S. relations, and the Russian-U.S. relationship. In the early 1990s, Kettering began hosting international fellows whose organizations felt that the deliberative process could help them develop democracy in the post-Communist period in Russia, in East-Central Europe, and in Latin America after the fall of military dictators.

This work—and much else like it—has been impressive. What is its impact on the conduct of national politics? As in many such ventures, this may be unknowable, at least for a considerable period of time. In a community, one may be able to discern differences in the way a community does its work, but on a national scale, change may be the work of generations. Given that citizens outside government are disillusioned by the disconnect between them and their governments and are hungry for ways of making a difference, most practitioners feel that success is measured by laying down one achievement after another.

The West Virginia Center for Civic Life

One organization that seems to have made significant progress toward establishing statewide citizens' networks is the Center for Civic Life in Charleston, West Virginia. They have consciously gone beyond a collection of local activities to think on a statewide scale. The accomplishments of the organization in its first decade reveal a sense of citizens working within the context of the relational paradigm. Although they would not refer to a paradigm, they repeatedly use its vocabulary. I tell their story largely in their own words.

Their story begins around the turn of the 1990s, although it reaches back into the mid-1980s for some of the original actors and is closely related to the growth of the NIFs. The Center, although quite independently breaking new ground, maintains a close working relationship with the Kettering Foundation. I record their story first in the words of Betty Knighton, who eventually became the Center's founding director.[15]

When Betty Knighton first became involved with deliberative forums, she was working part-time with the Humanities Council in West Virginia while raising three children. The Council became aware of several women engaged in adult literacy programs who were using abridged versions of the NIF guides to engage high school dropouts, prison inmates, and residents of a housing project.

How did those programs begin? In the words of one of these women, Jean Ambrose, whose focus as director of the Commission for National and Community Service for ten years is citizen engagement and citizen leadership: "I had a specific goal. I think that's how many people come to this work. I was working with an issue that I really cared about—adult illiteracy. I was working statewide at the time with adults who were functionally illiterate. I was always looking for processes, materials that would appeal to adult students, that would be written in simple, clear language, and that would treat them like adults. In 1986 or '87, I became aware of the Kettering Foundation's abridged NIF guides and went for moderator training to their Summer Public Policy Institute. I became very excited about the process. Our students used the issue guides with their tutors and then had a forum with other students. They worked up to a public forum where they could participate like anyone else. I was a member of the Humanities Council board at that time. I approached the Council for a little grant for a pilot project in my community to see how it would work. I convened a steering committee and used all the NIF issues. I found that people were really drawn to the process. Since then, I've taken it wherever I've gone as one of my basic tools—whatever the issue. You need the wisdom of people."[16]

The director of the Humanities Council, according to Knighton, saw public discourse as a way of immersing people in the humanities and thought in terms of connections and political process. "The situation was ripe because people in West Virginia were questioning why their condition was what it was," said Mary Virginia DeRoo, then working with the Council of Churches.[17] On the basis of Ambrose's experience, the Humanities Council's director asked Knighton to build on this program.

She learned about the NIF and began acquainting herself with organizations such as the Library Association and the Council of Churches, which had broad networks. She attended their meetings to learn their interests and to see how the NIF might fit into their work. "I've never tried to sell NIF to anyone," Knighton says. "The question always was whether we had common interests." Her approach was to listen, to learn, and to connect people where useful. "We were building relationships."

Meanwhile, Ambrose moved to a job in public housing working with very low income people who are not part of the political process. She occupied an office in a housing project. "I worked every day with people in dire straits. Knowing that there were whole areas of life that I knew nothing about, I realized that the only way I could learn would be to create an environment in which people felt safe enough to be honest with me. The issues forums provided a place where people could be treated with respect and I could show that I was a person in the housing authority administration who wanted to treat them with respect and wanted them to feel able to trust me. At that time we were working on the concept of resident management. We needed mechanisms for getting people together to build trust. Using the abridged issues guides, I held a few forums. Beyond that, I transferred the process to the larger issue of affordable housing that I was also working on. In all of this, my goal was to encourage West Virginians to become involved in their communities. The missing piece of moving to action has always been this thought piece where people can seriously sit down with each other as citizens and understand how they can't delegate responsibility for their problems to officials."

"In those early days," Knighton says, "we didn't set out with a strategy of building a network. If we had a strategy, it was the practical thought that connecting with organizations that had a statewide presence would give us the best chance of covering the state. If we could learn how to connect with their work, we could extend our work." At a certain point, she reflects, "Once partners became interested, the connections became a dynamic force that began moving us from our individual efforts to a statewide presence."

From the second year of their effort, "we had always had a steering group including representatives of most of the organizations using deliberation in their work," Knighton recalls. As the number of those engaged in the work increased, the idea of creating an organization began to take shape. From Knighton's vantage point, this coincided with a change in leadership at the Humanities Council and a decline of interest in these programs. In 1997, they decided to create their own tax-exempt, not-for-profit organization. In searching for a name, they first considered a descriptive title such as "The Coalition for the Promotion of Public Deliberation" but settled for the less precise but more usable "Center for Civic Life."

For Ambrose, what precipitated the formation of the Center was the dynamism of the deliberative process. "When the Humanities Council decided that it was not interested in supporting this any longer, there was not any question that it was going to stop. We needed to figure out ways to encourage people to understand what their role as citizens is and to form new habits. It's not hard to get people interested in this work. What is more difficult is forming habits—actually incorporating those habits into the way we do business. That required continued effort."

In 1995, Julie Pratt was director of the Governor's Cabinet on Children and the Family. "I saw in the newspaper an ad for a series of four forums on 'the troubled American family.' I had been listening a lot to how policymakers talked about this problem. I felt I needed to hear how other people talked about it. It was quite a diverse group, and the talk was quite contentious. I was surprised that people came back for the second meeting, but they did. I doubt that anyone changed their minds, but relationships changed. The biggest difference in the forum from the way policymakers talked about the issue was that citizens were speaking from their own experience; facts, ideology, and party line were less important. Then I went to one of Betty Knighton's summer institutes and participated in a Kettering Foundation program to learn more about the process for constructing engagement. I left government in 1997. I found the process instrumental in work that I was trying to do and understand better. I became interested in my own neighborhood."[18]

As they formulated the mission statement for the new organization, they thought systematically about what it would take to build a statewide network. When is a series of haphazard connections transformed into a network? As they took stock of what they had done, they identified four important insights.

First, people are "hungry" for a different way of talking that they can engage in. "People were looking for ways of talking to one another in public. That's what those first four women in the pilot NIF project latched onto," Knighton reflected. "The reason I think I was met with open arms almost everywhere was because people were ready for it—they were hungry for it. A lot of people in the state were disillusioned by other forms of public interaction that were unsatisfactory. We were meeting a need."

Knighton tells the story of a local forum. A University of Charleston student had engaged actively in the deliberation, but at the end of the forum, she said, "I'm really frustrated. I'm 19 years old. I'm a political science major. And this is the first conversation I've ever had like this." A white-haired lady responded: "Don't feel bad, honey. I'm 80, and this is my first time, too." This hunger seemed to be demonstrated everywhere from the poorest communities to the university students and even to state legislators who seem uneasy that they may be missing something important. "People find that their views are not just tolerated; they are welcomed."

Paul Gilmer, an African American member of the Center board who has divided his career among business, local government, and NGOs, explains this hunger in a more urgent way: "It's crisis-driven. People feel that high-level policymakers are in denial. Those of us in the trenches understand how severe the situation is. I've been in houses with no floors and two families living there. People in the gated communities don't see that. We see a state in crisis. Doing the things we've always done will just produce the same results. People want to try something different."[19]

"People have a real need to be listened to," said Neal Newfield, professor in the School of Social Work at the University of West Virginia working in family therapy. "In deliberation, at least portions of their positions are validated by other people. A forum is a place where you will be respectfully listened to." He continued: "Human beings are story-generators. After we've told a story, it becomes truth. I'm not a policy person or an administrator. Deliberative forums provide interface between stories and help us organize ourselves to make changes." As a photographer providing illustrations for the Center's issue book, "Making Ends Meet," he found hunger of a different kind: "I thought it might be difficult to get people to allow me to take pictures of their poverty. My experience was exactly the opposite: they came up to me and kissed me because they don't think anybody cares."[20]

Second, critical in responding to this hunger has been their discovery of the impact of contextualizing issues—presenting them not in remote national terms but in terms of West Virginian life. In Knighton's words, this permitted participants in forums to say, "This is about and for us." Knighton and her colleagues learned to engage West Virginians in framing their own issue books or to localize books on national issues so that citizens could identify with them. "People need to see a place for themselves. They need to see their role in the process."

In addition, Ambrose observed, in her work with volunteers and citizens doing national service, the connection between experience and the reflection that deliberation provides: "What these people learn in their volunteer work is that their actions can make a difference. They can no longer say that a situation can't be changed or that one person can't make a difference. If they've worked in a well managed volunteer or service program, they know that's not true. But they also need to have the conceptual base in terms of having had the opportunity to apply critical thinking to issues that concern them. Those two pieces don't always go together. There are lots of volunteer programs that are doing what they did fifty years ago without having engaged in any process that asks whether this is the best leverage for the amount of energies they were expending."

A corollary of giving citizens a sense that they can make a difference, in Ambrose's thinking, is her own sense of political process as providing "reliable opportunities for citizens' input into the decisions that affect their lives. We have very few opportunities for that. Here in West Virginia, people particularly feel disengaged from the political power structure. I work with many people in communities who really don't believe anything will change. We have an uphill battle in persuading them that this has a lot do to with their attitudes. The public forums can be a vehicle for making that connection."

Pratt seconded that view: "We have done a number of forums framed for West Virginian issues. People came to them to learn about the issues from other angles and to have their voices heard through the reports that were written on the forums. They felt connected to the public policy process in a way they never had before. People felt: 'I can understand these issues; they're not rocket science. I can form a position, and I can express a position.' The downside, of course, is that it focuses on what someone else should do. The public policy emphasis can undermine other initiatives."

Third, they discovered that the work of producing an issue book can become part of a larger process of engaging citizens in tackling problems. "The process of research, the interviews with people affected by an issue, the naming and framing of issues through a range of dialogues—all of these steps begin to give people a sense that this problem is theirs. They feel a part of creating an issue book. This is much more valuable than any form of outreach or publicity." Framing teams, Knighton explains, are only "conduits to the community." In preparing an issue book on a very sensitive issue—domestic violence—team members and others whom they involved talked with about 400 strategically placed citizens from victims to perpetrators.

Fourth, although citizens were hungry for a different mode of public talk and were making their own attempts at finding ones that worked for them, the existence of a self-conscious catalyst was critical in deepening their capacities and in connecting like-minded efforts. Without some group working at the Center, "there would not have been as much order in the chaos," Knighton said, referring to Dee Hock's description of a "chaordic" ("chaos" plus "order") network as a self-generating organism.[21] Indeed, she described the challenge of the new organization as "how to build a hub out of mini-hubs." In identifying further potential partners, they became more rigorous in their criteria: "Do they have the energy and the capacity for regenerating themselves? Are they interested only in one-time events, or do they want to share with others? Will they teach others? Do their networks connect with others?" The process of helping others to connect can lead to what Knighton calls "spontaneous regeneration."

Ambrose refined the point: "What's proving most successful is connecting with people who are really well organized in their own issue networks—the Coalition Against Domestic Violence and the Prevention Resource Center—and really understand the power of the process but recognize that they are not reaching out and tapping the wisdom of people as deeply as they want to be. It's a way of making really good practitioners even better and of being more effective in promoting the issue that they care about. Those are turning out to be the contacts that will be enduring. That will be the best way of spreading the work and helping people form habits of deliberation, which is our main purpose."

Since the Center formally began work, they have framed issue books on a range of problems. In one instance, an outline of the issue guide was published in both the morning and the afternoon newspapers. In other instances, they started with NIF books and customized them to the West Virginian situation. They have held training institutes in issue framing so that the specialized organizations Ambrose spoke of could frame their own issues as well as moderate forums. On several occasions, they held a series of statewide forums on issues of current concern to the governor and the legislature, wrote a report distilling how the public was thinking about these issues, and held public meetings to report to legislators. Some of these reports were also presented on television. In one case, they framed an issue for West Virginians called "Making Ends Meet," only to find users in the national network. They have also developed both a statewide and then a national book on healthcare, working on contract with the National Issue Forums Institute. From this diverse effort, citizens gained a sense that they were part of a larger process through which their voices were being heard.

The Center regards as especially promising the fact that, over a period of four years, the administration and faculty of the University of Charleston have "embedded deliberative dialogue and NIF at all levels of what we do at the university," explained dean of Student Life Doug Walters.[22] That means four years of exposure for some 200 students per year. The University provides office space for the Center. "Right from their orientation program, students become familiar with NIF. Faculty, where possible, have drawn the deliberative process into their pedagogy. Students are learning a way of thinking and talking that enables them to engage in logical ways with questions about race, sexuality, American politics, and international conflict. Students frame their own issues and hold forums. And besides, civic dialogue was the process by which the faculty reached their consensus on this emphasis. Students may not change their drinking habits, for instance, but they are much more aware of their responsibility toward fellow students whom they see sliding toward alcoholism. It has also provided a way of reducing tension on campus as the student body has become more diverse. This approach is spreading to some of the other smaller colleges in the state." Knighton also cites a group of university students in Campus Compact who have conducted a series of forums around the state and then returned to their own campuses to sit with members of the surrounding community to design joint actions.

Paul Gilmer sees the students meeting a variety of needs through their deliberative experiences: "They're looking for themselves. Who am I, and where am I going? They want to feel impactful. They want to feel, 'I can change this; I can make it better.' They're also looking for answers to other questions that are ticking around in their heads."

Their Conceptual Framework

In all of this, citizens have developed a philosophy of politics that is quite different from the conventional view that they were taught in school and grew up with. Most of them attribute the evolution of their thinking to their experience.

When asked what her view of politics was before she became involved in the deliberative work, Knighton described her picture as one of traditional processes: each citizen has a responsibility to follow political affairs, to learn about the issues and candidates, and to vote thoughtfully. Debate was the mode of exchange. "I did understand how the Parent Teachers Association and my church government worked, but I didn't relate that to politics."

When asked the same question, Ambrose began by noting that her view had been formed through her work for two degrees in American history: "We're a representative democracy; we elect people who have more time to study the issues; we expect them to make good decisions; if they don't, we don't vote for them again. As a student of history, I was impressed with the profound influence of individual leaders and their domination of the process. My role as a citizen was to decide who I thought would be the best leaders and delegate that responsibility to them. Actually, I grew up in a town with active town meetings during my childhood, but somehow that didn't enter my adult consciousness as an alternative—focusing on citizen engagement—to the representative model. As a student of American history, I was aware of the interaction between leaders and popular movements in certain periods, but I guess I didn't see myself in that context."

Neal Newfield at the University of West Virginia described the common public view of politics more bluntly: "People when they talk about politics see it as mean, nasty, and brutish. One side takes a position where there is no middle ground; your streets are lined with gold and anyone who disagrees with you is an ass and has no right to think that way. Then you debate and polarize the situation further. I find that absolutely painful. I hate it. I'm pretty good at debate, but I don't like it as a way of getting at workable truths. For me, the Center's philosophy allows for seeing 'the good, the bad, the ugly' in any approach to an issue; their notion is to get a group of people together to dissect what beliefs are organizing people's action and what the trade-offs are. It's the only way I can comfortably be involved in politics. It seems that most people see politics as entertainment and enjoy the spectacle of people going at each other with no sensibilities for the other's position."

Where did power fit into this picture? "On the negative side, I would have considered it to be amassing money or back-room deals," Knighton says. "On the positive side, I thought power came from building public support for a decision rather than thinking of citizens as doers. Today, on the other hand, in moderating a forum, I can almost see dotted lines among people, thinking that these are people who can work together. *I now see power as a potentially shared force field* (emphasis added)." Recognizing the potential of citizens working together, she says: "I'm even more frustrated and maddened by decisions made without reference to public views or public knowledge than I would have been before I became involved in this work because I have seen how much people can handle, how wise they are, how reflective they can be, and how nuanced their thinking is. Before, I wouldn't have been so hurt by the missed opportunities."

"It has certainly been proved to my satisfaction," said Ambrose responding to the same question, "that when people come together for the common good, power springs up there. Those experiences when people really do see each other as human beings change their relationships. The power that comes from those experiences has a wisdom to it that I don't see in other expressions of power. We have these indelible images from the past 50 years—the Civil Rights movement, the people overthrowing Marcos in the Philippines,

Tiananmen Square with the man standing in front of the tank, the fall of the Berlin Wall, South Africa which could have been a terrible bloodbath. That's the sort of legitimate—and real—power that I'm talking about."

A perspective on power originating in a quite different perspective was expressed by Sue Julian, team coordinator of the West Virginia Coalition Against Domestic Violence. She put the pieces together conceptually this way:

> I became a co-director in a shelter for battered women and their children in the heart of the coal fields in the southern part of the state. A part of the analysis of the battered women's movement was that violence in the home and eventually violence in the world is essentially an issue of power and control and an arbitrary belief in the right to maintain that power and control. I made this incredible connection—which I think is the gift of the battered women's movement to the world—between the various forms of violence in intimate relationships and war; they're all connected.
>
> The alternative is looking at relationships—it's all about relationships in my understanding now—based on equality, mutuality, accountability, input, access to decision-making, shared and accountable stewardship of resources. Decisions must include those most affected by the decisions. We must listen to the people for whom our services are developed. We must listen to the staffs of the organizations that we shape. We must prioritize relationships and look at the spokes of the power and control wheel—isolation, withholding of emotional support, economic control over resources, the threat or reality of sexual or physical violence. Opposite to that, the spokes in the equality wheel are respectful dialogue, listening to the voices, mutuality. . . . In looking at domestic violence, we had to figure out how best to respond to the need, what services to develop. We could only create that safe space in our homes, in our communities, in our state, in our country by listening to the people who were directly affected.
>
> Somewhere along the line, I learned of forums being held on 'the troubled American family.' I was impressed by the process, by the challenge—I thought I was a good listener—of sitting in a room with people with different perspectives, a different take, different belief systems. The challenge was how to take these differences and to commit to living side by side. It also changed my thinking about how do deal with people who perpetrate violence.[23]

She came to a different view of the source of power.

What Has the Center for Civic Life Achieved?

Is something being created that is changing political culture in West Virginia—that in some way is changing how West Virginians relate to each other? Is the practice of deliberation reaching a point of critical mass?

In asking the questions, I am quick to recognize that they are unanswerable in a definitive way. I am acutely aware from experience that, in a complex social and political context, cause and effect can rarely be completely understood. Where there are many inputs to a decision or action, one can rarely know which input can claim decisive credit. Nevertheless, one can identify changes in behavior in smaller settings and at least begin to judge how far-reaching they may be.

"I actually think that we are on that path," Knighton responded. "There have been effects like that in parts of the state, but certainly not in all. I don't know that that will ever be possible because there will always be people who will resist or not be interested." The record of statewide issues framed and forums held speaks for itself. The number of diverse organizations—including universities—using the process is concrete. Reports written on the forums and presented to the governor, to the legislature, and to the public on television are a matter of record. The capacity of the Center to be the engine for producing issues books for the NIF enlarges their contribution. Impressive as the record is, Knighton and her colleagues probe for the underlying indications of fundamental change.

"Here's a major shift I've noticed," she reflected. "In the early days, those of us involved were the ones making contacts, reaching out, visiting new places, thinking about connections with potential partners. Now when people who have heard about the process ask for help, we can connect them with others nearby rather than acting ourselves. There are communities or parts of communities that use this process as an integral part of their public life—part of their normal way of doing their work."

In addition, she added, "Individuals have told me the experience has changed their political thinking. There are certainly organizations that would say their organizational culture has changed. Also, all these students are graduating from the University of Charleston with deliberation as an integral part of their education; we can't really know for some time how that will affect their performance as citizens. The issue framing work that the Center has done with existing organizations to enable them to frame their own issues is very important."

Ambrose provided an example from her own work of how partners can extend their learning about the deliberative process well beyond the Center. "For me as both a board member of the Center and head of a partner network, being able to connect thinking in a forum and actual work in the community has been critical for me. The development of people who understand what facilitative leadership and its skills look like is important. The typical West Virginian's picture of a leader is not them. It's a special person and usually a member of a particular family. Letting people know of a process that taps into the wisdom of the group takes the burden off them. It permits them to step forward and say: 'I can't do all of this, but this is the piece I can do.' People can get together that way. It gives people courage."

"Ten years aren't very long," Ambrose continued. "Even so, there are hundreds of people who have changed their way of thinking and lots of organizations that understand that they are not as effective as they could be in tapping public wisdom. Because West Virginia is a small state where lots of people know each other, more and more we hear people saying, 'We need to frame this issue.' There's a change in the way people approach problems. We're seeing people building issue framing and deliberation into their planning and program development processes. The hope is that, over time, it will be a common experience to have enough people in a given room who will turn to this process to deal with their problems. That's where we are getting into some deep learning. It's building that community that is our real work. We have more requests for help than we can respond to."

Sue Julian's answer is even more subtle: "I respond with great humility. The work of ending violence, of building freedom are ongoing and always will be. The domestic violence network in West Virginia was organized in the early 1980s. There was one law on the books; we felt we were out there alone; it was hard to speak to others because our perspectives were so different. There was no open talk about the issue. Over the years, the state has seen many laws passed and strengthened; there are multiple opportunities for training, education, advocacy. There is increased awareness that domestic violence happens, that it is a crime, that there are options, that there's help for victims. That part of the record is clearly visible.

"That would be a nice place to stay. But through our public deliberation project we heard what people in communities are saying about law enforcement response, about our public awareness materials, about the lack of services, about lack of responsiveness in the courts, about being revictimized in doctors' offices or in health care clinics, about the fear that keeps people entrapped in violent relationships. We have to address what we're not doing. The public deliberation project—having these conversations in groups of ten all over the state—helped us hear what we're not hearing. It provided a space to figure out together what needs to be done. We need a shift in decision-making processes from Roberts Rules to something that really does value the voice of the minority and struggles to come to decisions that value that voice. It's a shift in listening and caring—and not naively."

That participants in the process can analyze progress, judge shortcomings, and identify further steps in the light of experience through the deliberative process itself may be the most significant measure of what citizens are learning in relationship through dialogue. The bottom line is not only what has changed but whether citizens are demonstrating a capacity to direct change with greater sensitivity.

Where Is the Center Going?

The answers fall into two arenas: First, practices *are* changing in a growing number of organizations and communities, and it is essential to go on embedding these practices in more institutions and networks. To do that will require more attention to building the Center institutionally. This will require money. Second, the Center needs to catalyze the establishment of stronger links between deliberation and action because that is where citizens become convinced of the efficacy of the deliberative process.

"We are at a point where there are so many opportunities," Knighton answered. "We want to take advantage of the opportunities that these last ten years have given us in terms of public interest, public awareness, public desire to participate in this network."

"In program terms," she said, "we're ready to move into some of those areas that we've only experimented with briefly." For instance, the Center could work more with media and with policymakers on a variety of issues "over time in an ongoing way." "We have done enough of this to know that it can be really fruitful, but I don't even know what is possible in working with the legislature over time. We also know that it's fraught with potential difficulties in a partisan climate."

On another front, Knighton felt their work with college students is very promising and wanted to follow up seriously on programs already developing, for instance with Campus Compact. The purpose in that project is to have students design contexts in which they become public actors with community members based on public deliberation. "Then we want to follow this experience and others like it where public deliberation leads to action. We want to be more aware. We want to know more about how that works, when it doesn't work, what the obstacles are. Are there steps that these students and community members develop that could be taught to others?"

Ambrose added focus on West Virginia's economic development: "I don't know how many studies we've had on why we're so poor. One of the latest says, in effect, 'We have an oligarchy here. That's one of the reasons we're so poor. People feel disengaged. We need more diverse, more participatory leadership.' A lot of readers didn't like that analysis, but it's given credibility to the latest report called, 'Building Bridges and Empowering Citizens.' They don't have any bridge-building or empowering processes except what we're doing. That has created an entering wedge for us."

"To do any of this, we have to grow institutionally. Up until now," Knighton reflected, "we've just built solid relationships, and everything seems to have worked out. But I know that we have to think more systematically about making ourselves sustainable. If we had a full-time program officer, for instance, we could double what we could do in terms of follow-up and support for communities. We've been reluctant to focus on that because our main effort has been helping people develop skills that they can use and sustain themselves. Now we've reached a point where there is so much going on out there that if we are going to be a training provider, a connector, a networking workhorse, we have to have the time and staff to do that."

Pratt pointed to one practical point—the perennial importance of financial support. "We were really fortunate that the launching of the Center coincided with West Virginia receiving a five-year grant from the Kellogg

Foundation—not to the Center as such but for a number of the activities that the Center and its partners were engaged in. Ideally, in the spirit of an engaged public, funding should come from West Virginia's citizens and organizations that value the Center's contribution to productive public engagement."

The Center team knows they have to give much more attention to the link between deliberation and action. "The critical piece," Ambrose said, "is people's experience in linking talk to action—the discovery that they can make a difference."

In creating this link, the Center feels it can only take the first step. To preserve their neutral position, they feel they have to restrict their focus to the process of issue naming, framing, and deliberation—not on the substance of issues and not on moving to action.

"The purpose of groups that we have convened is to provide citizens with a new experience of citizenship, but I think we do leave people hungry for figuring out what the next steps are," Ambrose continued. "In some ways, the first next steps are their sharpened awareness and continuing education. They start to listen to the news differently, they read more critically, and they reach out for information they weren't interested in before. To begin with, we don't have a way to track even that effect in most instances. In any case, we know that a series of community forums alone is not likely to lead to action because participants don't necessarily have any bonds to the issue."

Beyond that is the more difficult challenge of actually moving systematically from deliberation to action. In providing that link, Ambrose says, "The Center has imposed some barriers on itself. What we have done is to work with networks of engaged partners who are the ones who carry on the actions. We have defined the Center for Civic Life as aggressively neutral. That is a barrier to action. We don't even convene the forums. As we've defined ourselves, it's inappropriate for us to lead the move to action. We hope that someone else will do that. A strong network does have that capacity."

Knighton constantly struggles with the problem. For instance, she expressed being wary of getting too close to media. "In a city with two newspapers—one more conservative, one more liberal—working with one could send the wrong message. Working with the legislature also risks putting us in partisan settings."

She repeated Ambrose's point: "We wanted so desperately to be this non-partisan, neutral presence for people. We wanted to be trusted." Mary Virginia DeRoo adds, "We don't want to muddy the waters—to tarnish our image."

Nevertheless, the challenge remains. "If we don't help people move to action, there's all this missed opportunity," said Pratt, "but worse than that it causes people to feel more despair and more likely to sit on their couches rather than go to another community meeting that they don't see going anywhere." Although the Center, like the Kettering Foundation, is concerned to protect its neutrality and is therefore wary of getting involved in action, they do understand that not pointing a way to move to action can lead to disillusionment with the whole process. There is no reason, they acknowledge, why they could not add to their training—and to the deliberative process itself—steps for designing action and involving the larger community in it.

In all of this, they demonstrate what it is to be a community of engaged citizens who learn together.

CHAPTER NINE

Citizens Talk about the Russia-U.S. Relationship

Harold H. Saunders
Philip D. Stewart[1]

We move now to one of the major international relationships the United States must learn to conduct more effectively as the Citizens' Century unfolds. In this study, we have the unique opportunity to look at the dynamics of the Russian-U.S. relationship through the eyes of citizens of each country deliberating among themselves on the relationship and their perception of the other country. The next challenge will be how to engage policymakers with citizens' views.

As the Soviet system became more flexible under Mikhail Gorbachev and as the Cold War wound down in the late 1980s, Soviet colleagues increasingly began talking about civil society. In our experience, this was dramatized in 1988 at the plenary of the Dartmouth Conference at the Lyndon Baines Johnson Library at the University of Texas in Austin. The Soviet delegation was a panoply of the "stars" of their civil society. After that meeting, the group met in California with conveners and moderators from the U.S. NIFs—an early effort to connect citizens of the two civil societies.

After the Soviet Union dissolved at the end of 1991 and the new Russian Federation moved toward a Russian form of democracy, Russians could begin drawing a wider range of citizens into political life, broadly defined. For instance, a few young Russians among the earliest international fellows in a new program at the Kettering Foundation in the early 1990s designed and conducted citizens' deliberative forums on issues important in Russian communities. Two of them registered their own NGOs in Russia.[2]

In 2001 and 2002, three Russian organizations[3] conducted 75 public forums across Russia on citizens' attitudes toward the United States and the conduct of the Russia-U.S. relationship. U.S. citizens in the NIFs initiated 25 mirror-image forums. In April 2003, an American–Russian group met in Washington, DC, to share insights into the relationship emerging from these forums and to discuss their implications for policymakers. They called themselves "the New

Dartmouth Conference"—a re-formation of the longest continuous bilateral dialogue between Soviet then Russian and American citizens, beginning in 1960, that played a remarkable role during the Cold War.[4]

The concept of relationship presented in this book is rooted significantly in our experience in Soviet-U.S. dialogue in the 1980s—especially in the Dartmouth Conference Regional Conflicts Task Force. Whereas in chapter ten this concept is used to organize the insights from dialogues among members of the policy-influencing communities in China and the United States, it is used here to organize insights from citizens entirely outside the structures of government and power. In short, it demonstrates that these citizens, more than governments, tend to think in terms of the relationship between whole bodies politic without explicitly using those terms. They feel strongly that the future of the Russian-U.S. relationship may depend more on their interactions than on the behavior of governments.

No one arranging these forums argues that this is a "scientific" report from a demographically representative sample of the two countries' populations, although 100 groups involving some 2,500 citizens from widespread geographic areas are not insignificant. The insights are not the results of public opinion polls or surveys. They are, rather, thoughts from two–four hour deliberations in which citizens in active dialogue around a structured and tested agenda weighed various possible approaches to the conduct of the Russian-U.S. relationship a decade after the end of the Cold War. The separate issues guides were framed by and for the citizens of each country.

Participants' objectives were not to formulate specific recommendations for policymakers, or even concrete decisions. Rather, these deliberations served primarily to clarify the difficult choices citizens must make among things they hold valuable in setting the most desirable path for the future development of this relationship. The products of their deliberations are a sense of direction and the thinking behind it—not an action plan. Such a sense of direction should be—but too often is not—the starting point for policymaking. A deeper understanding of the trade-offs they weigh is what distinguishes this form of citizen deliberation. This quality of public deliberation is what makes the records of these forums a uniquely valuable resource, as opposed to opinion polls, which are only snapshots of a quick reaction to questions formulated for a purpose. These forums permit a tentative analysis of the kind of relationship that two peoples are prepared to support.

What follows reflects how citizens talk and think about the relationship, often in their words, organized within the framework of our concept of relationship. The picture that emerges underscores the usefulness of thinking in terms of the relational paradigm and the concept of relationship.

Why Focus on Citizens' Perspectives?

Is it not sufficient to focus on the "real" actors in the relationship—policymakers, the policy-influencing community, and perhaps the international business community?

In broadly democratic societies—and today we include both Russia and the United States in this category despite significant differences in their political cultures—legitimacy and authority derive ultimately from citizens. Citizens today are sometimes not content to exercise this sovereignty solely at the ballot box. Indeed, we have gone so far as to conceptualize international relationships not only as state-to-state relations, but rather as "a process of continuous interaction among whole bodies politic across permeable borders." On the one hand, relatively few citizens, either American or Russian, give much daily thought to their relationship. But, the relationship does become particularly salient on at least three occasions.

First is when governments act in ways that counter what citizens hold most valuable about their own nation or their relationship with another. For example, the impression that the Bush administration created on many, probably most, Russians while these forums were taking place was that he was prepared to attack Iraq in 2003 despite the decisions of the U.N. Security Council and whether Iraq disarmed or not. For many Americans, this raised doubts about whether this kind of behavior was consistent with the values we hold as a nation. It also raised questions in both countries about the worth of the Russian-U.S. Strategic Partnership, signed by the two presidents less than a year before in Moscow.

When the public believes government actions go beyond citizens' views about a relationship, it may set limits. If these limits are exceeded grievously over time (e.g., the Vietnam War for the United States and the Afghan War for the Soviet Union), governments can lose the authority to continue their policies, and ultimately the legitimacy of the political system itself can be compromised.

Not all governmental action in the Russian-U.S. relationship transgresses these limits. In fact, the end of the Cold War, developing democratization in Russia, increasing economic cooperation, and greatly expanded business contacts all generated U.S. citizens' permission for our government to develop and intensify cooperation across a growing range of areas. These included arms reductions, Central Asian security, oil and natural resource development, and the war against terrorism, to name only a few. How fully Russian citizens support these developments, after having experienced a collapse of their way of life that posed security and identity issues for citizens of the former superpower, remains to be seen.

Second, citizen-to-citizen interactions between Americans and Russians are ever more frequent. Ordinary Russian citizens come to the United States to study, to work, to rest. Thousands of American citizens work in Russia on a regular basis in governmental projects, private enterprises, NGOs, and foundations, among others. Many more meet through study, tourism, sister-cities, and other programs. These contacts give the relationship life, make it concrete and real, and lead to complex webs of relationships. These interactions shape, reinforce, or change perceptions, beliefs, and expectations about oneself and about the other side. We need to understand these more fully.

For Russians as for most peoples outside of the United States, there is one form of nearly constant contact with America that most Americans are either totally unaware of or only dimly perceive. Yet this contact has a profound impact on images of the United States and consequently on the kind of relationship others find acceptable or not. It is the pervasive presence of American films and music on Russian TV and radio, CDs, and tapes—the most invasive form of American "culture." While this is a long-standing global phenomenon for many, for Russians denied any but the most carefully controlled contact with the West or America for more than 70 years, the sudden flood of American mass culture into their homes has a special impact. It confronts a proud and deeply rooted culture that is a significant part of their identity. Nearly every Russian household's exposure to American mass culture is a powerful if unexpected illustration of our hypothesis that relationships are formed by a "continuous process of interaction among whole bodies politic." These interactions are beyond the reach of democratic governments.

A third moment, salient for the American–Russian relationship for citizens of each nation is the act of deliberating about options for this relationship. One of the most uniform post-forum results in both countries was the unsolicited observation that the deliberations themselves had created a new interest in learning more about the other side. They seem to raise awareness of the ways that multiple things citizens value are affected by this relationship and of the complexity of the issues involved. They also bring to light significant differences in what American and Russian citizens might expect and value in a relationship. We see as one of the most promising areas for study the opportunity to reflect upon how these differences might be addressed. We can also expose the implications for both policy and the relationship should these differences remain or deepen.

The heart of this approach is the idea presented in this book—that power and influence derive as much from the conduct of relationships as from control over material and intellectual resources. Good relationships create greater and more effective capabilities to accomplish objectives than simple coercive power. Mutually advantageous relationships, in turn, are the product of cumulative, multilevel, open-ended and continuous interaction, engaging significant clusters of citizens either within or between countries.

The Russian-U.S. Relationship in Citizens' Words

The five components of relationship presented in chapter four provide the framework for the following analysis of insights from the forums.[5] Ultimately it provides an operational framework through which the relationship may be more effectively managed and strengthened.

Identity

What Is Russia? Who Are the Russians?—Russian Perceptions

Russia is a great power but was once a superpower. Being a citizen of a great power is one of the most commonly heard expressions of Russian self-identity.

"Russia is a great source of natural, cultural and intellectual resources; therefore there are strong reasons to respect her, and therefore America might be interested in her friendship." As one participant said of Russia and the United States: "These are two leading powers, military powers, who possess great military potential. How their bilateral relations develop will determine the life of the entire planet." At the same time: "With the collapse of the Warsaw Pact, the USSR as a superpower ceased to exist." Some express a strong sense of national and personal "loss" as a result of this sudden change. Others, however, noted the costs of this former superpower status: "The reality was that then our country constantly lived in a state of war."

When asked to list those parts of Russian life they would not be willing to sacrifice in order to improve relations with America, a participant listed in order of priority: Russian culture, Russia's independence, the nation's resources, both natural and intellectual, and Russian patriotism. The preservation and enhancement of these aspects of identity, then, define some of the limits of any relationship with America. More particularly: "To some degree we are a special country, a special people—Slavic, Orthodox, and Christian. We have our own traditions, our own customs, and therefore [in developing relations with America] we need to be very cautious. We need to take our mentality into account. Our soul, our way of life cannot accommodate everything that they have." Another Russian: "Let us simply reject the negative in American culture."

Many Russians, during their deliberations, pointed to the pervasive presence of American films on Russian television as not only creating a poor image of America, but as a threat to Russian culture. "Sometimes, I'd like to borrow an awful lot from America. But sometimes I really want to resist them. For example, the way they impose themselves upon us through the broad dissemination of American mass culture, the overwhelming presence of their films on television to the point that it is impossible to acquaint oneself with our own national films."

It is important for our understanding—and makes it more complicated—that while American companies certainly produce these films, it is Russian television executives who choose to show American films. These decisions are normally made on commercial grounds, that is, the anticipated audience the film can draw, and thus the advertising revenues. In this case, the influences on a most sensitive aspect of relationship—Russians' pride in their culture—are multisided, complex, and not subject to direct or central control by either side.

Although love of country is very strong among Russians, they are not blind to the nation's imperfections. Illustrative is the following comment by a mature Russian woman when asked whether she would like to move to America: "No, because everyone should have a homeland, and be proud of her homeland. If you are dissatisfied with something in your homeland, then do something to fix it or to improve it. Don't just run away, because you can hardly expect things to be better in America anyway." Other participants looked to re-armament as a means of stimulating the growth of

Russian patriotism, and with it a new national ideology that could bind together the various peoples of the Russian Federation.

This deep and abiding pride in their great power status, their world-class culture, and their intellectual capacity—integral parts of their identity—raises the salience of any elements of the Russian-U.S. relationship that directly or indirectly demean, challenge, or simply ignore these core aspects of the Russian identity.

One simple example illustrates how even the best-intentioned foreigners—in this case American missionaries—can deeply injure Russian pride. Regarding fundamentalist missionaries working in Russia, one Russian forum participant observed with sadness: "I would like to add a comment regarding the Christian missionaries. For a great country, this is simply insulting. They appear certainly to be well-intentioned, but they treat us Russians as if we were uneducated aborigines."

Even when pride of country is not very deeply felt, many Russians appear to feel guilty about this and consider that something should be done to strengthen Russians' ability to take pride in their nation. "You know, so long as we do not respect or take pride in ourselves, no one will take us seriously. Everyone should sense that we respect ourselves. Often, of course, we do not respect ourselves. Rather, we praise Western culture and the Western way of life, the striving to become Western."

Again and again, Russian forum participants spoke of how, in their view, the Russian character differs from the American as well as that of other Western peoples. "We have a different mentality," was one frequent refrain. Another put the differences starkly: "We are different peoples. The Americans are businesslike. Russians are kind-hearted." A woman who had recently visited Sweden contrasted her feelings upon leaving Russia for the first time, and upon returning. "As I left Russia for a trip to Sweden a few years ago, I said to myself, 'Goodbye to unwashed Russia, country of slaves.' But when I returned just two weeks later, I said to myself, 'What happiness that I am returning home. What happiness that I can go to my neighbors to share a cup of tea.' " Russians see themselves as more socially oriented and generally less concerned about material matters, even material well-being, than their American counterparts—and they see these traits as central and valued elements of the Russian identity.

Related to this mentality, some Russians contrast their dependence upon their circle of friends with American individualism—differences noted long since by Americans but now self-consciously observed by Russians as an important part of being Russian. These differences were concisely summed up by the following Russian comment: "[Americans] live just for themselves, and nothing else around them is of any concern. This individualism would oppress us. . . . This material security is simply not so important to all Russian people. For us, socializing, social connectedness, our community is still important. Material well-being is not our highest priority. . . . Our lives are sustained primarily by our social relationships, by our friends, by our families."

A related quality of character that Russians see as distinguishing them from Americans is the degree to which Russians instinctively look to government for answers to their problems. Some see this as a normal and desirable Russian trait; others believe here is where Russians can learn from Americans. Taking the latter view, one stated his position as follows: "We still need to learn to rely upon our own strengths. We all admit that love of work is not a driving force in our lives. However, we do know how to work. But, somehow in this process, we rely more upon the state for help, whereas [Americans] count on themselves. They believe a person should rely primarily upon himself; if the state helps, so much the better."

Russians, then, appear to have a quite clear sense of their identity as Russians. That some of these key factors appear to Russians to be threatened by elements of the relationship with America is also clear. Complicating any conscious efforts to strengthen the relationship in ways that respect this identity is the pervasive and perhaps uncontrollable presence of American mass culture in Russia today. At the same time, it appears that the opening of Russian borders in the late 1980s has helped the Russians not only to clarify their own sense of identity, but also to gain a more balanced and well-defined sense of who the Americans are.

What Is America? Who Are the Americans?—Russian Perceptions

As many Russians use contrast to describe themselves, we have already discussed some elements of a Russian sense of the American identity. Additional thoughts reflect how Russians interact with this American identity.

These include Americans' business-like approach to the world, their individualism, and self-reliance. For some Russians, this individualism can have a direct impact on our relationship, as it seems to be associated with a general American trait reflected in the way the American government also behaves. As one Russian put it: "Americans act solely on the basis of their own interests, not considering the interests of other countries." While this is probably the predominant view, even after public deliberation, at least one Russian insisted, "It is possible to be friends with Americans; they know how to listen and to hear." Regarding American culture, another Russian urged his codeliberators not simply to accept or reject it. "We should simply accept its existence as a fact, accept it not as our own culture, but rather accept that it exists, parallel, together with ours."

Aside from a sense of the identity of Americans as individuals, Russians, as yet, do not appear to have reached a new consensus on what America is as a political entity, as a state. For most, America is still seen as a superpower. For many Russians, this status seems to derive primarily from America's nuclear capabilities. As Russia continues to have rough parity in nuclear weapons, this enables some Russians to see Russia's and America's fates as still inextricably intertwined, as illustrated by this comment from a Russian forum: "These are the two leading powers, military powers, which possess enormous military potential. And, indeed, the condition of life in the entire

planet depends upon how relations between these two countries develop."
Some Russians continue to see competition between our two nations as
inevitable. "The USA is our traditional competitor in economics and in
culture." And: "There is a competitive struggle between Russia and the
USA over resources." Others take a broader view of the basis of American
power: "The USA is a powerful social-economic, political, and cultural subject. She is worthy of respect. We can make friends with her."

Based on these differing perceptions of what America is, we can conclude that the United States as a nation and as a state still has opportunity,
through its policies and behavior, to influence the formation of a broad,
positive Russian consensus on what America is. One Russian participant
indicated openness among Russians: "This is above all an issue of my own
internal psychological level of comfort. Since my childhood, I was taught
that Americans are people just like us. We celebrate the same holidays. We
did not develop the feeling that these are our potential competitors or that
America is some great superpower."

What Is America? Who Are the Americans?—American Perceptions

Americans in their deliberative forums on the Russian-U.S. relationship
tended to focus less on the question of their own or Russian identity.
However, the traits they did observe are important because Americans' self-
image seems quite different from Russians' perception of Americans. The traits
most often ascribed by American participants to Americans included: "com-
passion, caution, concern not to appear arrogant, highly self-critical, concern
not to impose, ignorance of other cultures." While it is probable that the traits
Russians most often associated with Americans would also come out in a study
of American self-images—especially "individualism and self-reliance," "businesslike" as contrasted with "social"—it is noteworthy that few if any of the
traits explicitly noted by Americans were found in the Russian forums.

While emphasizing his view that "Americans are a compassionate people,"
an American forum participant balanced this against the caution that "it is
important to use wisdom in dealing with Russia. Be compassionate but
prepared." This suggests what may well be an important limit for the
American public in this relationship—the fear that those we seek to help
will "take advantage" of American generosity. This was made concrete in
concerns that the Russian mafia probably has been the largest beneficiary of
American aid to that nation. Americans see themselves as ready to help, but
if they feel that help is illegitimately diverted then they may well withdraw
with injured pride.

In discussing the option of providing substantial humanitarian aid to
Russia, many Americans, in the deliberations, expressed twin concerns:
"Who are we to help when we too have similar problems" and "Russians
are a proud people; they may not respond well to this."

At least one American did draw attention to the idea that "Americans are
pretty preoccupied with their own lives," but drew a different implication

from the Russians: ". . . and therefore we don't have any understanding of Russian culture, literature, or history." That is, our concern for our own interests tends to blind Americans to interest in other cultures.

The contrast to Russian perceptions bears noting again, as it points to a profound asymmetry in our relationship. Whereas Russians are bombarded daily with images of American life through American films, music, and literature, Americans are exposed nearly exclusively to their own films, music, and literature. Russia enters most Americans' consciousness, if at all, through occasional reports appearing on TV or in the press. It is not a daily presence as for Russians. From a policy perspective, this probably means that Russians will always be more aware of whatever America does or does not do, and particularly of the values America is communicating than will Americans of Russian behavior or values.

Who Are the Russians?—American Perceptions

The Russians are a proud people. Russian pride in their history, culture, and traditions was noted with respect by many Americans. They also emphasized Russian intellectual accomplishments as a source of national pride. Most participants recognized the need to act in our relationship with Russia, as individuals and as a nation, in ways that do not injure this sense of pride. They stressed the need always to treat Russia as an equal for both moral and pragmatic reasons: "This will lead to greater cooperation in the long run."

Interests

If two peoples or nations believe they can only realize their most important interests through their relationship, then they have strong incentives to consider the potential impact of all their actions on that relationship. On the other hand, if they believe they share no important interests, when difficult choices must be made, little tends to support sacrifice or compromise of one's interests for the sake of the relationship. Reality for most relationships tends to be somewhere between these two positions.

Core Russian National Interests—Russian Perceptions

Each state has its own interests, and government's role is to defend them. While one Russian speaker suggested that a full range of cooperation should be developed between ordinary American and Russian citizens, he cautioned, "Relations between the two states are an entirely different matter. Nations are led by specific individuals, politicians, who must act on their own concrete national objectives, not general interests. Every country has its own national interests and it is to defend these that the government is elected." This growth in Russian society of a concept of individual interests as potentially separate from state interests suggests a surprising development of the idea of individual rights in the short history of post–Soviet Russia.

Most Russian forum participants favored pragmatic cooperation with the United States. In fact, nearly 90 percent, in post-forum questionnaires, felt that it is in the fundamental national interest of Russia to join in a coalition with the United States to "defend peace, to struggle against crime, and to preserve the environment." Russians' support for these interests appears to be based both on pragmatism and on idealism. One Russian commented: "We need to live in friendship with America because we comprise a single human civilization, because we need to preserve peace, because together we can deal with the ecological problem, low birth rates, and the problem of armaments. We have many concerns that bring us together, and where, irrespective of differences in political structures, social life and so forth, we need to work together, that is at the level of our governments."

Among pragmatic arguments in support of this view were heard such statements as: "A cold peace is better than a good argument. . . . One head is good, but two are better. . . . Partnership never hurt anybody. . . . We want no more conflicts, nor wars." Many Russians were also able to link this sense of Russia's national interests with their own personal interests, noting in particular that such intergovernmental cooperation would lead to expanded personal possibilities, and greater opportunities for personal growth.

Other Russians point to our common social problems as creating a motivation for cooperation. "Cooperation among ordinary people like you and me, among children, this would be very helpful." Possibilities for mutual economic benefit were not frequently mentioned, but some Russian forum participants did recognize that there is at least a potential for mutually beneficial economic cooperation not only in Russia, but on the scale of the global economy.

For some Russians, restoration of the military balance with the United States at all levels is a matter of pride as well as interest. Quite naturally, many Russians regret the passing of the former Soviet empire, and particularly the decline in Russian military power that followed. One participant explained: "You don't even need to connect this with America. In any case, we must strengthen our military foundation." Others link this to the need to be able to resist what is perceived as American "diktats," for example in the bombing of Serbia in 1999 and the war in Iraq. Asked one Russian, "Why have they taken upon themselves the right to dictate to people the conditions in which they must live? Their ambition promises nothing good for world society." These views found some support among about 70 percent of Russians completing post-forum questionnaires.

However, this is only one side of the story. For many Russians, experience has persuaded them that "it is impossible to resolve any serious issue by means of force." Beyond this, there is a profound Russian concern for the consequences of any remilitarization of Russian society and politics, which, they fear, could all too easily accompany a concerted effort to restore full military parity with the United States. The same Russian who argued that rearmament must be undertaken "in any case," continued with the following warning: "For such a long time we were a fully closed society, and why?"

Russians defined the conditions within which they believe Russian interests require rearmament to be contained. First, any rearmament should be within the context of agreements negotiated with America. Second, severe constraints on financial resources were noted. "An endless military build-up is only a waste of money. We don't have sufficient financial resources for education, for medicine, nor for many other basic needs." Third, Russian citizens see preserving the gains of democratization and a market economy in Russia as important reasons to limit the role of military power in their society. The key words here are "adequate" military power that cannot threaten "freedoms."

Russians also show strong awareness that unbridled Russian military power might increase the likelihood of any Russian-U.S. or other conflict leading to war. Even in the absence of war, excessive military power and even the implied threat of its use can create unnecessary, new enemies.

Russia should "contain" America diplomatically not militarily. What appears new in Russian thinking about its interests is a clear rejection of the use of force to deter or contain America. Balanced military power should exist to serve as an implicit threat, they said, but the primary means of ensuring that the United States takes the interests of other nations into account as it contemplates actions on the world stage should be diplomatic. Working together with other leading European and Asian states and through the institutions of the United Nations, Russian policy should be to "entwine" America in legal and moral undertakings that oblige her to act in concert with Russia and other major powers. This position was supported by more than 80 percent of all forum participants completing questionnaires.

We noted earlier the profound Russian concern with losing their identity through the American embrace of friendship and cooperation. Participants emphasized Russia's interest in maintaining a sufficient distance from America, so as "not to lose our own character," or worse "to become enslaved to America" psychologically.

These discussions brought up an even deeper reason for Russia to reject trying to become too much like America: the danger of a profound split in Russian society, perhaps even leading to civil war. For us, this represents one of the most important insights on the limits of the Russian-U.S. relationship.

Russian society has been deeply scarred by past efforts at embracing Western ways and thought. Peter the Great created a lasting split in Russian society when he tried to introduce Western customs and practices into the Orthodox Church. The introduction of Western Marxism into Russian society led to the most costly civil war in all of Russian and perhaps European history. Even many pro-Western Russians today are aware that an excessive closeness with America, or even Europe, could lead to a reopening of old wounds in a society that has not resolved whether it is part of the West, the East, or uniquely in-between. Any policy of close cooperation must respect this most salient of limits on American behavior.

On the other hand, this does not mean that there is in Russia significant support for what might be called Russian isolationism. The issue, rather, is one of Russia pursuing its own path, striving for more independence, and less one of a psychological need to see whether "Uncle Sam" approves.

In short, Russian citizens see Russian interests as providing a sound basis for the development of closer relations with America. But Russians are also very clear that there are real limits to just how close such a relationship can or should become. A productive American–Russian relationship must consciously and consistently respect these clear limits, as should any healthy personal relationship.

In addressing the question of Russian interests, forum participants noted that certain realities of Russian life, not dissimilar to American, hindered a fuller discussion. Among these is the fact that for most Russians the issue of American–Russian relations is not a particularly burning question. Second, there is a particular lack of interest in political issues among the youth, and this makes it difficult to judge the longer term. Finally, Russians feel they possess inadequate factual information about America, about its actual culture—not what they see on the screen—to come to fully sound judgments.

Core American National Interests—American Perceptions

American security cannot be achieved solely by military means. Americans, like Russians, believe that it is in the interest of the United States to maintain a strong military capability. They do not see this strength directed toward Russia but "against whatever threats may arise, e.g. terrorism today." At the same time, many participants emphasized that "it is not in our interest to focus primarily on our own security through military means, as this is only a part of security, and can lead to a cycle of conflict." In addition, in the interest of economic security, "the U.S. should not overspend on security as did the Soviet Union, leading to its collapse."

As do Russians in their forums, Americans perceive an overriding U.S. interest in maintaining allies and acting multilaterally. Forum participants are concerned that if the United States focuses solely on its own security, it might isolate itself from the rest of the world. "Maintaining allies like Russia is important for economic and political reasons." This interest shared by our peoples contrasts sharply with what was perceived by many at the time of these forums as an excessive readiness by the Bush administration to "go it alone" on crucial issues affecting not only U.S. security, but that of the entire Middle East as well as of our European and Russian allies.

"I heard during the deliberations," said one moderator, "a good deal of concern for the Russian people as fellow human beings; we were struggling with just how to go about helping to improve our relationship . . . and helping the Russian people, while not sacrificing our nation's security."

Americans do not see Russia as a threat. When faced with the option of dealing with Russia by putting U.S. military preparedness always in the first place, most Americans in the forums found this approach "excessive" because "it assumes Russia is still strong and a threat. We need not be so hawkish. Russia needs time to get its house in order. . . . With order and stability, democracy will grow strong."

This does not mean that all fears and underlying tensions in the relationship have vanished. Rather, deliberative Americans reach the pragmatic conclusion that these tensions are better managed through a closer relationship with Russia. "Tensions exist over the fear that Russians will sell weapons and ideas to terrorists or nations not friendly to the U.S. The existence of this circumstance makes developing friendly relations with Russia essential, not just convenient."

"We need Russia as an ally" was a common refrain. "Russia is a potential superpower no matter whether we help them or not, so what concerns me is our relationship, our social relationship, with Russia because in the future if they do become a superpower we want to be their allies; we don't want to be their enemies this time." Note that for this American citizen, creating such an allied relationship will depend at least as much on the quality of our citizen-to-citizen, that is, our "social," relationship as on government-to-government relations. In both America and Russia, the forums showed that citizens already have a well-developed awareness of their critical role in this relationship. American citizens at least have a decided preference for citizen initiatives over governmental initiatives.

Americans want Russia's political and economic transformations to succeed. "Even though Russia is currently struggling with its transition from Communism to a free market economy, forum participants agreed that a robust Russia might be the best way to ensure our own nation's security." For other Americans, Russia's natural geostrategic position in the world makes her a major actor. A weak Russia is seen as a more dangerous Russia. "Russia's stability is in the U.S. interest."

While wanting a strong Russia, Americans are cautious about what they can or should do to support strengthening the Russian economy. Some Americans are prepared to go so far as establishing a "Marshall Plan" for Russia, but most would not support such a step. Most recognized that Russia is still a risky place to invest. "Investment in Russia is a long-term investment. Businesses that are looking to make a quick buck are not interested. Investors want there to be protections for their investments from within Russia."

One of the key reasons for these concerns is fear of corruption. A participant in one forum noted that "there has already been a great deal of business investment by U.S. firms in Russia, and some of these companies have been 'burned' because of the differences in cultures and business practices." This observation parallels the numerous Russian statements regarding the different work ethic and business cultures in the two countries. Interestingly, this was one of the things—a better work ethic—that Russians felt they could borrow from Americans.

Some participants expressed concern about American businesses becoming too fully involved in the Russian economy, fearing that "economic cooperation might be too exploitive of the Russians and more to Americans' advantage." They also expressed concern for "potential corruption at our end."

Mutual respect for each other's identity and interests forms the heart of a productive relationship. "The group agreed that treating the Russian people with respect in whatever we do is essential." Such behavior is seen as particularly essential in the post–Cold War world. "Russia was a leader in a bipolar world that is now unipolar. They still want to have their place. They want to have their power and influence, though it's not what it used to be."

If Americans see themselves as having a national interest in friendship and alliance with a robust and strong Russia, this interest is predicated upon Russia's continuing its democratic development. Americans' sense of their interests would probably change fundamentally were this trend not to continue. "People are adamant that a primary condition of a long-term relationship with Russia turns on Russia's commitment to be an open society and maintain democracy."

At the same time, just as Russians are chary of too much of an embrace by America, many Americans are concerned about an intimate relationship with Russia. "Most people are still wary about getting too close to Russia. Some even resent that we choose to help Russia while we still have many problems of our own." Others are not confident of Russia's path once her strength revives. "Is there a possibility that once the Russian economy grows strong again (presumably in part through American aid) that the nation and its people might turn against the United States again?"

Such caution on both sides, especially in light of our past history, is probably healthy. Both Americans and Russians feel we need considerable time to get to know and understand better each other's cultures, habits, ways of thought, and traditions before developing a more intimate relationship. A Portland, Oregon, forum participant seemed to sum up this interest well when he affirmed that "the bedrock for any approach to Russia is U.S. interests: look realistically at Russia's 'warts.' "

The preferred path to a new relationship, for most Americans, seems to be through greatly expanding citizen contacts and probably simultaneously reducing the level or at least dependence upon government-to-government activity. "There seemed to be a growing chorus for the need to increase the general exchanges of people. There was widespread agreement that this would be the most positive and least intrusive form of influencing Russian counterparts—and also letting them come to their own decisions by means of observation and experience. It is quite clear that the desirability of substantial government engagement, even for positive social goals, such as health, had almost disappeared from the forum's radar by discussion's end."

In short, Americans do not perceive their national interests to be in conflict, to any substantial degree, with Russians' perceptions of their interests. At the same time, both are cautious about too quick a rush to embrace each other.

Power

Americans and Russians sense the potential power of their relationship. Both American and Russian citizens seem to grasp that through cooperation we are each better off than through confrontation. The support for multilateralism, economic cooperation, and greater contacts and exchanges among our citizens all testify to this. But, the caution that citizens from each country raise about moving too fast, about too tight an embrace, about too intrusive American economic involvement, about the pervasiveness of American cultural influence in Russia, for example, all suggest that our citizens are not yet ready to fully embrace the power that seems inherent in this relationship. As of today, citizens do not fully grasp the potential of this power. Citizens are prepared, at this point, only to begin what could be a long path to where they are ready to imagine and then to grasp the power that can be produced by a more fully developed relationship.

Russian Perceptions

Russians, more than Americans, seem to feel that the preconditions are not yet in place to enable us, together, to move further in this relationship. They are acutely aware of the asymmetry of power. For many Russian citizens, Russia must first achieve military and economic equality with America.

The struggle going on in the minds of many Russians over these issues was aptly illustrated by one Russian speaker: "I think that on the question of relations with America, we first need to build up the strength of our state, the well-being of our people. But, concerning relations with other peoples and nations, we are in a position even today to live as good neighbors. America is a more developed country than Russia, so we need to create here conditions like in the United States; we need to exchange experience. I think that recently Americans already are beginning to speak of Russia as having achieved something important in the political and economic sphere. But it is still too early to trust the Americans."

Another Russian emphasized that Russia must first achieve equality so that in this relationship "it does not feel insulted." Others feel that before the relationship can develop further, "we need to change our consciousness." Finally, Russian participants came back to the idea that the next step should be the simple one of "coming to know each other better." "We need more direct interaction with Americans. We should have greater opportunities to travel to America more often, and this should encompass many, many of our citizens. They need to come here so that we can then begin, precisely at the level of citizens, to develop practical cooperation."

American Perceptions

Americans also perceived more people-to-people contacts as being essential. They emphasized the relational power that comes from such contacts.

For some the key is to develop a deep familiarity with Russian culture. "Anybody who has spent much time between the two countries knows that's one of the most attractive and wonderful aspects of Russia—connecting to Russian culture. Once there, you know all these things—the corruption and what might be by American standards a low standard of living—but then they become pretty secondary because it is such a rich culture. The people themselves are so warm and loving that these things become pretty secondary and you begin to relate on a people-to-people basis. That's the key to all of these issues—a two-way street of being equals, of learning together and becoming friends." Besides, citizen-to-citizen contacts reflect power of a relational kind. They are "the least intrusive form of influencing Russian counterparts—and letting them come to their own decisions by means of observation and experience."

Deliberative U.S. citizens came to the conclusion that governments, even with the best of intentions, are clumsy and unreliable when it comes to relationship-building. "Grass roots efforts seem to work better; they are at lower levels, smaller groups are helped directly. This is in contrast to government programs which we seem to lose control of, or where there is no accountability. Our heart is in the right place, but we cannot implement what we intend to do."

In short, for citizens of both countries, the essential next step is greater bonding among our peoples as a precondition to the development of the trust that is the foundation for an enduring relationship. "There is still no real bonding between the American and Russian people, and some needs to be worked out." "Words must be followed by actions to build trust at the state-to-state level and the people-to-people level." The next steps, as one American put it, are "to provide opportunities to the people so they can come together to feel empowered and able to work together to overcome some of the obstacles they are facing." Only then will they realize the power inherent in a strong relationship—power for the pursuit of common interests.

Perceptions, Misperceptions, Stereotypes

Both Americans and Russians were subjected for several generations to messages that often created and reinforced highly negative stereotypes of each other's political and social systems and perhaps most importantly their intentions toward each other. The deliberations held by Americans and Russians provided valuable insight into the current state of perceptions, misperceptions, and stereotypes.

Russian Perceptions of Western and Russian Culture

We have already seen that for many Russians, American mass culture is seen as unattractive, as foreign, and as threatening to Russian culture. There are alternative images, however. For example, one Russian forum participant observed: "When we speak of culture having in mind a sort of national culture, in this sense, the Americans have no unique culture of their own. Rather, American culture is an agglomeration, the combination of all cultural values that have been created in the world and esteemed by it. The greatness of America is that their culture has been able to appreciate and to preserve the best of global culture."

Personal contact and dialogue change perceptions—often in unpredictable ways. A young Russian woman, who had lived in America for a year, illustrated an important point about the impact of personal contact on perceptions. One cannot predict or plan how perceptions will be affected through long-term personal contact with another culture. What strikes one person may reflect more their own past than the points stressed in any familiarization program. "I liked America very much. When I returned home, I understood what a person must do for himself, at the entrance to his apartment, at school, and at work, in order to bring about some kind of order. I simply understood in the most elementary manner that Americans take care of their homes, are concerned whether their neighbors clean their yards. They even follow the rules of the road when driving, and if someone violates these rules, they don't say, 'It's none of my business.' "

Russian Perceptions of American Character

In Goncharov's novel *Oblomov*, the main character reflects upon his own tendencies to dream great dreams, but when it comes to the practical work of realizing them, he finds this to be beyond the typical Russian's capacities. To find a model of efficiency and hard work he has to turn to a foreigner, a German.

That some Russian citizens continue to hold such self-perceptions—now in contrast to Americans—illustrates that fundamental perceptions, perhaps national traits, resist change. One Russian forum participant used this perceived contrast to introduce his picture of Americans: "What I find attractive in Americans is their impressive capacity for hard work. They are not lazy as I learned when I visited America. Why do they live better than we? They are not possessed by illusions. They know that if they don't work hard, then they will have nothing. When we recall our history, it was those seeking adventure who were attracted to the new country, those who could no longer tolerate the limitations and the hopelessness of Europe, those who possessed a capitalist mentality. Such people could not find their place in Europe and they went to America. Often these were not the best people. But, even these were people unafraid of work and they developed a culture of hard work."

Building upon this example, another Russian participant drew on her perception of the Russian attitude to work, to professionalism: "As I began to live independently, I realized that we in Russia have very few people who are really professionals in their specialty. This is a great misfortune for our country. Of course, it is understandable why people take on so many different jobs at once, given our economy. But, this makes it more attractive to do business with professionals from America. Here we have something to learn."

Another Russian emphasized the "expansiveness" of Americans. "Their intentions are to do good everywhere, according to their own manner. In my view, we should not hold Americans at such a distance from us."

Russians tend to see American culture as based upon religion. "The Americans have no official state religion, but religion nevertheless forms the foundation of their society."

"What happened on September 11 revolutionized our consciousness. We saw that Americans are also people who can experience helplessness, and that state which we tended to criticize and oppose, this powerful state turned out not to be so powerful after all. Today our sympathy for ordinary Americans is probably quite strong."

It is hard to evaluate the relative weight of positive versus negative perceptions of America among Russians. But, as the earlier statement about the impact of the September 11, 2001, attacks suggests, both conscious policy behavior and unplanned events can influence this balance. The attacks in the United States may have temporarily brought positive human empathy to the fore. American policy toward Iraq, combined with a range of other policies, including NATO expansion into the Baltic states and U.S. withdrawal from the Anti Ballistic Missile (ABM) Treaty, are likely to reinforce negative stereotypes.

The most frequently found negative perceptions are illustrated by the following quotations from the forums:

> Friendship with America can never be unlimited. America wants to repress Russian spirituality, considering this the main support for our state.
>
> Even in friendship, America will attempt to dictate its own rules.
>
> America is an unreliable partner; they violate international agreements without taking account of their partners' interests.
>
> There is no need to idealize America. They also have their problems just as we do—a high level of crime, drugs, homelessness, etc.
>
> Americans have a better opinion of themselves than they do of us. When it comes to us, they don't offer us help.
>
> It is certainly true that America interferes in our affairs. But, if we ignore for the moment all factual and objective elements and simply speak of our emotional response. . . . When they bombed Yugoslavia [Serbia], I was just beside myself with anger. Then when they bombed Iraq, I just couldn't believe it.
>
> Friendship with America? These are unrequited feelings. This is friendship with a knife in the pocket—for example American withdrawal from the ABM treaty.

Perhaps more than any other element of relationship, the emotional component is most directly affected by actions. The examples cited suggest that it may be far harder to create positive perceptions through policy than it is to reinforce negative stereotypes. American actions, which appear to Russians to treat our relationship with little respect, seem capable at one stroke of reviving deeply negative images of the United States, and of reinforcing the idea that a positive relationship is impossible.

If governmental actions are powerful factors undermining relationships, it is important to note that no Russian forum participant could note a single U.S. government action that changed a negative image. Rather, whenever positive changes in perceptions occurred, the examples were personal experience with Americans. This underscores the case made by many Americans that the people-to-people path is the more promising approach to a healthy relationship. These conclusions are reinforced by American perceptions.

Americans See Russia as a Friend but not an Ally

The opposite may be true for Russia, at least in the short run. American opinion toward Russia appears to have moved from a generally unfavorable view of Russia to a majority now seeing Russia as an American friend. A critical factor in this change was the positive response of the Putin government following 9/11, and their active cooperation in the war on terrorism. Many Americans, in fact, now see Russia as a "dependable partner in the war against terrorism."

Despite this positive image, generalized distrust is perhaps the most pervasive perception. The American forums suggest that many negative perceptions of Russia persist. These perceptions cause deep cautiousness among Americans regarding getting too close to Russia; hence, Americans' uneasiness about accepting Russia as an ally. "I was very heartened by the Russian gentleman saying that Russia is not a threat to the U.S. We don't really embrace that as a society. It's hard to let go of what was drilled into us during the Cold War."

This lack of trust has a number of specific manifestations. One widespread perception is a fear that Russians exercise inadequate control over their weapons of mass destruction and associated technologies. The fear is not Russian use of these, but rather of their transfer to third parties. Related is the fear of an "accidental nuclear launch" from Russia.

The perception of corruption in Russian society, economy, and politics appears to be shared by most Americans who participated in the forums. For Americans, corruption is a manifestation of a lack of integrity, and as one participant put it, "That bothers me a great deal." Americans recognize lack of integrity in our own society, but most find corruption reprehensible wherever it is found because most believe that our economy particularly, but also our society and polity, ultimately depend upon people acting with integrity and honesty, and respecting rules and laws. Wherever evidence of corruption arises, Americans' distrust of the involved institutions and persons rises dramatically. The perceived pervasiveness, even normality, of corruption in Russia thus gives rise to a continuing unease with Russia that can undermine other positive elements in the relationship for many Americans.

We noted earlier that for Americans, the foundation of a healthy relationship is continuation of Russian democratization. Yet, Americans' uncertainty over democratization becomes another source of distrust. A number of Americans certainly understand that Russia may neither be ready for nor want "Western" democracy. But, then, will whatever develops in Russia encourage human freedom and development or repress it? Will "Russian democracy" reflect the fundamental values underlying the idea of democracy? Or, as some other American participants feared, will "Russia return to Communism or some form of dictatorial government?" These uncertainties are inevitable given Russia's history and the shortness of its current democratization experience. Yet, nevertheless, they will limit the depth of this relationship.

Deliberating on this issue, Americans took a typically pragmatic approach to the question of trust. "We misunderstand them, and they misunderstand us. . . . Distrust is dramatically lessened when Russian and U.S. citizens are able to visit each other's countries and experience professional or cultural exchange."

Patterns of Interaction

Most useful in helping us understand when and how interactions may affect the relationship is the concept of limits on behavior. Our analysis of the core elements of identity or interests shows that citizens can state clearly these core elements and are often acutely aware of transgressions of the limits they find essential to protecting them. A sense of power or powerlessness, positive or negative perceptions are formed, reformed, or transformed by these patterns of interaction. Those that respect the limits strengthen it. Similarly, every transgression leaves wounds that may last for years.

When we examine the patterns of interaction between Russia and the United States, among American and Russian citizens, we find first of all that they are highly asymmetrical. As we have noted several times, in their daily lives, Russian citizens are exposed to far more interactions with America than vice versa. In the economy, investments by American-owned companies rank number four after the leading European countries, or number two if we count Europe as one entity. Ordinary Russians experience this as a pervasive presence of American products on their shelves.

Other Russians have more direct experience with American commerce. In the major cities, American companies employ thousands of Russians, exposing them to American business culture. This includes firms engaged in advertising, marketing, production, distribution, finance, investment, oil exploration, charitable foundations, and manufacturing. The current level of Russian-U.S. economic interaction, while tiny by comparison with China-U.S. economic ties, for example, has tended to strengthen the tendencies of some Russians toward economic self-sufficiency, or autarchy, the policy pursued by and large during Soviet times. While this policy was supported by less than 20 percent of forum participants, it does suggest that the limits on American involvement set by Russian public perceptions may be far more restrictive than many Americans realize.

The Putin government appears also to show sensitivity to these limits by its actions to eliminate any legal advantages that American or other foreign firms have had previously over Russian firms. On the other hand, the Putin government has been responsive to Western business concerns respecting taxation, land ownership by Russians and foreigners, and improving the rule of law. As these policies also benefit Russian firms, they appear to have received quite widespread support within Russia. A Russian forum participant expressed what seemed to be a broad Russian consensus on the limits to economic cooperation with America: "Here there must be parity in cooperation, but not the expansion of the American economy into ours because there is no doubt that we need to support our own producers and develop our own economy."

How often do Americans encounter Russian products, technology, or services in their daily lives? Rarely, if ever. American exposure to the Russian economy is limited almost entirely to the media's discussions of corruption. Little wonder that this forms the core American image of the Russian economy. This limited exposure may also help to explain why some Americans feel that America should become even more deeply invested in the Russian economy, "because this is the way to make things happen."

What do Americans perceive should be the limits on economic and political involvement? One forum participant expressed what seems to be a common view among the deliberative public: "We do want to help them and we do want to give them advice because we have experience of a democratic free market society but we don't want to force anything on them . . . they are a very proud people . . . support them in the form of advice if they ask for it."

How to respect Russian concerns about the American cultural impact is a problem to which there are no simple answers. In the end this may be an issue that must be recognized and tolerated as part of Russia's becoming an open society. Russian TV stations select their own programming—responding to what they believe the public will watch. America may be the source of supply, but it has little or no control over marketing and distribution of the products of its mass culture.

Some Russians are very aware of this reality and urge fellow citizens to take control of their own lives and not simply blame America for Russia's ills. "Many of us adopt a negative attitude towards America not because we have any real reasons for doing so, but because this is convenient. We seek an enemy in order to account for our own difficulties, because we find it much more difficult to look at ourselves and to take personal responsibility for our misfortunes. . . . Yes, America influences our lives, but why do we permit them to influence us to such a degree?"

Another level of interactions are those at the citizen-to-citizen level. The frequency and intimacy of these contacts today, while significant, is probably less than at the height of the Gorbachev era and the beginning of Yeltsin's presidency in the late 1980s and early 1990s. During that period, hundreds of American foundations and civic organizations "discovered" Russia, and people-to-people programs covering every possible theme from civil society to mountaineering sprouted like mushrooms in the Russian forest following an autumn rain.

As the realities of the difficult transformation Russia was experiencing began to dawn on Americans and the first excitement diminished, so too did much of the momentum and resources being put into such contacts. Yet, even today, tens of thousands of Russians visit America each year, and perhaps even more Americans travel to Russia. While both Americans and Russians—especially those who have been to the others' country—believe that increasing the level of such contacts is the surest way to enhance the American–Russian relationship, there is little coordination outside of individual programs and little that either government can, or in many citizens' views, should do to facilitate these programs.

At the citizen-to-citizen level, the relationship is probably at its most chaotic. This is perhaps totally natural and positive, but it does raise the question as to how those interested in strengthening this relationship can help to assure that individual contacts less often transgress limits of behavior and more often reinforce positive images and perceptions. Here we are probably best advised to rely upon the assumption that with enough exposure to each other, ordinary citizens will develop sensitivity to what is permissible in a relationship, what detracts from it, and what builds it. Indeed, the deliberative forums that form the basis of this chapter demonstrate that citizens are capable of understanding their own identity and interests and of developing an awareness of where their limits lie.

One area where many Russians perceive citizen-to-citizen interaction to have passed acceptable limits is in the area of religion. Since the early 1990s, major religious organizations as well as hundreds of minor sects have sought to proselytize in Russia, drawing the ire not just of the official Russian Orthodox Church, but based upon comments in the Russian forums, of a broad spectrum of the Russian people as well. In the past few years, the Russian government has responded to these concerns by passing new laws restricting such activities. While Americans tended to view the Soviet Union as a "Godless" society, as it officially was, this led Americans to underestimate the depth of the ordinary Russian citizen's identity with Russian Orthodoxy and its long tradition.

We come finally to the level of government-to-government interactions and their impact on the relationship. We have already seen that large numbers of Americans and Russians feel that government is least well suited to manage this relationship. The truth is, however, that as the stronger power the U.S. government has many opportunities for shaping the relationship, for better or worse. Russia's government, especially its people, are highly sensitive to occasions in which the United States appears to overstep the bounds of what is deemed appropriate in the relationship.

For Russians, the question is how to constrain a more powerful partner. Unfortunately, if it wishes, official Washington can simply ignore today's much weaker Russia. Most Russians accept Putin's affirmation following 9/11 that today "there is no nation, no race, no peoples who are our enemies. Our only enemy is terrorism, and this is our common enemy." However, all Russians appear to be aware of their limited ability to constrain American official behavior. Most Russians conclude that for America to respect Russia's identity and interests, the latter should have sufficient power such that America dare not act otherwise in this relationship. As a Russian at one forum commented: "In my view, we should not keep America at a distance at least in some areas, such as the economic sphere. But, at the same time, we need to have a genuine military balance because the Americans conduct themselves insolently in relations with Europe and the Arab states."

In building a more effective relationship, most Americans, after deliberation, appear to support a style of American behavior that is characterized by "open lines of communication for all levels of conversation: military and security, trade partnerships, advancement of free market opportunities, movement toward democratic style of government, humanitarian projects, and educational and cultural exchanges—with travel in both directions."

What limits would the deliberative American public impose on American behavior toward Russia? From a Midwestern forum: American actions must be "respectful of Russia and Russian culture and again not the unilateral approach, not the overwhelmingly sentimental humanitarian approach, but more the realistic one based upon mutual cooperation and respect." Imposing American models is rejected by nearly all forum participants. Americans expect Russians to defend and act upon their own interests and urge Americans to exercise caution. "We should 'trust but verify.' If we find them trustworthy, OK, but we need to be cautious."

A Closing Reflection

Both Americans and Russians see their relationship as being of exceptional value to each side. At the same time, deliberative publics show a frank awareness of the complexity of this relationship and of the difficulties of moving this relationship to a level where the relationship itself begins to acquire genuine power and capacity. At the conclusion of one Russian forum, participants noted a number of factors that appear to complicate progress in the relationship. These include the following: "Political relations between these nations have always been complicated. . . . There is a certain underlying bitterness in each of our countries with respect to each other. . . . Our relations are complicated by the history of the Cold War."

For Russians, perhaps the most important obstacle is both psychological and material: "Russia has fallen behind other countries and we must first achieve a balance, and then build relations of partnership." Americans simply have not experienced the same trauma of loss of superpower status—and the dissolution of their country—and so have difficulty comprehending the importance of this factor. At all levels of interaction, therefore, this human reality is likely to complicate relations for some time.

While the relationship indeed faces challenges, however, we must note that today the positive aspects far outweigh the negative in the relationship. The Cold War and military confrontation are in the past. Soviet totalitarianism has been replaced by emerging democratic practices and institutions. Americans and Russians have come to know each other on a personal basis in significant numbers and to a better degree than ever in our past.

Perhaps most importantly, deliberative publics in both countries have begun the process of identifying for themselves and for each other—through dialogue—the critical elements of their identity and their core interests. Each public recognizes that respect for the other's interests and identity is the foundation for a future healthy development of this relationship. Old stereotypes, particularly the enemy image, are being replaced by much more complex and multisided perceptions that, for the most part, whether accurate or not, are reinforcing a more positive and constructive relationship. Citizens on both sides have identified direct contacts as the principal path to the fuller development of the relationship.

Russia, based upon insights from the American forums, appears to be acting well within the limits set by the American public, particularly in its pursuit of democracy and a law-based market economy—with the exception of corruption and mafia activity and potential backsliding on building a genuine democracy. Judging from pervasive comments in the Russian forums, the same cannot be said of the U.S. government, which is seen by Russians as habitually overstepping what they regard as appropriate limits.

Perhaps the two most critical challenges today are, first, how to address the issue of the sense of threat to Russian culture and traditions arising from the extensive daily presence of American mass culture and, second, how to create incentives to bring official governmental behavior into greater conformity with public desires for the Russian-U.S. relationship. Iraq was perhaps the most profound case in a generation of American unilateralism. In this context, the issue is how concerned citizens can encourage the American government to act more multilaterally, to take seriously the interests of its allies and friends.

Ahead lies the greatest challenge and the greatest opportunity. The challenge is how to stimulate in both of our publics an awareness of the enormous power for good in the world that can arise from the fuller flowering of our relationship. The opportunity, then, is together to begin this process of deliberation about how to move beyond the present, to begin the process of visualizing together the power for good of a soundly based and effectively conducted relationship.

In all of this, citizens seem well ahead of governments in their capacity to talk and think in ways that illuminate the overall relationship. They seem far closer to an awareness of limits in developing the relationship and the consequences of governmental actions. Above all, the richness of their deliberations makes the author of this book, who has served both in and out of government, wish that, like citizens outside government, political leaders could talk about how to develop the overall Russian-U.S. relationship—not just about policies for dealing with particular problems.

CHAPTER TEN

Conducting the China-U.S. Relationship: A Diplomat's View

We turn finally to what effect the relational paradigm and the concept of relationship could have on the conduct of a major interstate relationship. In the face of steadily increasing complex interactions between the bodies politic of China and the United States, experience since 1989 suggests that traditional ways of managing government-to-government relations will not serve the interests of a relationship that could shape the global community more than any other in the twenty-first century.

The quality of the relationship between two big countries depends heavily on the attention leaders and citizens pay to the overall relationship and its careful conduct. When the first steps toward reestablishing relations between China and the United States were taken in 1971 and 1972, close attention was possible because interactions were minimal and were in the hands of four leaders and a small number of advisers. By the beginning of the twenty-first century, the relationship involved numberless multilevel interactions between significant elements of the two bodies politic. Leaders struggled both to conduct the policies of the two governments and to conduct their relationships with elements of their own bodies politic with interests in the relationship between the two countries. The ups and downs of the relationship since 1989 illustrate the practical difference that focusing on the overall relationship can make.

The relationship between China and the United States has reflected an unusual mix of the interaction of citizens outside government and governments themselves. For the first half-century in the meaningful relationship between the two countries—from the late nineteenth century until 1949— it might be fair to say that interactions among citizens outside government dominated in a way that was not the case in most other relationships of either country.

From the 1880s until World War II, American missionaries in steadily increasing numbers took education and medical treatment to China in solid programs. Even though the involvement of Americans in World War II was clearly a governmental action, in many ways the relationships of American citizen soldiers with Chinese colleagues and citizens were an important part of the relationship. These interactions filled what is still a significant reservoir of goodwill between the two peoples, despite the actions of governments on both sides in the last half of the twentieth century. This reservoir has been drawn down, but it is not empty.

Governments, of course, were responsible for the rupture in the relationship in 1949 when the Communists took over in China, and governments were responsible for the reestablishment of a formal relationship beginning in 1971. It is interesting, however, to note that the American people seem to have been out in front of their government in the 1960s in looking toward resumption of a normal relationship. In a study of trends in U.S. public opinion over 50 years, Benjamin Page and Robert Shapiro wrote: "Despite hostile talk from the Eisenhower administration . . . the American public very gradually moved toward accommodation and reconciliation with the People's Republic of China. From the mid-1950s onward until the end of the 1980s, the main trend in public preferences about U.S.-China relations was a slow, uneven, but inexorable increase in desires for rapprochement. . . . long *before* Richard Nixon's 1971–1972 opening to China, the U.S. public had moved quite a way toward friendliness."[1]

The development of the renewed interactions flowing from then National Security Adviser Henry Kissinger's secret visit to Beijing in 1971 followed by President Nixon's visit in 1972 presents an interesting picture of the steady broadening of the relationship to the point where the relational paradigm presented in this book has become more applicable than the old realist paradigm. In the beginning, Kissinger and then Nixon conducted in-depth dialogues with Premier Zhou Enlai and Chairman Mao Zedong on the real intent and interests of both countries. They were scrupulous in managing every detail of the relationship. Interactions were limited. It may seem a paradox that leaders on both sides were quintessential practitioners of the realist paradigm in their global thinking; their relationship was cemented by their common sense of threat from Soviet expansionism. The relationship was still between two governments. Nevertheless, the centrality of power in their global strategy was played out in this situation as but one component of their attention to the overall relationship itself.

Within a decade, leadership changed, and a growing economic relationship between the two countries engaged increasing numbers of citizens outside government. Then Chinese students flocked to U.S. universities by the thousands. By the beginning of the twenty-first century, it had become both realistic and essential to think in terms of the overall relationship between the two countries—not just their governments. The relationship was increasingly a cumulative, multilevel, open-ended process of continuous interaction among significant parts of whole bodies politic. What would be the consequences of analyzing and conducting that relationship through the prism suggested in this book—or the dangers of not doing so?

Elements of the China–U.S. Relationship

The following picture is drawn from more than 15 years of experience in nonofficial dialogues between American and Chinese citizens now outside government, although a number of them have had government experience. One might call them members of the policy-influencing communities. These insights are drawn from careful notes on the meetings and recorded cumulatively in my style of "rolling drafts."[2] They are also drawn from separate conversations with Chinese colleagues ranging from philosophers and historians to diplomats and military officers to explore the concept of relationship. They are organized under the five components of relationship. Each discussion concludes by noting possibilities for change through sustained dialogue.

Identity

What are the primary life experiences that have brought each party to a relationship to the present moment? In what ways, if any, has each party defined itself in terms of the other?

China's historic challenge has been one of creating and sustaining a unified, centrally governed China with the world's largest population in a vast territorial area. Out of that experience, Chinese have learned to place a premium on the coherence and harmony of the whole group both locally and nationally and to fear any hint of fragmentation or chaos that would undermine that unity. In recent years, China has also focused on meeting the basic human needs of survival such as food, shelter, and clothing. China indeed defines human rights in terms of these basic human needs; they see what Americans call "human rights" as "civil rights."

The people of China are heirs of an ancient and continuous civilization. It is an essential part of their identity. Henry Kissinger spoke of Premier Zhou Enlai along with other Chinese colleagues as displaying an "inward security"—which he attributed in part to that ancient civilization—"that allows them, within the framework of their principles, to be meticulous and reliable in dealing with others."[3] These principles are deeply rooted in Confucian thought, which heavily influences their approach to relationship.

The history of the United States records the experience of people fleeing the arbitrary power of centralized governments and churches in Europe or seeking economic opportunity. Both experiences caused them to place high value on protecting the rights of individuals as the ultimate source of sovereignty in any human collectivity and their freedom to pursue their legitimate interests with minimal government interference. As did China, the people of the United States established a government to sustain the unity of the country, and that government fought a bitter and prolonged civil war in the 1860s to preserve the union. The unity of the people and the states of the United States, however, was a carefully negotiated balance between central power and a variety of constraints on that power.

This balance was thoughtfully defined in a written constitution ratified by the people of the original 13 states and constantly interpreted and reinterpreted in an independent judiciary and in deliberative legislative bodies over more than two centuries. The rule of law and access to these independent courts is viewed by American citizens as the key to protection of their individual and group rights.

Although the United States is a young country, its people reflect deep roots in a variety of civilizations. Through successive waves of immigration, Americans have constantly accommodated to new identities and energies.

To their principally European original heritage, Americans added a distinctly American flavor from their own experience of developing a continental territory. That experience enhanced traditions of individual self-reliance and self-assurance. That experience was also deeply marred by the institution of slavery and the uprooting and suppression of Native Americans. With the closing of the frontier and the coming of industrialization and urbanization beginning in the late nineteenth century, modifications of the extreme manifestations of individualism began, but the fundamental value remained.

Against that longer background, each country's more recent history provides more current ways for its people to think about themselves. These self-images color the relationship today.

The people of China understandably and repeatedly characterize themselves as the victims of a century of foreign intrusion and humiliation. The United States played a comparatively minimal role in that experience. Following the dissolution of the Soviet Union, Chinese citizens, like others, have seen the United States as the "sole superpower" and have increasingly projected onto it descriptions such as "arrogant," "hegemon," and "bully" from that earlier experience as well as from current interactions. Chinese complain that many of the international standards that the United States presses China to observe were written in the West; China in its present form did not participate in their drafting or ratification, although in becoming a member of the United Nations, China has technically if not politically subscribed to them.

The people of the United States have emerged from a half-century in which global leadership and responsibility with all of their attendant costs and consequences were thrust upon them. This left Americans with the habit of acting alone where others would not shoulder a share of responsibility and often angered by other countries—even allies—who pursued their own profit without much regard for the kind of world their self-centered actions were sometimes producing. Such international documents as the UN Declaration of Human Rights and the Helsinki Final Act embodied certain universal views on human rights. Other nations have subscribed to these standards but have often not joined the United States in taking responsibility for enforcing them.

At the same time, many Americans enjoy being seen as the "sole superpower" but are uncertain about how to use that power. They are rebuffed when they assert it and criticized when they fail to step forward. In addition, many citizens are tired of the responsibility and its costs in human lives and dollars and just want to focus on improving the quality of their own lives. If the United States must engage militarily abroad, citizens in dialogue with each other have expressed a strong preference for doing so only as part of a multilateral effort. The problems faced, they say, are the world community's problems—not just American problems. With all of that, they are quite alert to their self-interest in leading in the technological and economic transformations widely known as "globalization."

Both nations have reasons to be uncertain about their identity in today's rapidly changing world. This fact alone offers an opportunity for dialogue.

Chinese feel increasing confidence from China's economic success, but at the same time that very success raises questions about China's ideological base. The Chinese Communist Party and the government retain centralized political control while allowing major decentralization of economic control either by law or in fact. The government's struggle to retain political control often obstructs establishment of a rule of law that would provide a predictable environment for foreign investors and visitors. In addition, some Chinese elders are concerned that many young people are learning to value money and profit above traditional Chinese values.

Many Chinese have shied away from the prediction that China is becoming a major power and denied the global responsibilities that accompany this role. They have been feeling their way as a permanent member of the United Nations Security Council, but are often torn between resisting what they regard as U.S. pretensions to "hegemonic" power—that is, pretensions to rule the world—and real needs to prevent aggression or genocide.

The American people at the turn of the century were coping with severe disillusionment over the decline in economic opportunity in the economic streamlining of the 1990s, and the recession prolonged into the first years of the new century. They are increasingly concerned over a seeming fragmentation of their moral code. In the political realm over the past half century, they placed confidence in big government to solve their problems but increasingly recognized that many problems are beyond the reach of government. Many have not yet accepted their responsibility as citizens for making their own contribution to the solution of those problems—either at home or abroad. In addition, many Americans are also sensitive to the fact that some 20 percent of American society do not fully participate in the benefits of the economy.

The attacks by Islamic extremists on targets in the United States on September 11, 2001, seriously shook the foundations of Americans' self-image. Historically accustomed to seeing themselves in control of their own future, they were forced to question this assumption and to deal with hitherto unacceptable government intrusiveness into their lives. They were also forced to face up to the fact that U.S. influence in the world is deeply resented in many places and that Americans cannot be secure unless they pay attention to actions generated in the remotest corners of the world but with ever greater sensitivity to the identities of others.

Possibilities for change. If we were honest with each other in dialogue, Chinese might say to Americans that it is time for the United States to treat other powers as equal colleagues in shaping the international system and to act collaboratively rather than unilaterally and arrogantly. Americans might say to the Chinese that it is time to stop playing the role of victim and to accept responsibility for shaping the world of the future so others *can* work with China as an equal. They might also say, as they did to Soviet colleagues in the 1980s, that Americans will not regard as equal a government that arbitrarily arrests, imprisons, and even tortures its own citizens—not to mention visiting Chinese Americans.

One starting point toward a sounder relationship might be a dialogue on what kind of world we want to live in—on what kind of international system would best respect our identities and serve our most important interests. What responsibilities should big powers assume—both as restraints on their own behavior and as obligations in enforcing international standards of behavior? For instance, what are our responsibilities with regard to proliferation of weapons of mass destruction, in the face of impending genocide, terrorism, or aggression, or for the rights of individual human beings? Such dialogue would elicit fundamental statements of purpose and intent, which both Americans and Chinese regard as essential foundations for building a sound relationship.

As described below, the deeply probing conversations between Zhou Enlai and Henry Kissinger in 1971 and 1972 were conducted in the spirit of determining fundamental intent on both sides. Without that determination, a sound relationship could not have been created. Nevertheless, each side seems to approach relationship in a way—apparently rooted, perhaps unconsciously, in our identities—that puts off the other. This remains a difference to be examined together and hopefully to be overcome.

Interests

What does each party seem to feel are its greatest needs or interests? Why are they really important? To what extent is a party defining these needs as a function of the relationship—that is, in terms of what it wants to take from or deny to the other or who each perceives the other to be? Why?

It is important to remember that interests are often defined both analytically and politically and that, in a relationship, common interests are also defined in terms of how each side perceives itself in relation to the other. This is important to note because Chinese seem to think of interests as objectively defined by governments, whereas, in the United States, interests are often defined in the larger political arena as well as by government analysts. An open question is exactly how citizens' concerns affect policy in each country.

To quote David Lampton, former president of the National Committee on U.S.-China Relations and later professor at the Johns Hopkins University's Paul Nitze School of Advanced International Studies in

Washington, DC: ". . . the Chinese remain convinced that nations ultimately place primacy on economic and security interests. Beijing, therefore, tends to see Washington's idealistic pronouncements on human rights
as simply a smoke screen, or bargaining chip, to soften or weaken China so
that the 'real' American economic and security agenda can be advanced.
Only when the Clinton Administration in the last part of the first term
talked about a strategic dialogue, the need for priorities, and the necessity
of elevating security and economic interests, did Beijing begin to take the
administration seriously."[4]

At the same time, Chinese colleagues in nonofficial conversation say that
interests are "not always self-evident"—that it is "essential to understand the
thought processes through which interests are defined." It may be that individuals in both countries who work in the field of international relations
reflect traditional academic thinking about national interest—that it is
objectively defined by a state's geographical position, its economic and
industrial base, its resources, its demographic character, and its political
system. What seemed to creep into thinking at the end of the twentieth
century was some sense that, in addition to these objective facts, human
beings—some in leadership, some simply influential—can put these objective factors together in different ways with different priorities depending on
their purposes.

In analytical terms, we can say that both China and the United States
share an interest in an international system that would be conducive to
economic development and peace. But in the United States, how Americans
define specific interests with regard to China will depend on how they see
China defining itself. And Chinese will define their interests vis-à-vis the
United States partly in terms of how they read U.S. intentions toward
China.

China's paramount interest, it seems to thoughtful Americans, is to protect
and restore the unity of China. Americans feel that, by the Chinese government's definition, this interest overrides any consideration of whether the
use of all effective means is justifiable. At least some Chinese in 2001 seemed
to be stating the need for dialogue among Chinese on that question. To cite
a story in the *International Herald Tribune* following the September 11, 2001,
terrorist attacks on New York and Washington: "China Shows a Less-Than-
Warm Response to Disaster in America": ". . . more than 50 years of living
under the rule of a Marxist-Leninist party has contributed to creation of a
moral vacuum in China. 'China has never had a serious discussion of what
kinds of means can be justified to achieve what kind of end,' Mr. Shi
[Yinhong, head of the international relations department at People's
University] said. 'That is because in the history of Stalinist Marxist parties, a
glorious end can be justified by whatever means you like.' "[5]

Americans at the deepest level believe that they cannot protect what they
value most—their fundamental principles of political freedom and justice—in
a world in which others reject compatible standards of international behavior.
Americans on one level saw the terrorist attacks of September 11, 2001, as

a profound demonstration of the need for a commitment of governments and citizens around the world to some widely accepted standards of behavior based on full respect for the principles of different religious and civilizational traditions.

China—if for no other reason than economic—has a strong interest in the strength of the U.S. economy. Many Chinese in dialogue also recognize the importance of a stabilizing U.S. military position in East Asia to constrain what they see as Japanese militarism and to contain North Korea. On this latter point, they are conflicted by their concern over potential use of U.S. military forces to defend Taiwan's perceived movement toward independence.

The United States has no interest in the fragmentation of China; on the contrary, it has stated its interest in a unified and economically developing China. That said, Americans are conflicted on two points: First, many abhor the Chinese suppression of the Tibetan people and culture and oppose Chinese efforts to incorporate Taiwan by force into the People's Republic of China. Second, Americans will be repulsed by any Chinese governmental attempt at brutal repression to maintain its control. On the economic side, while the United States has a strong interest in China's economic success, Americans condition that with a strong concern for China's careful observance of international standards such as those explicit in the terms of China's membership in the World Trade Organization (WTO).

On the human level, serious questions arise about citizens' interests in the relationship. For instance, anyone who was in China, as my wife and I were, during the two weeks in April 2001 after a U.S. reconnaissance plane and a Chinese fighter aircraft collided, witnessed an outpouring of vitriol and hate directed at America in thousands of Internet postings. Or after the September 11, 2001, terrorist attacks: "I am happy because I hate America." In that medium, only a few Chinese expressed concern: "I weep for the cold-blooded Chinese." Again to quote John Pomfret:

> . . . China's security services, usually so quick to suppress the Internet when it is used for political purposes, have tolerated an avalanche of postings celebrating the attacks in message boards through the Chinese on-line world.
> . . . With the collapse of communism as an ideology, China's government has embraced nationalism and nationalist causes in its search for a new legitimacy. . . . China's state-run press has churned out a steady stream of anti-American articles that have succeeded in convincing many Chinese that the United States is out to get China, to contain it, overturn it or destroy it.[6]

Of course, many Chinese who have worked with Americans over the years for an improved China-U.S. relationship state strongly that they do not share these expressions of anti-American feeling.

In response, Chinese point to the bombing of China's embassy in Belgrade by U.S. warplanes in May 1999 and the April 1, 2001, plane collision as evidence of U.S. malevolent intent. They cite such events as reasons for anti-American feeling among Chinese citizens.

Possibilities for change. Fundamental questions for dialogue among American and Chinese citizens—as well as officials—are whether either side has a serious interest in a sound relationship—and why—and whether either is willing to examine its actions in light of that interest. Those Americans who would like to say that the United States has an interest in China's development depend for the credibility of their position on how China plays its role as an emerging great power. Is China potentially a partner shouldering its share of responsibility for a world in which each nation has larger interests than those defined by its own self-interests? Those Chinese who value the relationship would like to know whether U.S. leaders are prepared to act with greater concern for Chinese interests and to treat China as an equal rather than acting unilaterally. Can common ground be found between the seemingly conflicting interests of China and the United States? (1) China places a premium on protecting its unity and on group interests above individuals' interests while paying attention to meeting basic human needs. (2) The U.S. values individual freedom while respecting the unity of the state, both in China and the United States. How can Americans and Chinese talk about responsibilities they are willing to impose on themselves in the interests of an equitable world rather than a world where each country simply pursues its self-centered interests as defined by current leaders?

Power

What does each party see as the main elements of its own power vis-a-vis the other? In what areas does either see that it needs the other's cooperation to achieve its goals?

Chinese colleagues, in reflecting on the concept of relationship, begin by noting that the notion of hierarchy is inherent in any relationship. In a sense, it defines power in social relationships. Confucius defined the proper relationships between father and son, emperor and ministers, husband and wife, friend and friend, elder brother and younger brother. Within this philosophical structure, a Chinese child is taught to obey superior authority, to learn by rote, to respect elders. In contrast, Chinese colleagues observe, the American approach is that "a child learns"—not by rote but by experiencing. For the Chinese, essential elements of relationship are stated rules for dealing, for instance, with superiors and subordinates. Americans, they feel, tend to work out these rules as they learn to relate to others; how power works is defined pragmatically, whereas Chinese expect certain rules to apply. In international relations, Chinese recognize clear disparities of power but believe that a genuine relationship can be built only when one party deals with another as an equal and on the basis of reciprocity.

At the same time, I have heard repeatedly in China that "power defines a relationship" and that every state's main objective in the international arena is the quest for power. It is common in China to speak of the large gap between American and Chinese economic and military power, but power in today's world is not measured simply in military or economic terms. Power must be seen in many instances as the capacity to influence the course of events—not just to force change. In that context, the obvious disparity of material power between the two countries is not so decisive as it might otherwise seem.

First, China's mere geographic and demographic mass is a source of power to resist pressure. It essentially thwarts the conceivable use of U.S. military power to threaten the Chinese mainland, so this military might is no real threat to the integrity or sovereignty of China. Nor is it likely that the United States could muster the capacity to undermine the Chinese system as is commonly feared by many in China.

Second, China is not yet in a military position to confront the United States outside China's borders except perhaps in the Taiwan Strait. But at the beginning of the administration of U.S. President George W. Bush in 2001, the two countries engaged the question of how a U.S. program of national missile defense might render the Chinese nuclear arsenal irrelevant. This begged the question of how nuclear weapons might further the practical interests of either country.

Third, among the unexplored questions are whether the two governments and their peoples will decide that shared interests are so strong as to cause each to value their relationship highly enough to compel cooperation. This is an untapped source of power in causing each to change its behavior in the interest of both.

Possibilities for change. From the starting point of an in-depth discussion of our individual, shared, and conflicting interests, further dialogue could develop around such questions as the following:

- What interests of importance to both of us can be adequately achieved only if we cooperate? Would we recognize the enlarged capacity resulting from that cooperation as a form of power that benefits us both? What can we learn about power as it operates in our relationship?
- Can we define the potential role of military power in the China-U.S. relationship, especially the potential role of nuclear weapons?
- What are appropriate collaborative uses of military power on behalf of the international community in preventing atrocities, aggression, and genocide? What kind of Sino-U.S. relationship would that require?

A direct discussion of the nature, limits, and possibilities of power as it operates within the China-U.S. relationship could become a confidence-building measure as well as a practical contribution to collaborative ventures.

Perceptions, Misperceptions, and Stereotypes

How have each party's perceptions of the other evolved? What behaviors by the other reinforce these perceptions?

From 1989 to the present, the images of tanks suppressing young members of the democracy movement in Beijing's Tiananmen Square washed away U.S. perceptions from the previous decade of China as a reforming country. The 1989 image reawakened deep-rooted American fears of highly centralized and repressive government. The restrictions and harassment of U.S. journalists have reinforced these fears and have produced negative stories about China. The arbitrary arrests of Chinese Americans in 2001 caused some Americans to doubt that a relationship of mutual respect and cooperation could be possible.

China is perceived in the United States as a rapidly growing economic power and market, but fear of a longer-term, but inevitable, military buildup in China reinforces the image in the eyes of many Americans of a malevolent China bent on challenging U.S. power in the future. This fear was one of the major concerns expressed by Americans in some 50 public forums conducted in the United States in 2000–2001.[7]

At the same time, focus groups and public forums give evidence that the reservoir of goodwill steadily filled in the first half of the twentieth century is still being tapped. Americans recognize a historically great civilization and do not perceive the Chinese as necessarily enemies. Many acknowledge that they do not know enough about China and say they would like to know the Chinese people more directly.

One other point emanating from these public forums runs directly counter to the image widely held in China: Americans have zero interest in "ruling the world"—or being a "hegemonic power," to use the Chinese characterization. Americans are tired of the responsibilities of world leadership when they perceive so few others able or willing to share these responsibilities. The actions of President George W. Bush in Iraq in 2003 reinforced the Chinese perception, but the underlying feelings of American citizens seem likely to persist over the longer term.

The Chinese perceive the United States as an erratically hegemonic power, at best ambivalent about Chinese economic rise and reunification and at worst opposed. Chinese attribute powers to the United States that Americans do not feel they have or could exercise even if they wished.

As noted earlier, some U.S. actions have provided support for this Chinese perception—the war in Kosovo, the bombing of the Chinese embassy in Belgrade, deployment of U.S. destroyers in the Taiwan Strait, the collision of the U.S. intelligence plane and the Chinese fighter, Congressional resolutions supporting Tibetan independence, the invasion of Iraq. Reactions are exacerbated by those who project on the United States as today's leading world power the feelings of deep resentment and victimization rooted in the nineteenth-century humiliation of China by the then imperial powers.

One point that seems to emerge from early research on Chinese perceptions of the United States is that such perceptions are not monolithic. While the United States does seem to be widely regarded as "arrogant," many openly acknowledge the interdependence between the two countries and would not jeopardize that. There is enough variety in opinion to suggest the possibility for change.

Possibilities for change. These perceptions can be changed by a steady series of steps designed to reassure the other side of compatible long-term interests and intentions. This will require, first, identifying together the key misperceptions and designing steps that could erode them and then committing ourselves—both officials and citizens outside government—to a scrupulously conducted campaign to change perceptions. This can succeed only if it is deeply rooted in a systematic effort to change and strengthen our overall relationship. Citizens in and out of government will need to work through questions such as these:

- In what direction do we want to move our relationship?
- What are the obstacles to moving in that direction—political, perceptual, economic, military?
- What steps might be taken to overcome these obstacles?
- Who will take such steps?
- Can they be organized as a complex of mutually reinforcing steps that could build steady momentum for change?

Patterns of Interaction

How have the two parties habitually interacted? How can negative patterns of interaction be changed?

How two countries interact is a combination of traditional approaches to relationship, choice, leaders' styles, and the way their respective political systems work. This combination can be changed to some degree over time.

Let me begin by laying out what I have heard Chinese colleagues say about the conduct of relationship in Chinese culture. They generally accept my picture of the five elements of relationship presented in this book, but they elaborate on them in several interesting ways.

In addition to the ideas described in previous sections, Chinese stress the importance of patterns of interaction as a "space"—"not a physical but a cultural space"—where all other tracks in the relationship come together. Most start with two concepts rooted in the thought of Confucius. The first ("Li") is the necessity of rules that govern how a person deals with others. The second ("Ren") refers to a good relationship between two persons based on kindness to others and paying attention to others according to a moral standard—rules—that everyone should obey. Chinese colleagues say it would be natural for them to give high priority to principles that capture this moral standard.

Chinese cite the Five Principles of Peaceful Coexistence as a paramount example of these rules. Other principles that might govern interaction include: Don't force or impose; persuade—Chinese are ready to listen. If one party to a relationship cannot do what the other asks, he or she should explain why. "Do not do to others what you would not want them to do to you." Reciprocity is a key principle. Mutual respect—not putting another in a position of "losing face"—is essential. A relationship must be governed by the principle of equality.

While Americans would agree with most of these, they have found serious difficulty—in relations with both the Soviet and the Chinese governments—in accepting general principles stated by governments using traditional principles of international relations against the background of a Communist vocabulary that assigns particular ideological meaning. For instance, "democracy" loses common ground when appropriated by a highly centralized government. That is why Americans want to test what principles mean when applied to concrete situations.

In addition to principles to govern an interaction, this "space" where the elements of relationship come together must also include a common body of knowledge and shared understanding, an understood acceptable style of behavior, and contain institutions embodying these. A relationship is "mature" when all elements impart a significant measure of predictability. Specifically referring to the China-U.S. relationship, several Chinese colleagues pointedly say that the relationship would be mature when it survives political transitions in the United States, when it is no longer "a political football," when it is more stable and "suffers fewer ups and downs," and when one party does not interfere in the other's internal affairs. With regard to the last, one colleague cited Americans' tendency to tell others what to do. Taoism says, he recalled: "Just mind your own business; if you do not have a relationship, you should not tell others what to do." Or: "Confucian culture is not aggressive; it does not challenge others."

Against this general background, we can identify differences in approach to developing a relationship. They may not be as different as they first appear to be.

First, a Chinese friend succinctly capsuled the difference between Americans and Chinese in their approaches to the relationship between the two countries: "We Chinese want first to reach an understanding on what the relationship will be; then we can deal with particular problems. We focus on interests and intentions to establish the fundamentals of the relationship which will provide the framework for dealing with particular problems. Americans, on the other hand, feel that talking generally only about interests and intentions will lead to misunderstanding. They believe that generalities not concretely tested by seeing what they mean when linked to real problems and situations can be meaningless. Only when Americans understand what kind of actions generalities will lead to can they understand what value the relationship will have."[8]

A retired Chinese ambassador, speaking not for attribution in a nonofficial dialogue, made the point in a slightly different way: "Maybe both [countries] want to put bilateral relations on a solid basis. But their approaches are not identical. China would like to make bilateral relations more stable, while the United States would like to do constructive work in meeting so-called common challenges."

This difference in approach certainly has roots in experience, but the gap between the two sides' approaches does not seem as wide as these comments suggest. Reflecting on his earliest talks with the Chinese leadership in 1971, Henry Kissinger was deeply impressed by the Chinese approach to building a relationship:

> [Our approach was] to discuss fundamentals: our perceptions of global and especially Asian affairs in a manner that clarified our purposes and perspectives and thereby bridged two decades of mutual ignorance. Precisely because there was little practical business to be done, the element of confidence had to emerge from conceptual discussions. . . .
>
> [My talks with Zhou were] longer and deeper than with any other leader I met during my public service, except possibly Anwar Sadat. Two ideological enemies presented their respective views of the world with a frankness rarely achieved among allies and with a depth that one experiences only in the presence of a great man. . . .
>
> [Through the conversations with Zhou and Mao, including Nixon's] was built a structure that [has] withstood many stresses and has emerged as one of the foundations of contemporary international relations.[9]

Other Americans, too, have focused on the overall relationship. Former U.S. Secretary of Defense James Schlesinger headed a study group for the National Committee on U.S.-China Relations in 1996: "The central problem to be addressed is the overall character of the relationship, most particularly the absence of mutual confidence and the lack of a sense of shared interests. In this circumstance, each particular friction will have the potential of seriously disrupting the relationship. *Ad hoc* responses on both sides to irritating issues become the content of the relationship. Strategic understanding can help restore mutual confidence and a sense of common interests."[10]

David Lampton wrote in 1997:

> . . . working with Beijing on most individual issues will be unproductive without an overall framework for the relationship. The Chinese are preoccupied with ascertaining an interlocutor's *intentions* and *interests*. Unlike Americans, the Chinese are less concerned with "capabilities." Once intentions are determined to be basically "friendly" and interests found to be compatible with China's, Beijing will address most individual issues productively. This predisposition flew in the face of the first-term Clinton approach, which was to focus on problem areas, without first having established mutual confidence in intentions and interests.[11]

In terms of the paradigm presented in this book, I need to point out that all those quoted are focusing mainly on the positions of two governments—not on the overall relationship between two bodies politic. In a few instances, small groups in nonofficial dialogue through much of the 1990s learned slowly that individuals can speak from a perspective that may be different from official positions. A few even began looking into the implications of reflecting the feelings of citizens outside government in our pictures of the overall relationship.

A second difference in approach results from the difference between the two political systems. The Chinese normally focus on state-to-state relations, while Americans must factor special interests and a centrist public into the relationship. China does not ignore the role of the public in the United States in shaping U.S. participation in the relationship, but the U.S. political system is not well understood in China. The reverse is also increasingly true. While Americans know they are still dealing with a highly centralized, nondemocratic government, they are also wondering to what extent that government is fully in control, especially in the economic arena. It is too early to speak of the interaction between two whole bodies politic, but the borders are far more permeable than they once were. Interactions among citizens—however circumscribed—are far more open, and with tens of thousands of young Chinese having studied in the United States, total thought control is impossible, although it still is a strong factor.

Today's relationship is clearly different from the carefully conducted relationship of the 1970s in that both governments in different ways suffer a certain lack of control in assuring careful formulation and implementation of agreements. China has decentralized its economic program to a point where it can no longer assure local compliance with internationally negotiated agreements. In the United States, many perspectives can influence U.S. policy toward China. How to conduct such a complex relationship in a coherent way is a challenge in both countries.

Possibilities for change. Although it seems impossible to recapture the patterns of interaction that characterized the relationship in the 1970s, it is not at all impossible to restore greater care to the conduct of the relationship. This would need to begin with will and commitment at the highest levels on both sides. That commitment would need to be followed by more frequent and closer communication at all levels of government and among significant groups of citizens outside government.

These steps—important as they are—will be meaningless mechanical moves unless they are taken explicitly within a concept of the overall relationship such as that presented in this book. Only then will participants recognize the full range of what must be involved in changing an overall relationship as complex as this one.

Options for Conducting the Relationship

With this picture of the elements of the overall relationship in mind, what is the range of options for conducting the China-U.S. relationship? Toward one end of the spectrum is ignoring the overall relationship, selecting specific issues, and pursuing them either individually or according to some priority. Toward the spectrum's other end is an effort to design a broad-gauged policy taking into account as much of the overall relationship as possible.

To reflect on what difference it makes to work in the context of the overall relationship, two experiences are presented briefly below. My purpose is not to present a full picture of the relationship in the years since 1989; the point is to offer two limited analyses to explore the hypothesis that seeing the relationship through the lenses of the relational paradigm would make a difference. The point is not that anyone in these examples explicitly invoked the concept of relationship or the relational paradigm as offered in this book; the point is that it makes a difference to operate in some such broader context. The two experiences are (1) the eight-year evolution of policy in the two terms of President Bill Clinton and (2) the much more contained incident triggered by the collision of a U.S. intelligence plane and a Chinese combat aircraft in April 2001.

The Experience of the Clinton Administrations

Ever since the Chinese government's brutal crackdown on the democracy movement in Tiananmen Square in Beijing on June 3–4, 1989, significant elements in the Congress had favored sanctions against China. Committed as he was to a strong relationship with China, President George H. W. Bush had expressed the outrage Americans felt while he sought to minimize the long-term damage to that relationship. Through the rest of his administration, the issue between the Congress and President Bush became increasingly contentious. From his time as second head of the U.S. Liaison Office in Beijing (1974–1975), Bush had developed a deep feeling for the China-U.S. relationship. "I take this whole relationship very personally, and I want to handle it [that way]," Bush wrote in his diary on June 24, 1989. As National Security Adviser Brent Scowcroft told Chinese leader Deng Xiaoping shortly thereafter during a then secret trip to Beijing, "The president shares the feelings of the American people with regard to the recent events in China, but he also believes deeply in preserving the relationship between our two countries." From a second visit emerged a "road map" for moving the relationship a step at a time toward a sounder footing. In Lampton's words, this was "a careful minuet of reciprocal bilateral moves. Beijing would take small strides forward and Washington would favorably respond."[12] This is what I have called a scenario of interactive steps.

During the presidential election campaign of 1992, Clinton had taken up the issue, criticizing Bush for his policy of "coddling dictators" even though he recognized the U.S. interest in the economic relationship with China. Now, as president, he had to try to square that circle in a difficult political context he had contributed to shaping. He had little of Bush's sense of the overall relationship. My purpose here is not to rehearse the history and complexity of Sino-U.S. interactions, but to contrast a policy of public, diplomatic ultimatum to the policy that emerged of trying to reestablish a functioning multilevel relationship that involved interactions in many areas of interest.

The Clinton administration's first effort to articulate policy toward China was driven by the need for the president to report to the Congress by June 3, 1993, his decision on whether to renew Most-Favored-Nation (MFN) trading status for China. The challenge as Clinton put it to Winston Lord, his nominee as assistant secretary of state for East Asian affairs, was to find a balance between U.S. economic interests and China's performance on human rights that would produce consensus in the Congress.[13] The Clinton administration's first effort to shape policy toward China was focused much more on America's own domestic political interests than on developing a sound overall relationship with China.

The resulting policy was an effort to link renewal of MFN status to the requirement that the Chinese meet certain conditions for extension of MFN beyond June 3, 1994—a linkage that ignored fundamental aspects of the overall relationship. In the words of David Lampton: "This search for conditions . . . was fatally flawed, driven as it was almost entirely by domestic politics. The search represented a failure to come to terms with the reality that the mere public articulation of such conditions would be construed in the PRC as an *ultimatum*, therefore unacceptable to the Chinese whose national identity revolved around safeguarding national sovereignty."[14]

Over the next year, President Clinton very quickly began to doubt the wisdom of this linkage. In September 1993, he approved a policy of "constructive engagement" that had been outlined in a memo by Winston Lord. On May 26, 1994, Clinton explained his decision to "delink human rights from the annual extension of Most Favored Nation trading status for China":

> I believe the question, therefore, is not whether we continue to support human rights in China, but how we can best support human rights in China and advance our other very significant issues and interests. I believe we can do it by engaging the Chinese. . . . We will have more contacts. We will have more trade. We will have more international cooperation. We will have more intense and constant dialogue on human rights issues.[15]

The concept of "engagement" implicitly recognized a process of continuous interaction, but it was still a good distance from sensitivity to the elements of the relationship.

While this was a step toward focusing on the overall relationship, Lampton points out that "the bilateral relationship would not be on a relatively more durable footing until security considerations were elevated further, in Beijing as well as in Washington." That next step was forced by the dangerous confrontations in the Taiwan Strait between July 1995 and March 1996. "This friction," Lampton writes, "reminded both sides that the U.S.-China relationship concerned more than trade and human rights. It is a relationship that, first and foremost, is about war and peace."[16]

Again my purpose is not to recount history. Suffice it to recall that a sequence of events surrounding moves by Taiwan's leadership seemingly to assert greater independence for Taiwan led to a series of dangerous escalating military moves by both China and the United States. Chinese missile-firing exercises around Taiwan ultimately caused the United States to send two aircraft carrier battle groups to the waters near the Strait.

It is worth noting that the November 1994 elections had put both houses of the U.S. Congress in Republican hands for the first time since 1954. In the words of Congressman Ben Gilman of New York, the new chairman of the House International Relations Committee: "[O]ne-half of the Congress has less than four years of institutional memory and little experience in foreign affairs."[17] This was just one more cause for making China policy indeed the product of the whole body politic, as the actions of that new Congress played an increasingly significant role in contributing to significant misperceptions in Beijing of U.S. intent.

At the peak of the Taiwan Strait crisis, by happenstance the visit of the Chinese vice foreign minister and director of the State Council's Foreign Affairs Office to Washington provided an opportunity for intense dialogue. The outcome was a decision for more active mutual engagement and to begin a "strategic dialogue." National Security Adviser Anthony Lake visited Beijing in July, and an agenda of high-level exchanges was announced.

Perhaps even more important were some of the conclusions Lake drew from his visit. As Lampton describes them from personal conversation: "He found that one could not expect much from senior Chinese leaders unless one treated them with respect and spoke with them directly—face mattered. Second, China's economic transformation was truly phenomenal. Thus Beijing could not be pushed around. Finally, before issues could be effectively addressed with the Chinese, relations had to be put into a larger strategic framework." Lampton comments: "These were sound judgments, even though they came three and one-half years late."[18]

Gradually, the administration had discovered that the overall relationship mattered and that the careful conduct of major aspects of an important relationship was essential. They were still far short of understanding the depths of the relationship: identity, interests, power in different forms, perceptions, and patterns of interaction. As Secretary of State Warren Christopher finally put the point in a speech in New York on May 17, 1996, before the National Committee on U.S.-China relations and other organizations:

> The United States and China share many interests that can only be served when our two countries deal constructively and openly with each other. . . . On some critical issues, we have deep differences. Our focus must be on the long term and we must seek to resolve our

differences through opportunities to advance common interests whenever possible and avoid deterioration to open rivalry.[19]

Lampton concludes: "Unfortunately, the president's own comprehensive statement was not to come for about another year and a half in a speech delivered on the eve of President Jiang Zemin's fall 1997 visit to the United States."

Exchanges in 1999 further dramatized the extent to which the Congress could derail the President's course. In April, Premier Zhu Rongi arrived in Washington hoping to reach an agreement that could lead to China's accession to the World Trade Organization (WTO). His visit took place in the face of domestic objections to economic concessions he was prepared to make and opposition to the U.S.-led war in Kosovo. Despite Clinton's initial intentions to proceed, he backed away from the agreement during Zhu's visit because he understood he could not count on the necessary support from Congress. The decision hit the Chinese leadership hard after they had faced down their own domestic opposition. A month later, a U.S. aircraft over Belgrade bombed the Chinese embassy and triggered angry demonstrations against U.S. offices in China. Again a "road map" of steps was prepared to calm relations. On November 15, China and the United States finally agreed to terms for China's accession to the WTO, but only in the context of an increasingly complex collection of pressures on the relationship.

In January, 2001, George W. Bush assumed the presidency having called China a "competitor" during his campaign. Once again, the "immature"— to use the Chinese characterization—China-U.S. relationship had become a "political football." Once again, events would drive a new president—this time early in his term—toward the center in recognizing the importance of the relationship, although still unable to master the art of conducting the overall relationship. His first test came on April 1.

The Spy Plane Collision

The collision of a U.S. intelligence aircraft and a Chinese fighter plane near Hainan Island early on Sunday, April 1, 2001, provides a simple example of the relevance of keeping the overall relationship always in view. It also provided another example of how important it is to reach beneath the surface of events to understand the deeper dynamics of the relationship.

U.S. aircraft have for years flown missions over international waters to collect electronic intelligence. Chinese fighter aircraft had adopted a practice of flying close to them and "buzzing" them. On this Sunday morning, according to the U.S. crew, one of them flew under the U.S. plane and then pulled up ahead of it, hitting it hard enough to damage both planes. The Chinese plane went down, and the pilot was lost. The U.S. plane made an emergency landing on Hainan Island in Chinese territory. The plane was impounded and the U.S. crew held.

A public exchange of recriminations at the highest levels of the two governments followed. President Jiang said the U.S. plane had rammed the Chinese plane and violated Chinese air space. He demanded an apology. President Bush replied, in effect, that the United States would not apologize for what it had not done.

Visiting Beijing and Nanjing through the two weeks of the crisis, I had the opportunity to meet with Chinese citizens: university students in large and small audiences, historians and philosophers, and high-level diplomats and military officers. During this whole time, I refused to engage in debate over exactly what had happened in the air because I had no authoritative account. This response tended to push the more thoughtful interlocutors to say: "I don't know exactly what happened either, but that's not the most important point. The main point is that your plane should not have been there at all."

A senior Chinese scholar of the United States later put that point in an even larger perspective. She was offering her definition of what Chinese mean when they accuse the United States of acting as a "hegemon." It is not necessarily that the United States wants to rule the world, she suggested. It is that the United States assumes that it can act any way it wants, even while it condemns others for doing the same things. For instance, a committee of the U.S. House of Representatives in May 1999 (the "Cox Committee") had charged China with spying in the United States for many years and stealing nuclear secrets.[20] Americans could be upset, she pointed out, by thinking that China had spied on the United States while flying spy planes against China. In short, the underlying feelings had much more to do with unequal treatment—a double standard—than with what had actually happened.

I was interested when, at the end of the week, a senior military officer echoed what had been going on in my mind all week:

> [Our countries, peoples, press, and officials] could have handled this in either of two ways.
>
> What we did was to begin trading charges and demands. That turned the incident into a confrontation right from the start.
>
> What should have happened: One of the top leaders on either side should have called his counterpart and said: "I understand there has been an accident. I am told a pilot has been lost; I am deeply sorry. I don't know exactly what happened. Do you? Let's each name a small group to go together to the site to question those involved together. Let's each bring any flight tracking information we have. Let's stay in close touch."[21]

I was interested that my Chinese interlocutor, whom I expected to take a very hard line, favored the second approach. Such an approach could have strengthened the collaboration between the two militaries, would have provided a nonconfrontational setting for the Chinese to voice their concerns about the intelligence flights, could have allowed U.S. participants to try to find an appropriate response, and would have avoided the public outpouring of anti-American feeling that added one more burden to an already weakened relationship.

A Concluding Reflection

It does indeed make a difference when officials and citizens of two great countries act with sensitivity to their overall relationship and when they pay close attention to the conduct of the relationship. One of the problems in the Clinton administration was that the president paid attention to the relationship with China only sporadically, making his first comprehensive speech on U.S.-China policy only after more than four years in office. One of the president's many obligations is to help the American people understand important challenges facing our country.

A complex relationship such as that between China and the United States will be buffeted constantly by forces and events beyond anyone's control. One way to limit damage and to stay as closely on course as possible is to keep a daily finger on the pulse of the relationship. Having spent 25 years in the U.S. government, I am no believer that changes in bureaucratic structure necessarily improve anything. Improvement in whatever structure exists happens when people within those structures think differently and relate differently. I would charge appropriate officers to come together across bureaucratic and departmental lines—and to find ways to include involved citizens outside government informally, regularly, and frequently—to focus on the overall Sino-U.S. relationship as a whole or in some significant part. I would seek agreement of Chinese counterparts to meet regularly with U.S. participants and to conduct frequent e-mail conversations. I would make the thoughts suggested in the sections above titled "possibilities for change" the subject of intensive nonofficial dialogue. Again, I believe that the concept of relationship would provide a working analytical and operational framework for these efforts. It would make a difference.

U.S. citizens in two sets of separately framed public forums across the country in 2000–2001 came to comparable conclusions. "We need to develop trusting relationships," said one woman in a forum in Michigan. "We really need to develop an interdependence to create a truly secure world." To quote further the report on those forums: ". . . several of the participants suggested that, in the end, Cold War enemies found common ground once they physically got together to talk things through. This idea of talking together, weighing directions together, getting to know each other on a human level in an environment that would promote mutual respect and cross-cultural understanding was underscored in every forum held throughout the United States."[22]

The Citizens' Century

CHAPTER ELEVEN

What Difference Does It Make? What Makes This Difference?

Citizens in many places yearn for a role in shaping their own futures. Many demonstrate remarkable capacities to play that role. What is missing is a view of politics that includes, encourages, nourishes, and supports them. Many—if not most—politicians, funders, theorists, journalists are stuck in a paradigm that marginalizes them. In the face of exclusion or disregard, many feel helpless, but others are finding their voices and the tools to improve their lives. They are living the relational paradigm. They are engaging as whole human beings in whole bodies politic.

The experiences recounted in the preceding chapters demonstrate that citizens *are* engaging in public life and that their engagement *can* produce results where their reach extends. The next step is extending that reach to influence larger arenas. That work is still in its early stages. We need to recognize and support solid achievement—not hide behind the pretense that it is not important unless we can measure its impact. *The future of the democratic revolution depends on our substantive and financial support.*

What Difference Does a Different Way of Thinking Make?

What have we learned from the stories in the previous five chapters? With the questions posed in chapter five as our framework, let's reflect on the experiences of these citizens and listen again to their words.

First, citizens can and do engage in public work—the work of improving the quality of their collective lives. They have "reconceptualized themselves as citizens"[1]—as political actors. They speak a different view of politics. As they build relationships in their communities, they generate "bonding social capital"—reliable patterns of interaction among people who know and trust one another.

"The government has neither the capacity nor the resources to put every town in our country on its feet economically," said a Tajikistani citizen in 2001. "If anyone is going to do that, the citizens of those towns will have to do it."[2] "People who were disillusioned by other forms of interaction were looking for ways of talking to one another in public," says Betty Knighton in West Virginia. "I have seen how much people can handle, how wise they are, how reflective they can be, and how nuanced their thinking can be."[3]

South Africans, particularly in the decade after 1984, engaged first in communities and ultimately in a nationwide effort to transform the political system and the relationships among racial and ethnic groups—the patterns of interaction in the country. After 1992, the National Peace Accord—negotiated by nongovernmental groups—established a framework for citizens to create what amounted to dialogue groups in hundreds of communities to address violence and, in the end, to begin transforming relationships.

Small groups in Tajikistan helped by their own NGO, the Public Committee for Democratic Processes, experimented with Economic Development Committees in poor towns deeply divided during the civil war. Sustained Dialogue groups in seven regions are dealing with relational problems raised by the integration into their democratic, secular polity of the only legitimate Islamic party in Central Asia and by the presence of Islamic extremists returning from neighboring Afghanistan and Pakistan.

West Virginians turned to deliberative forums to tackle specific problems such as promoting adult literacy, availability of health care, sound family life, preventing domestic violence, and workable options for families dealing with economic pressures. They created the Center for Civic Life to deepen citizens' capacities and to develop statewide influence. They learned that their job as citizens, even under representative government, goes well beyond traditional duties of voting.

American and Russian citizens initiated public forums in both countries to learn how citizens think and talk about the overall relationship between these two great powers. They agree broadly that hope for a sound and durable relationship lies more in citizens' hands than in government institutions. They learned that they can talk insightfully about the relationship between two peoples, traditionally the province of governments.

Even in the China-U.S. relationship, citizens show themselves to be potential actors. The economic development that is rapidly changing the character of China is driven by citizens outside government, although still within the Communist political system. U.S. citizens in public forums more clearly articulated principles to govern the relationship than has a government whipsawed by interest groups and weakened by leadership without focus on the overall relationship.

In short, citizens have demonstrated capacity to deal in nuanced ways with complex problems and to build the relationships necessary for public work—the capacity to concert. They have demonstrated the capacity to work through well-designed, systematic, disciplined social processes toward goals they define. They have learned to judge their achievements, and to make mid-course corrections. Frequently they accomplish what is beyond the reach of governments. Above all, they demonstrate a capacity to engage citizens in public work in ways that most governments are not even considering. They think of themselves as political actors. They are.

Second, some citizens recognize and experiment to find ways to meet the next challenge—how to extend their reach to influence the larger social, political, and economic systems that restrict or enlarge their opportunities. This is "bridging social capital." They interact—engage—in steadily widening social and political arenas. They build networks on local and regional levels, but this work is still in its early stages. They seem instinctively to understand the power that emerges from the relationships and the multilevel process of continuous interaction among citizens outside government.

"We didn't set out with a strategy of building a network," recalls Betty Knighton in West Virginia. "If we had a strategy, it was the practical thought that connecting with organizations that had a statewide presence would give us the best chance of covering the state. If we could learn how to connect with their work, we could extend our work. Once partners became interested, the connections became a dynamic force that began moving us from our individual efforts to a statewide presence. . . . Until now, we've just built solid relationships, . . . but I know that we have to think more systematically about making ourselves sustainable."[4] Parviz Mullojanov in Tajikistan writes similarly: "The final goal [of the Economic Development Committees] is to create a network of community-based committees that would be able to make an essential contribution to interethnic and intercommunity relationships in the country."[5]

Again, in our stories, South Africa stands out. South Africans moved their country from minority to majority government in a structural constitutional transformation. They know their next challenge is extending networks to help citizens address more deeply and widely those relationships in communities where tensions often block collaboration that is essential for economic growth, justice, and hope. The Truth and Reconciliation Commission established a common picture of the past, but the work of reconciliation is unfinished.

Tajikistan's Public Committee is helping citizens achieve local results. They recognize, as a citizen in one of the Economic Development Committees said: "First of all, we have to prove the effectiveness and usefulness of our EDC for the rest of the community. In order to reach this goal, we have to implement successfully at least two or three of the designed projects."[6] They must also demonstrate that the capacities of citizens to change the course of life constructively can strengthen, not threaten, government. When they can demonstrate economic and social accomplishments in enough places, they may aim to develop networks for change in larger arenas. That is the point of reaching critical mass.

The citizens who are the sinews of the West Virginia Center for Civic Life have built a solid organization with statewide impact. They recognize that their primary opportunity is to connect established organizations using the deliberative process for their own purposes to build statewide networks. A corollary is to build and fund their Center to take full advantage of these opportunities, while still nourishing the deliberative process in budding community organizations and academic settings.

Public forums on the Russia-U.S. relationship across both countries awakened interest in the relationship among larger numbers of citizens, especially interest in expanding citizen exchanges between the two countries. But on neither side has this yet produced any systematic movement in that direction.

The China-U.S. dialogue has likewise extended its reach by engaging a larger number of citizens in its research on the relationship. A significant circle of citizens in both countries has thought about how the relationship might evolve most productively in the interest of citizens in both and in the larger interest of developing a more effective community of nations. Given the size of the two countries and the habits of government in both, however, the impact of this work is still confined to a relatively small circle.

In short, citizens recognize the importance of developing networks to extend their reach into whole bodies politic and are learning to build them. The West Virginia Center for Civic Life has demonstrated a progression of learning that works through these steps: citizens master a particular instrument such as the deliberative process; they apply that process to problems that affect them directly; they form their own groups to spread learning about that process and to help likeminded groups connect; encouraged by the results they achieve, these groups reach out to others with similar interests, forming networks to influence their larger political environment. They see themselves as engaging in a political process where relationships are changed. The Public Committee in Tajikistan is building the foundations by increasing the number of Economic Development Committees. The New Dartmouth Conference is studying how to move the learning from Russian and U.S. forums into wider arenas.

Not among the studies in this book are dramatic examples in the United States such as the Civil Rights Movement, the feminist movement, and the movement against the Vietnam War. The South African example is in this category as are movements in the former Soviet Empire. The budding civic renewal movement in the United States described in chapter eight is the larger context to which the West Virginia achievement contributes.

Third, experience suggests that an organization—a catalyst—at the heart of this process can help citizens (a) to find an appropriate instrument that they can use to deal with their immediate problems and then (b) to broaden their influence beyond their limited settings by connecting with others who share their goals. Behind such connections is recognition that developing relationships generates the power that citizens need to reach their goals. Ideally, the initiative and the first steps emerge from the spontaneous actions of citizens. At a certain point, capacities can be deepened, and these efforts can be multiplied and connected more quickly with others by groups formed to be catalysts in facilitating these connections. These catalytic groups build on experience to develop analysis of processes, provide training in them, and serve as connectors, usually preserving their neutrality by not engaging in the substance of issues or in advocacy. They are catalysts, not managers.

Parviz Mullojanov, executive director of Tajikistan's Public Committee for Democratic Processes, describes the Committee's role as creating spaces for citizens to learn to do the work that only they can do. This was the role of the Dartmouth Conference Regional Conflicts Task Force when in 1993 it offered its space for the Tajiks to talk about their civil war. In Mullojanov's words: "The best mechanism to assure wide civic engagement in the peace process is the public deliberative dialogue approach as practiced in the Dartmouth Conference and the Inter-Tajik Dialogue. The Public Committee's main idea is to create public spaces in the form of committees of 10–12 people representing different factions of society where citizens can deliberate on pressing problems. In the course of dialogue, a sense of trust and cooperation, as well as a sense of cohesiveness grows among participants. Dialogue changes conflicting relationships not only within the group but also intercommunal and interethnic relationships beyond the group."[7]

The Public Committee has made processes for change available to citizens in communities. It has trained citizens to frame issues for public forums, moderators for those forums, moderators to organize and conduct Sustained Dialogue groups, and moderators to organize and lead Economic Development Committees. It has worked under an agreement with the Minister of Education with three professors from each of eight universities to develop a text and a curriculum for courses in conflict resolution and peacebuilding rooted in Tajik culture and Western scholarship and practice. The Public Committee's work has combined initiating, monitoring, and supporting programs with the purpose of generating local capacity to sustain them.

On a national scale, the United Democratic Front in South Africa after 1984 became a coalition of organizations ranging across the political and racial spectrum. It was not so much the hub of a management wheel as a web of communication through which practices and experiences were shared and adapted to developing situations. In 1987, the Institute for Democratic Alternatives in South Africa (IDASA) was formed to organize meetings across the lines of apartheid when that contact was still illegal. As noted above, the National Peace Accord created a framework and encouragement for communities to bring groups together in dialogue to reduce violence. Since the structural change, IDASA has become in South and southern Africa one of the preeminent trainers in practices designed to improve relationships in communities. At the same time, the South Africans are immensely proud that it was all done without the help of outsiders. In the words of Roelf Meyer: "We developed joint ownership of the process. . . . [That] may distinguish the South African process because we never allowed outsiders to come in. . . . We knew we had to do it ourselves."[8] This was possible, in part, because their internal catalysts worked so well.

The West Virginia Center for Civic Life was created from a growing circle of individual initiatives in areas of interest to these individuals: adult illiteracy, domestic violence, troubled families, health care. What brought them together was their use of deliberative processes to deal with these very different problems. In developing their own capacities, they drew on the research, training, and materials of the National Issues Forums and the Kettering Foundation, which themselves by the mid-1990s had a nation-wide reach through amorphous networks of likeminded groups. The Center for Civic Life purposefully provides training in the deliberative process to enable organizations to use it in pursuing their own interests and to connect them in what the Center hopes will become statewide net-works. They are also making their own contribution to the nationwide community of organizations using the deliberative process. As Betty Knighton said pointedly: "Without some group working at the center, there would not have been as much order in the chaos."[9]

The Russia-U.S. forums are a product of the longest continuous bilateral dialogue involving Soviet, now Russian, and American citizens—the Dartmouth Conference—and of the Kettering Foundation's experience in developing the deliberative process. The Russian forums resulted from the initiative of three NGOs, and the American forums were organized under the auspices of the National Issues Forums Institute. In both countries, each forum was held in collaboration with a local organization. The Dartmouth Conference has also demonstrated its convening power in providing space for citizens of Tajikistan to engage in dialogue about their conflict and, much later, for those living in Armenia, Azerbaijan, and Nagorno Karabakh to discuss their stalemated conflict.

The China-U.S. Dialogue and the public engagement it has produced result from the work of a quasi-governmental research organization in Beijing—the Institute of American Studies in the Chinese Academy of Social Sciences—and the Kettering Foundation and the National Issues Forums networks in the United States. Both organizations use research as the vehicle for enlarging the circle of engagement in the China-U.S. relationship.

In short, catalyzing organizations work across a carefully defined spectrum. At one end, some actively enter the citizens' environment to find people who recognize a need to act and introduce these citizens to practices they can use. Next, some of them train citizens and monitor their perform-ance over time as a continuation of that training. Toward the other end of the spectrum, they may even provide limited support for a first project to enable citizens to learn through experience that their actions can make a difference and that their process can be sustained as a way to tackle new problems. Their objective is the creation of sustainable, self-generating clusters of citizens and networks.

Fourth, what is only beginning to happen in most places is to improve connections between citizens outside and inside government and to create whole bodies politic. Some experiments have begun on the local level, but the gulf at higher levels remains wide and probably in most cases unaddressed.

"The Center for Civic Life," says Betty Knighton, "could work much more with policymakers in an ongoing way. We have done enough of this work to know that it can be very fruitful, but I don't even know what is possible in working with the legislature over time. We also know that it's fraught with difficulties in a partisan climate."[10]

The moment of South African constitutional transition was, of course, unique, and the transition from minority to majority government certainly increased the number of citizens interacting with government. Many of IDASA's programs enhance constructive, problem-solving interaction between citizens and their local governments. Beyond the local level, much work remains to be done. Behind the transformation was a "holistic" view of change in some minds, but the challenge remains enormous because this relationship is unfamiliar for most citizens both inside and outside government.

The Economic Development Committees in Tajikistan and the regional dialogues of the Public Committee have made a careful effort to gain the acquiescence of municipal officials in their work but not normally their official collaboration. It is essential to reassure government that such activity is not a threat, but there is the danger that government will take over any effort. Formal interaction is less common on the national level, but at that level there have been, since the early days of the Inter-Tajik Dialogue, informal connections through individuals who played roles on both official and nonofficial tracks.

The West Virginia Center for Civic Life has produced reports from statewide forums and has presented these reports before the state legislature, to the governor, and on statewide television. Discovering how this might be done more consistently and effectively is one of the areas slated for further experiment and development.

In the Russian-U.S. dialogue, members of the New Dartmouth Conference are experimenting with ways of causing governments to take seriously what citizens say in their forums about the relationship. During the Cold War, Dartmouth Conference task forces introduced ideas at governmental and Communist Party levels, but with the end of the Cold War, neither government has shown as much interest. As one Russian colleague said at the fortieth anniversary reunion of the Dartmouth Conference in 1990, "The market for our product is no longer there."[11]

The China-U.S. dialogue has occasionally opened doors for conversations between participants and government officials. Results of some dialogues have been reported to government. But both sides continue to struggle with the challenge of producing findings that compel government attention.

In short, this is a challenge being addressed in pragmatic ways in local situations, but it is still a major hurdle at national levels. Even at local levels, citizens in some places must cope with officials who want to take over any effort, leaving little outside their realms of control. But evidence suggests that collaboration or at least coexistence between citizens and government is most possible at lower levels. At higher levels, there are numerous examples of individual citizens from the policy-influencing community who can interact with policymakers. The Inter-Tajik Dialogue discussed mechanisms for this purpose: the proposed Consultative Forum of the Peoples of Tajikistan and the subcommissions of the National Reconciliation Commission, which oversaw implementation of the peace agreement. The challenge now is to develop regular mechanisms for interaction between citizens in and out of government. Policymakers sometimes join citizens' forums in West Virginia and a growing number of other places. A small number of officials play a significant role in Sustained Dialogue in Tajikistan. But we are far from developing, testing, and sustaining workable mechanisms for this interaction.

Fifth, a most striking revelation in these stories is the depth and breadth to which citizens, engaging their own problems in different settings, have instinctively reached—through experience—comparable conclusions about the nature of politics and the instruments they use. Their vocabulary reflects—in their own words—that of the relational paradigm and the concept of relationship. They have naturally resorted to dialogue in some form. They have become political actors, believing that they can generate a form of power that some political scientists have not defined as power but that nevertheless produces results. It seems we can be confident that the relational paradigm captures what comes naturally to citizens—that it is not just a theoretical construct.

"There was a picture of change made up of more than just who sits in power," to repeat the words of Pravin Gordhan in South Africa. "There was a complex understanding about what the nature of change would be. If you see your objective as dismantling one system and replacing it with another, change is of a holistic order. In the first instance, yes, you have to have access to political power; in the second instance, that access would allow you to have the resources, the authority, and the legislative means to introduce other changes; third, that would have to be underpinned by changes in the economy; fourthly, there would be a social element to this change which involved a change in relationships—the development of a nonracial culture, reconciliation of sorts between black and white, introducing a new set of values which would enable people to respect each other, to accept each other as equals, etc."[12] And the African philosophy of *ubuntu* is a profound and beautifully simple statement about relationship: "A person is a person through another person."[13]

South Africans who played leading roles in the transformation often explain their actions in terms of their way of thinking. In addition to the above statement, Judge Richard Goldstone reflected: "It's not a linear process. It's not a process of us and them. . . . there must be for a successful rapprochement dialogue, readjustment, reconciliation, an appreciation that two people share more than divides them—a common destiny."[14] Roelf Meyer, principal negotiator for the apartheid government, reflected on the unique ability of citizens outside government to reduce violence through the National Peace Accord and its implementation: "How important civil society can be! New people came into the picture. The process widened. . . . Personal interactions became more important."[15] Susan Collin Marks, one of those "new people" recalled: "Instead of seeing ourselves locked in a zero-sum, win-lose competition in which only one side could win, we started to see ourselves as partners in a problem-solving relationship."[16] "We are intensely critical of power-based negotiation in a civil war. . . . The application of coercive force won't last," said a scholar of negotiation and conflict resolution.[17]

In Tajikistan, the Public Committee's leaders are deeply committed to a citizen-centered view of politics. "Democracy means that every view must be heard, even those with which we fundamentally disagree. Only when everyone feels that her or his views will have a full and fair hearing will dialogue begin to be taken seriously by the community as a whole. Only when dialogue is taken seriously can a community begin to come to terms with its most serious and fundamental problems. . . . To the degree that these conditions are sustained over time in public dialogue, Tajikistan will move forward in its democratic development."[18]

In West Virginia, beyond connecting networks in the process of continuous interaction, Betty Knighton says, "I now see power as a potentially shared force field." Jean Ambrose reflected, "It has certainly been proved to my satisfaction that when people come together for the common good, power springs up there. Those experiences when people really do see each other as human beings change their relationships. The power that comes from those experiences has a wisdom to it that I don't see in other expressions of power."[19]

American and Russian citizens naturally fall into talking about their relationship as a human interaction in which respect for the other's culture and identity are often more important than issues governments deal with, and dialogue may be more important in many instances than negotiation. They reveal a deep desire to relate on a human level and a feeling that increasing exchanges among citizens is essential.

The China-U.S. dialogue has demonstrated the usefulness of analyzing the overall relationship as a basis for efforts to change it. Experience suggests repeatedly that governments do not conduct the relationship in a productive way when they focus on isolated issues rather than on conducting the whole relationship. Citizens in both countries are comfortable thinking about the relationship in terms of mutual respect.

In short, citizens outside government in these widely dispersed countries speak the language of human interaction, not the language of political institutions. They recognize the importance of relating constructively with government but seem to say that will happen when government officials see themselves as citizens inside government rather than as officials. In most instances, citizens outside government are far closer to a philosophy of whole human beings acting in whole bodies politic than those inside, and they see more acutely than those inside how essential their engagement will be in accomplishing what is beyond the reach of government.

What Makes This Difference?

First, to engage, citizens must believe (a) that resolution of a problem depends on them and (b) that there is something they can do that will make a difference.

In the experiences we have probed, individuals have in some instinctive way begun to "reconceptualize themselves as citizens" and to recognize that they are responsible in many instances for dealing with collective problems. They do not refer to a *paradigm shift*, but the vocabulary and the worldview underlying their words and actions reveal that they are thinking beyond the traditional state-centered theories of politics to see themselves as potential actors.

That shift happens in several ways. Most commonly, it seems, they are drawn into situations where they learn that they as individuals can make a difference. Or once removed, they may see other citizens' accomplishments and seek to learn the processes that have worked for others. One strategy of civic organizations is often to engage citizens in situations where they experience making a difference.

Citizens must also find tools they can handle. The various instruments in the Citizens' Political Process such as the deliberative process, Sustained Dialogue, and variations such as the Economic Development Committees in Tajikistan are examples. They need to feel: "That is something I can do." Or: "I can't solve the whole problem, but I can work on this piece of it." Training programs and, in a few instances, university curricula are making these tools more accessible.

Second, experience demonstrates that the key to achievement is citizens developing relationships with others and finding a process that enables them to relate productively in doing the work they must do together. Experiencing this "capacity to concert"[20] and realizing that it can generate power is often decisive in citizens committing to collective work. As their work continues over time, a next step is often to focus on beginning to broaden relationships by stitching together a network of likeminded groups in an ever-widening scope to pursue a common purpose on a broader stage.

Third, I return to the words of David Bohm: "A proper world view, appropriate for its time is generally one of the basic factors that is essential for harmony in the individual and in society as a whole."[21] The conceptual lenses we use to bring the world into focus determine how we act. The stories recounted in this book suggest that people in widely differing circumstances and places have instinctively embraced the essence of the relational paradigm, both in word and in act. A paradigm shift is taking place and is often articulated or is at least implicit in the minds of those who have become political actors. In South Africa, activists describe coming to a new worldview in the years of their maturing under apartheid and learning how to resist it. In Tajikistan, leaders of the Public Committee are deeply committed to a philosophy in which the citizen is the focus of political life. In West Virginia, citizens say that their experience has led them to a new view of politics. Experiencing relationships built in pursuing common purposes seems to lead citizens to a nontraditional understanding of the essence of politics. What will it take to achieve broad common acceptance of the new?

Fourth and most difficult, citizens need to demand different political behavior from their leaders. They have yet to do this effectively in most instances. Then we need a courageous response—a demonstration by a few leading politicians of a different way of conducting politics—and journalists perceptive enough to recognize the difference. While citizens are learning dialogue, deliberation, and collaboration, most political leaders are honing skills of being more divisive and more corrosive of the whole body politic. This is an explosive example for politicians to set in any country. It is wasteful, destructive, and even immoral. To repeat Havel's words, "We need to behave differently."[22] The hope is that citizens who have learned and demonstrated conclusively the effectiveness of a different way of thinking, relating, and acting might demand the same of their leaders. To apply President Dwight Eisenhower's words to the political arena: "I think that people want peace so much that one of these days governments had better get out of their way and let them have it."[23] Indeed, in a democracy that may be the most effective—if not the only—way to change the practice of politics.

Fifth, funders often do not recognize the pivotal role of citizen organizations that play the role of catalysts in the transformation. Funders often require administrative structures that are unnatural for organizations of citizens outside government or they fund through government agencies that are unresponsive to citizens or are even corrupt. These organizations model a view of politics that is unfamiliar to bureaucratic structures; they fashion and embed through training the tools citizens need; they serve as the connectors that create networks and stitch them together; and they open public spaces where citizens outside and inside government could work together. Most of these organizations are living hand-to-mouth. The challenge before funders is to see them as critical to the next phase in the democratic revolution. Failure to respond generously but in nonintrusive ways reflecting "a world view appropriate for its time" is a major threat to the democratic revolution.

Sixth, governments have an opportunity to conduct major international relationships instead of managing intergovernmental relations. To do so, they must learn to listen thoughtfully to citizens outside government and to engage with them as equals in dialogue. The voices of citizens reflecting on the Russia-U.S. and the China-U.S. relationships reveal a perspective and wisdom in thinking about these relationships that is often not found in government. The Dartmouth Conference and the China-U.S. Dialogue witness that citizens can talk seriously in dialogues sustained over time about the conduct of the relationships between their countries. Few of them believe that governments can listen. Experience in government tells me that there is no reason—except habit or arrogance—why governments could not join with citizens outside government to create a complex of ongoing dialogue groups on our major international relationships and problems. Structural changes in government rarely solve problems; the main obstacle to good policymaking is not structure but the way citizens inside government interact. A simple mechanism to bring citizens in and out of government together in dialogue would not require structural change. It would simply require "a different way of thinking—another way of relating."

The Citizens' Century

Politics is about relationship—citizens connecting to improve the quality of their lives together. Dialogue is their instrument, enhancing their capacities to concert. Human beings will not be whole until they learn to relate through open and honest dialogue. To create a just and compassionate political environment, they constitute government. Citizens inside and outside government must learn to relate peacefully and productively for the benefit of all. Polities will not be whole until all citizens—inside and outside government, scholars and practitioners—are engaged collaboratively in serving the whole.

Engaging whole human beings in whole bodies politic is the great project of the Citizens' Century.

NOTES

Acknowledgments

1. Martin Buber, *I and Thou*, a new translation with a prologue, "I and You" and notes by Walter Kaufmann (New York: Simon & Schuster: A Touchstone Book, 1996).

Preface

1. Harold H. Saunders, *The Other Walls: The Politics of the Arab-Israeli Peace Process* (Washington, DC: American Enterprise Institute, 1985). Second edition: *The Other Walls: The Arab-Israeli Peace Process in a Global Perspective* (Princeton, NJ: Princeton University Press, 1991). It is out of print but available from ProQuest Information and Learning—UMI, 300 N. Zeeb Rd., PO Box 1346, Ann Arbor, MI 48106–1346; tel.: 1-800-521-0600; e-mail: info@il.proquest.com.
2. Harold H. Saunders, "We Need a Larger Theory of Negotiation: The Importance of the Pre-Negotiating Phases," *Negotiation Journal* (Vol. 1, No. 3, July 1985), pp. 249–262.
3. It is one of the rules of the Inter-Tajik Dialogue that remarks will not be attributed to individuals. The quote is from the author's notes on the meeting. After earlier meetings of the Dialogue, academic participants had asked my colleague and me to conduct sessions to acquaint them with the Western discipline of conflict resolution. We had used John Paul Lederach's triangle illustrating three levels of society engaged in conflict resolution. See John Paul Lederach, *Building Peace: Sustainable Reconciliation in Divided Societies* (Washington, DC: United States Institute of Peace Press, 1997), p. 37.
4. Harold H. Saunders, *A Public Peace Process: Sustained Dialogue to Transform Racial and Ethnic Conflicts* (New York: St. Martin's Press, 1999; Palgrave paperback, 2001).
5. Thomas S. Kuhn, *The Structure of Scientific Revolutions* (Chicago: The University of Chicago Press, Second Edition, Enlarged, 1970).
6. David Bohm, *Wholeness and the Implicate Order* (London, Boston, Melbourne, and Henley: Ark Paperbacks, an imprint of Routledge & Kegan Paul plc, 1983; first published, 1980), p. xi.
7. Richard P. Feynman, *The Meaning of It All: Thoughts of a Citizen Scientist* (Reading, MA: Addison-Wesley Helix Books, 1998), p. 3.

Introduction

1. James D. Wolfensohn, president of the World Bank, Address to the Annual Meeting of the Board of Governors, September 28, 1999, in words used to introduce Deepa Narayan, with Raj Patel, Kai Schafft, Anne Rademacher, and Sarah Koch-Schulte, *Voices of the Poor: Can Anyone Hear Us?* (Oxford: Oxford University Press for the World Bank, 2000), before the title page.
2. Thabo Mbeki, president of South Africa; Henrique Cardoso, president of Brazil; Goran Persson, prime minister of Sweden, "Only One Earth: We can do this good work together," *International Herald Tribune* (August 28, 2002), VIEWS: Editorials & Commentary, p. 6.
3. James D. Wolfensohn, "Trends can be changed: What kind of world for our children?" *International Herald Tribune* (August 23, 2002), VIEWS: Editorials and Commentary, p. 8.
4. Barry James, "Talks to tackle threat to biodiversity," *International Herald Tribune* (August 23, 2002), pp. 1, 9.

5. Václav Havel, "The End of the Modern Era," *New York Times* (March 1, 1992), p. E1223d in David Mathews, *Politics for People* (Urbana and Chicago: University of Illinois Press, 1994), p. 163.

6. Kofi Annan, Nobel Lecture, Oslo, December 10, 2001, copyright The Nobel Foundation, available at http://www.nobel.se/peace/laureates/2001/annan-lecture.html.

7. These thoughts were originally formulated and published as "Opening Remarks" in *Communicating What Works: Addressing Change & Conflict in Developing Democracies*, a Report on a Conference, July 17, 2000, prepared by Partners for Democratic Change (San Francisco, CA) and the Kettering Foundation (Dayton, OH).

8. I first used the phrase in print as the title of an article, "Whole Human Beings in Whole Bodies Politic," in *Kettering Review* (Dayton, OH: Kettering Foundation, Fall 1998), pp. 66–73.

9. See, e.g., Deborah Tannen, *The Argument Culture: Moving from Debate to Dialogue* (New York: Random House, 1998).

10. A. H. Maslow, "A Theory of Human Motivation," *Psychological Review* (Vol. 50, 1943), pp. 370–396, reprinted in Richard J. Lowry, ed., *Dominance, Self-Esteem, Self-Actualization: Germinal Papers of A. H. Maslow* (Monterey, CA: Brooks/Cole Publishing Company, 1973), pp. 154–163.

11. For an account of the shift in thinking after 1960 about methods of resolving conflict, see John W. Burton, *Resolving Deep-Rooted Conflict: A Handbook* (Lanham, MD: University Press of America, 1987), pp. 14–17.

12. James D. Wolfensohn, Peter A. Seligmann, and Mohamed T. El-Ashry, "How Biodiversity Can Be Preserved if We Get Smart Together," *International Herald Tribune* (August 22, 2000), p. 8.

13. Among the scholars are Jacob Bercovitch, Morton Deutsch, Martha Finnemore, Ted Robert Gurr, Margaret Hermann, Margaret Keck, Ronnie Lipschutz, David Little, Marc Howard Ross, Jeffrey Rubin, Kathryn Sikkink, Janice Gross Stein, Mary Ann Tetreault, I. William Zartman. Among the scholar-writer-practitioners with whom I have worked are Edward Azar, Andrea Bartoli, John Burton, Chester Crocker, Louise Diamond, Herbert Kelman, John Paul Lederach, John McDonald, Christopher Mitchell, Joseph Montville, Nadim Rouhana, Vamik Volkan. For a list of suggested readings, please see Harold H. Saunders, *A Public Peace Process: Sustained Dialogue to Transform Racial and Ethnic Conflicts* (New York: St. Martin's Press, 1999; Palgrave paperback, 2001), pp. 319–323.

14. The speaker wishes to remain anonymous. This comment was made in private conversation. See chapter seven.

15. Pravin Gordhan, taped interview in his Pretoria office, September 28, 1999. See chapter six.

16. Jean Ambrose, in a taped interview in her Charleston office July 6, 2004. See chapter eight.

17. Thomas S. Kuhn, *The Structure of Scientific Revolutions* (Chicago: The University of Chicago Press, second edition, enlarged, 1970), p. 11.

Chapter One   Politics Is about . . . ?

1. Thomas S. Kuhn, *The Structure of Scientific Revolutions* (Chicago: The University of Chicago Press, second edition, enlarged, 1970), p. 77.

2. John A. Moore, *Science as a Way of Knowing: The Foundations of Modern Biology* (Cambridge, MA: Harvard University Press, 1993; first Harvard University Press paperback edition, 1999), pp. 2–4.

3. I am grateful to Katharine Wheatley, my assistant at the Kettering Foundation, 2000–2002, while she pursued her M.A. at the Elliott School in The George Washington University, for her research in the political science literature of the latter half of the twentieth century in support of my analysis in this chapter.

4. Hans J. Morgenthau, *Politics Among Nations: The Struggle for Power and Peace* (New York: Alfred A. Knopf, Inc., 1978), p. 42.

5. Hans J. Morgenthau, *Politics in the Twentieth Century: The Decline of Democratic Politics* (Chicago, IL: The University of Chicago Press, 1962), p. 13.

6. Hans J. Morgenthau, "What Is Political Power?" in Sam Sarkesian, and Krish Nanda, *Politics and Power: An Introduction to American Government* (Port Washington, NY: Alfred Publishing Company, Inc., 1976), p. 69.

7. Harold D. Lasswell, *Power and Society* (New Haven, CT: Yale University Press, 1950), p. xiv.

8. Harold D. Lasswell, *Who Gets What, When, How* (New York: Meridian Books, Inc., 1958), p. 13.

9. Bertrand Russell, *Power* (London, UK: Unwin Books, 1960), pp. 9, 179.

10. Morgenthau, *Politics in the Twentieth Century*, p. 48.

11. Kenneth E. Boulding, *Three Faces of Power* (Newbury Park, CA: Sage Publications, 1990), pp. 9–10.

12. Erwin A. Jaffe, *Healing the Body Politic: Rediscovering Political Power* (Westport, CT: Praeger, 1993), pp. 5, 67.

13. Joseph S. Nye Jr., *Soft Power: The Means to Success in World Politics* (New York: Public Affairs, 2004), p. x. Chapter one, "The Changing Nature of Power," presents a beautifully subtle and much needed discussion of the dimensions and nuances of power in the context of states and world politics.

14. Anne-Marie Slaughter, *A New World Order* (Princeton and Oxford: Princeton University Press, 2004), p. 207.

15. Adrian Leftwich, "Politics: people, resources and power," in Leftwich, ed., *What is Politics? the activity and its study* (Oxford: Basil Blackwell, 1984), pp. 62–63.

16. Robert O. Keohane, ed., *Neorealism and Its Critics* (New York: Columbia University Press, 1986), p. 7.

17. James D. Morrow, "A Rational Choice Approach to International Conflict," in Nehemia Geva and Alex Mintz, eds., *Decision-making on War and Peace: The Cognitive-Rational Debate* (Boulder, CO: Lynne-Rienner Publishers, 1997), p. 12.

18. Mary E. Clark, *In Search of Human Nature* (London: Routledge, 2002), pp. 6–8. I am also indebted to her for an earlier description of the evolution of the Western worldview in *Ariadne's Thread: The Search for New Modes of Thinking* (New York: St. Martin's Press, 1989), especially on this subject in Chapter 9, "From God to Man: Origins of the Western Worldview," pp. 245–272.

19. I am deeply indebted to my friend and colleague, Ramón Daubón, for the elegant and powerful phrase, "capacity to concert," and for the thinking that denotes it the long missing ingredient in economic development theory—the essence of what is now commonly referred to as "social capital." He says that the verb that we translate into English as "to concert" is in Spanish more commonly used and has more powerful social connotations. He first presented this line of thought in *All of the Voices: an Alternative Approach to Development Assistance* (Arlington, VA: Inter-American Foundation, 2001). It was then published in an article that we wrote together, "Operationalizing Social Capital: A Strategy to Enhance Communities' 'Capacity to Concert,'" *International Studies Perspectives* (Vol. 3, 2002), pp. 176–191. As vice president of the Inter-American Foundation, he leads an effort in the funding community to focus grant-making first on the capacity to concert—the political process that produces ideas and projects for solving community problems—rather than only on the projects. It is the political process, he argues, not the money that makes the projects and economic growth sustainable.

20. Leftwich, "Politics: people, resources and power," p. 65.

21. David Mathews frequently makes this comment in public presentations.

22. The "Citizens' Political Process" has been central to my work with international colleagues at the Kettering Foundation since the mid-1990s. It was first presented in published form in Saunders, *A Public Peace Process: Sustained Dialogue to Transform Racial and Ethnic Conflicts* (New York: St. Martin's Press, 1999; Palgrave paperback, 2001), pp. 59–66. This discussion draws heavily from that presentation. It has been further developed in Harold H. Saunders, "A Citizen's Political Process," *Kettering Review* (Spring 2004), pp. 37–46.

23. David Mathews, *Politics for People: Finding a Responsible Public Voice* (Urbana and Chicago: University of Illinois Press, 1994), pp. 167–168. He cites Daniel J. Elazar, and John Kincaid, "Covenant and Polity," *New Conversations* (Vol. 4, 1979), pp. 4–8.

24. Mathews, *Politics for People*, pp. 151–152. He cites Stanley J. Hallet, "Communities Can Plan Future on Their Own Terms," *Regeneration* (Vol. 6, January 1990), p. 8.

25. Daniel Yankelovich has made this point in conversation.

26. My earlier statements on scenario-building have listed only four steps. I have added this new first step—listing resources—in response to comments by a number of colleagues and in the spirit of starting on a positive note.

27. Robert D. Putnam, with Robert Leonardi, and Rafaella Y. Nanetti, *Making Democracy Work: Civic Traditions in Modern Italy* (Princeton, NJ: Princeton University Press, 1993).

28. Michael Woolcock, "Social Capital in Understanding Social and Economic Outcomes," *Canadian Journal of Policy Research* (Vol. 2, No. 1, Spring 2001), p. 13.

29. Daubón and Saunders, "Operationalizing Social Capital," p. 176: "This paper addresses a concern increasingly being voiced in the donor establishment: fifty years of development assistance programs have failed to produce conclusive evidence that they can foster sustainable economic and social development in poor countries. The nature of donor programs is such that it emphasizes economic remedies and orients aid to finite projects. Yet recent evidence suggests that sustained development may be more a continued civic process whereby communities form their capacity to come to their own understandings about public ways of behaving and relating, whereby they develop their capacity to concert. This translates into a practical capability to pinpoint underlying problems, assess alternative approaches and devise solutions most likely to be sustained."

30. Meeting this need has been one purpose of those who founded and have sustained the International Society of Political Psychology. Efforts have been made through summer institutes to introduce young scholars to the methods of both disciplines. After receiving the Society's Nevitt Sanford Award "for professional contributions to political psychology," I delivered a lecture calling for the creation of "non-disciplinary spaces," where established scholars from different disciplines and their advanced students might come together as concerned citizens to develop as instruments for citizens such ideas as the concept of relationship. See "Two Challenges for the New Century: Transforming Relationships in Whole Bodies Politic," *Political Psychology* (Vol. 23, No. 1, March 2002), pp. 151–164.

Chapter Two   "A Proper World View, Appropriate for Its Time"

1. David Bohm, *Wholeness and the Implicate Order* (London, Boston, Melbourne, and Henley: Ark Paperbacks, an imprint of Routledge & Kegan Paul plc, 1983; first published in 1980), p. xi.
2. Mary E. Clark, *In Search of Human Nature* (London: Routledge, 2002), p. 5.
3. Shirley M. Tilghman, "Biology's Changing Landscape," *PAW: Princeton Alumni Weekly*, (Vol. 103, No. 16, June 4, 2003), p. 12 (www.princeton.edu/paw).
4. Bohm discussed the Eastern view of "wholeness" in *Wholeness and the Implicate Order*, pp. 19–26. See also Clark, *In Search of Human Nature* (London: Routledge, 2002), pp. 8–11.
5. For a brief assessment of the Newtonian revolution, please see Bernard J. Cohen, *Revolution in Science* (Cambridge, MA: The Belknap Press of Harvard University Press, 1985), pp. 170–175.
6. Marquis de Pierre Simon Laplace, *Celestial Mechanics*, 4 vols. Translated by Nathaniel Bowditch (New York: Chelsea Publishing Company), corrected facsimile reprint of the volume published in Boston, 1829, p. xxiii, quoted in Cohen, *Revolution in Science*, p. 172.
7. Edward Speyer, *Six Roads from Newton: Great Discoveries in Physics* (New York: John Wiley & Sons, Inc., 1994), p. 9.
8. Clark, *In Search of Human Nature*, p. 6.
9. Cohen, *Revolution in Science*, p. 173.
10. Cohen, *Revolution in Science*, p. 169.
11. Cohen, *Revolution in Science*, p. 174.
12. Cohen, *Revolution in Science*, pp. 153–154.
13. Cohen, *Revolution in Science*, p. 174.
14. Isaiah Berlin, *Personal Impressions*, ed. Henry Hardy (London: The Hogarth Press, 1980), p. 144 cited in Cohen, *Revolution in Science*, p. 174.
15. John A. Moore, *Science as a Way of Knowing: The Foundations of Modern Biology* (Cambridge, MA: Harvard University Press, 1993), p. 131.
16. Charles Darwin, *The Origin of Species* (New York: Gramercy Books, 1979), pp. 100, 133.
17. Ernst Mayr, *This Is Biology: The Science of the Living World* (Cambridge, MA: The Belknap Press of the Harvard University Press, 1997; first Harvard University Press paperback edition, 1998), p. 21.
18. Moore, *Science as a Way of Knowing*, pp. 253, 260, 267, and 272.
19. Mayr, *This Is Biology*, p. 69.
20. Albert Einstein and Leopold Infeld, *The Evolution of Physics: From Early Concepts to Relativity and Quanta* (New York: Simon and Schuster, Inc., 1938; republished in 1966), pp. 52 and 65.
21. Einstein and Infeld, *The Evolution of Physics*, pp. 125, 151, 244.
22. Bohm, *Wholeness and the Implicate Order*, pp. ix–x.
23. Bohm, *Wholeness and the Implicate Order*. pp. 9, 11, 48. On p. 48, Bohm comments further: Philosopher Alfred North Whitehead "[i]n more modern times . . . was the first to give this notion [of process] a systematic and extensive development" in his book, *Process and Reality* (New York: Macmillan, 1933).
24. Darwin, *The Origin of Species*, pp. 117 and 115. I originally read these words as quoted in Moore, *Science as a Way of Knowing*, pp. 131–132, who quoted them in this order from a facsimile of the first edition, with an introduction by Ernst Mayr, published in 1964 by Harvard University Press, Cambridge, MA, pp. 61–62.
25. Mayr, *This Is Biology*, p. 18 quotes Alex Novikoff, "The Concept of Integrative Levels and Biology," *Science* (No. 101), pp. 209–215.
26. Mayr, *This Is Biology*, p. 67.
27. Mayr, *This Is Biology*, pp. 207, 221–222.

28. James Gleick, *Genius* (New York: Pantheon Books, 1992), p. 5. I am grateful to Robert Durkee, vice president and secretary of Princeton University, for calling this to my attention.

29. Gary Zukav, *The Dancing Wu Li Masters: An Overview of the New Physics* (Toronto, New York, London, Sydney, Auckland: Bantam Books, 1980; first published by William Morrow & Company, Inc., 1979), p. 199.

30. Henry Stapp, "S-Matrix Interpretation of Quantum Theory" (Lawrence Berkeley Laboratory preprint, June 22, 1970; revised edition: *Physical Review*, D3, 1971, 1303), quoted in Zukav, *The Dancing Wu Li Masters*, p. 71.

31. Zukav, *The Dancing Wu Li Masters*, p. 72.

32. Zukav, *The Dancing Wu Li Masters*, pp. 95, 93.

33. Bohm, *Wholeness and the Implicate Order*, p. 11.

34. Zukav, *The Dancing Wu Li Masters*, p. 304. The quote from David Bohm appears in Zukav, *The Dancing Wu Li Masters*, p. 305; he cites a lecture given by Bohm on April 6, 1977, at the University of California, Berkeley.

35. Bohm, *Wholeness and the Implicate Order*, pp. xi, 1–2.

36. Bohm, *Wholeness and the Implicate Order*, pp. 1, 2, x, and 3.

37. Darwin, *The Origin of Species*, pp. 127, 130, 156.

38. Michael R. Rose, *Darwin's Spectre: Evolutionary Biology in the Modern World* (Princeton, NJ: Princeton University Press, 1998), p. 51.

39. Darwin, *The Origin of Species*, p. 75.

40. Rose, *Darwin's Spectre*, pp. 29–30.

41. Mayr, *This Is Biology*, pp. 16, 17, 18, 307, 309.

42. Bohm, *Wholeness and the Implicate Order*, p. 1.

43. Donald E. Stokes, *Pasteur's Quadrant: Basic Science and Technological Innovation* (Washington, DC: Brookings Institution Press, 1997), pp. 3–6, 74, 87, 102. Stokes works from Vannevar Bush, *Science—The Endless Frontier: A Report to the President on a Program for Postwar Scientific Research* (Washington, DC: National Science Foundation, reprinted 1990) as the definitive statement of what he calls the "postwar paradigm." He cites the quote from Conant as: "Report of the Panel on the McKay Bequest to the President and Fellows of Harvard College" (1950), p. 7.

44. Zukav, *The Dancing Wu Li Masters*, pp. 47–48 and 92–93.

45. Bohm, *Wholeness and the Implicate Order*, p. 6.

46. Zukav, *The Dancing Wu Li Masters*, p. 111.

47. Zukav, *The Dancing Wu Li Masters*, pp. 28, 29, 30.

48. Bohm, *Wholeness and the Implicate Order*, p. x.

49. Richard P. Feynman, *The Meaning of It All: Thoughts of a Citizen Scientist* (Reading, MA: Addison-Wesley, Helix Books, 1998), pp. 26–27, 18, 16–17.

50. Feynman, *The Meaning of It All: Thoughts of a Citizen Scientist*, pp. 24–25.

51. Mayr, *This Is Biology*, pp. 26, 27, 64, 69.

52. Moore, *Science as a Way of Knowing*, p. 135.

53. Mayr, *This Is Biology*, p. 26.

54. Henry Pierce Stapp, "The Copenhagen Interpretation," *The American Journal of Physics*, (Vol. 40, 1972). Quotations in this section except where otherwise noted are from pp. 1098, 1103, 1104.

Chapter Three   The Relational Paradigm: A Multilevel Process of Continuous Interaction

1. Ernst Mayr, *This Is Biology: The Science of the Living World* (Cambridge, MA: The Belknap Press of the Harvard University Press, 1997; first Harvard University Press paperback edition, 1998), pp. 99–101.

2. As I recall, it was Kenneth Hansen, then director of the international division of the Office of Management and Budget.

3. Thomas S. Kuhn, *The Structure of Scientific Revolutions* (Chicago: The University of Chicago Press, second edition enlarged, 1970), p. 111.

4. Kuhn, *The Structure of Scientific Revolutions*, p. 77.

5. Dee Hock, *Birth of the Chaordic Age* (San Francisco: Berrett-Koehler Publishers, 1999), p. 30.

6. Hock, *Birth of the Chaordic Age*, pp. 141, 191.

7. Hock, *Birth of the Chaordic Age*, pp. 137–139.

8. Mayr, *This Is Biology*, pp. 16–19.

9. Albert Einstein and Leopold Infeld, *The Evolution of Physics: From Early Concepts to Relativity and Quanta* (New York: Simon and Schuster, Inc., republished in 1966), p. 244.

10. Ludwig Von Bertalanffy, *General System Theory: Foundations, Development, Applications* (New York: George Braziller, 1968), p. 4. In a concise account of the history of systems theory (pp. 10–17), he places its modern roots in the mid-1920s and identifies the involvement of scholars across disciplines. Noting the founding of the Society for General System Theory (later the Society for General Systems Research) in 1954, he writes: "Meanwhile another development had taken place. Norbert Wiener's *Cybernetics* appeared in 1948, resulting from the then recent developments of computer technology, information theory, and self-regulating machines. It was again one of the coincidences occurring when ideas are in the air that three fundamental contributions appeared at about the same time: Wiener's *Cybernetics* (1948), Shannon and Weaver's information theory (1949) and von Neumann and Morgenstern's game theory (1947)," p. 15.

11. Robert Jervis, *System Effects: Complexity in Political and Social Life* (Princeton, NJ: Princeton University Press, 1997), pp. 6, 7, 10, 12–13, and 34. A number of Jervis' footnotes on these pages provide extensive and helpful bibliographic references.

12. One exception is a relatively recent book written to place systems thinking before a broader audience: Joseph O'Connor and Ian McDermott, *The Art of Systems Thinking: Essential Skills for Creativity and Problem Solving* (London: Thorsons, 1997).

13. In my book, *A Public Peace Process*, published in 1999, I spoke of six components of relationship. Soon after publication, I reduced the number to five. I decided that "limits on behavior" should be incorporated as part of "patterns of interaction," thus somewhat simplifying presentation of the overall concept.

14. Daniel Yankelovich, *The Magic of Dialogue: Transforming Conflict into Cooperation* (New York: Simon and Schuster, 1999), draft manuscript of the Introduction that he shared with me.

15. The National Issues Forums, as discussed more fully in chapter eight, is a nationwide network of community organizations in the United States that annually conduct public forums on issues of national importance. The overriding purpose of these forums is to engage citizens in a deliberative process in the hope that they will learn to use that process—the Citizens' Political Process—in coping with their everyday problems, thereby enhancing and spreading the essence of democratic process.

16. See Paul Salem, "Deconstructing Civil Society: Reflections on a Paradigm," *Kettering Review* (Fall 1998), pp. 8–15.

17. These thoughts amplifying the new paradigm were first formulated in print in Harold H. Saunders, "Whole Human Beings in Whole Bodies Politic," *Kettering Review* (Fall 1998), pp. 66–73.

18. Einstein and Infeld, *The Evolution of Physics*, p. 152.

Chapter Four   The Concept of Relationship

1. For Einstein's words, please see chapter two, note 21, in this book. Martin Buber's poetic book of philosophy, *I and Thou*, is essentially about relationship. It is difficult to extract short statements, but two capture the point: "Spirit is not in the I but between I and You. . . . love . . . is between I and You. . . . What has been said earlier of love is even more clearly true at this point: feelings merely accompany the fact of the relationship which after all is established not in the soul but between an I and a You." Martin Buber, *I and Thou*, a new translation with a prologue, "I and You," and notes by Walter Kaufman (New York: Simon & Schuster: A Touchstone Book, 1996), pp. 89, 66, 129.

2. See chapter two, note 27, in this book.

3. Susan Collin Marks, *Watching the Wind: Conflict Resolution during South Africa's Transition to Democracy* (Washington, DC: United States Institute of Peace Press, 2000), p. xvii.

4. My first attempts to formulate the concept of relationship in the context of observations about our changing world were two papers: (1) "Beyond 'Us and Them'—Building Mature International Relationships," a draft monograph prepared in 1987–1988; (2) a version of that paper published as a work in progress, "Beyond 'We' and 'They'—Conducting International Relationships," *Negotiation Journal* (Vol. 3, No. 3, July 1987), pp. 245–277. I experimented in applying the concept to different conflictual relationships in: "The Arab-Israeli Conflict in a Global Perspective," in John D. Steinbruner, ed., *Restructuring American Foreign Policy* (Washington, DC: The Brookings Institution, 1988), Chap. 8; "The Soviet-U.S. Relationship and the Third World," in Robert Jervis and Seweryn Bialer, eds., *Soviet–American Relations After the Cold War* (Durham, NC: Duke University Press, 1991), Chap. 6; "The Concept of Relationship: A Perspective on the Future Between the United States and the Successor States to the Soviet Union" (Columbus, OH: The Mershon Center at The Ohio State University, begun in 1990 but not published until 1993 because of the dissolution of the

Soviet Union); the new Epilogue to a second edition of my 1985 book reflecting its new subtitle, *The Other Walls: The Arab–Israeli Peace Process in a Global Perspective* (Princeton, NJ: Princeton University Press, 1991). The last sets the Arab–Israeli peace process more fully in the context of international relationships as political processes. A broader thesis statement appeared in "An Historic Challenge to Rethink How Nations Relate," in Vamik D. Volkan, Demetrios Julius, and Joseph V. Montville, eds., *The Psychodynamics of International Relationships, Vol. 1: Concepts and Theories* (Lexington, MA: Lexington Books, 1990), Chap. 1. Harold H. Saunders, *A Public Peace Process: Sustained Dialogue to Transform Racial and Ethnic Conflicts* (New York: St. Martin's Press, 1999; Palgrave paperback, 2001) focuses on the use of sustained dialogue to change relationships.

5. For a thorough discussion of large-group identity see Vamik D. Volkan, "Psychoanalysis and Diplomacy: Part I. Individual and Large-Group Identity," *Journal of Applied Psychoanalytic Studies* (Vol. 1, No. 1, 1999), pp. 29–55; "Psychoanalysis and Diplomacy Part II: Large-Group Rituals," *Journal of Applied Psychoanalytic Studies* (Vol. 1, No. 3, 1999), pp. 223–247; "Psychoanalysis and Diplomacy: Part III. Potentials for and Obstacles against Collaboration," *Journal of Applied Psychoanalytic Studies* (Vol. 1, No. 4, 1999), pp. 305–318; "Individual and Large-Group Identity: Parallels in Development and Characteristics in Stability and Crisis," *Croatian Medical Journal* (Vol. 40, No. 4, December 1999), pp. 458–465. Volkan, a Turkish Cypriot by birth, was long-time director of the psychiatric hospital in the University of Virginia's Health Sciences Center and in 1989 was founder of the Center for the Study of Mind and Human Interaction, also located within the Health Sciences Center. He is now retired.

6. I first made this proposal in detail in the Nevitt Sanford Award lecture at the annual conference of the International Society of Political Psychology in July 2000. It was published as "Two Challenges for the New Century: Transforming Relationships in Whole Bodies Politic," *Political Psychology* (Vol. 23, No. 1, March 2002), pp. 151–164.

7. Vamik D. Volkan, *Bloodlines: From Ethnic Pride to Ethnic Terrorism* (New York: Farrar, Straus and Giroux, 1997), pp. 81–82.

8. A most helpful capsule discussion of the evolution of the concept of individual identity appears in Erik H. Erikson, *Identity: Youth and Crisis* (New York: W.W. Norton, 1968), Chapter I, "Prologue." See also Erik H. Erikson, *Identity and the Life Cycle* (New York: W.W. Norton, 1980; originally International Universities Press, 1959).

9. See Vamik D. Volkan, *The Need to Have Enemies and Allies: From Clinical Practices to International Relationships* (Northvale, NJ: Jason Aronson, 1988).

10. Georgi Arbatov, director of the Institute of USA and Canada Studies in the Soviet Academy of Sciences, made the comment in the sixteenth meeting of the Dartmouth Conference in Austin, Texas, in 1988. The Dartmouth Conference has been the longest continuous bilateral dialogue between American and Soviet—later Russian—citizens, having started at Dartmouth College in 1960. See James Voorhees, *Dialogue Sustained: The Multilevel Peace Process and the Dartmouth Conference* (Washington, DC: United States Institute of Peace Press and the Kettering Foundation, 2002).

11. As noted in the Introduction, Psychologist A. H. Maslow in the 1940s, for instance, called attention to basic human needs as physiological (food); safety; love, affection, belongingness; self-respect and the esteem of others that grows from capacity and achievement; and self-actualization (self-fulfillment). Maslow "A Theory of Human Motivation," pp. 370–396.

12. See, e.g., Harold H. Kelley, Ellen Berscheid, Andrew Christensen, John H. Harvey, Ted L. Huston, George Levinger, Evie McClintock, Letitia Anne Peplau, and Donald R. Peterson, *Close Relationships* (New York: W.H. Freeman and Company, 1983), pp. 12–13: ". . . the term *relationship* . . . essentially refers to the fact that two people are in a relationship with one another if they have impact on each other, if they are 'interdependent' in the sense that a change in one person causes a change in the other and vice versa." My own view is that—important as this sense of interdependence is—it is essential (1) to define relationship in terms of the larger range of elements presented in this chapter and (2) to reserve the word *interdependence* for application to those situations in which parties begin to depend on each other to achieve aims that are important to them both.

13. Salem, "Deconstructing Civil Society," in an analysis of civil society in Lebanon says that civil society organizations are vibrant but many are authoritarian within and exclusivist without.

14. The findings of this research are reported in English in Zhao Mei and Maxine Thomas, eds., *China–United States Sustained Dialogue, 1986–2001* (Dayton, OH: Kettering Foundation Press, 2001).

15. See Harold H. Saunders, *The Other Walls: The Arab-Israeli Peace Process in a Global Perspective*, especially pp. 1–5.

16. Edward Luttwak, "Franco-German Reconciliation: The Overlooked Role of the Moral Re-Armament Movement," in Douglas Johnston and Cynthia Sampson, eds., *Religion: The Missing Dimension of Statecraft* (New York: Oxford University Press, 1994), Chapter 4.

17. Kelley et al., *Close Relationships*, p. 14.

18. Robert Axelrod, *The Evolution of Cooperation* (New York: Basic Books, 1984) provides a very thorough analysis and interpretation of an extensive series of computer tournaments that tested experience in a number of models of interaction. It is an outstanding example of how two parties might learn a productive pattern of interaction.

19. See, for instance, George Breslauer, "Ideology and Learning in Soviet Third World Policy," *World Politics* (Vol. 29, April 1987), pp. 429–448; or Joseph S. Nye, Jr., "Nuclear Learning and U.S.-Soviet Security Regimes," *International Organization* (No. 4, Summer 1987), pp. 371–402. James Voorhees drew my attention to this work.

20. Professor I. William Zartman at the Paul Nitze School of Advanced International Studies, Johns Hopkins University.

21. Albert Einstein and Leopold Infeld, *The Evolution of Physics: From Early Concepts to Relativity and Quanta* (New York: Simon and Schuster, Inc., republished in 1966), p. 31.

Chapter Five   A Different Way of Thinking—Another Way of Relating

1. Harold H. Saunders, *The Other Walls: The Arab-Israeli Peace Process in a Global Perspective* (Princeton, NJ: Princeton University Press, 1991).

2. Harold H. Saunders, *A Public Peace Process: Sustained Dialogue to Transform Racial and Ethnic conflicts* (New York: St. Martin's Press, 1999; Palgrave paperback, 2001).

Chapter Six   Transformation in South Africa: A People Engaged

1. Allister Sparks, taped interview in his Johannesburg home September 30, 1999. He is the author of two of the most insightful books on the South African mind and experience: *The Mind of South Africa: The Story of the Rise and Fall of Apartheid* (first published 1990 in the United Kingdom by William Heinemann, Ltd.; London: Arrow Books, 1997) and *Tomorrow Is Another Country: The Inside Story of South Africa's Negotiated Revolution* (first published 1995 by William Heinemann, Ltd.; London: Arrow Books, 1997).

2. Pravin Gordhan, taped interview in his Pretoria office, September 28, 1999.

3. Leon Wessels, taped interview in his Johannesburg office, September 30, 1999.

4. Charles Villa-Vicencio, taped interview in his Cape Town office, October 6, 1999. He is the author of *Civil Disobedience and Beyond: Law, Resistance and Religion in South Africa* (Cape Town: David Philip, 1990).

5. Villa-Vicencio, taped interview, October 6, 1999.

6. This is a classic description of what the scholars of conflict resolution have called a "hurting stalemate"—the point at which both sides of a conflict recognize that their interests are being intolerably hurt and that there is no prospect of their getting their way by force. For instance, please see I. William Zartman and Maureen R. Berman, *The Practical Negotiator* (New Haven: Yale University Press, 1982), pp. 54–57. Zartman used the phrase in his seminars throughout the 1980s.

7. Laurie Nathan, taped interview in his Cape Town Centre office, October 6, 1999.

8. Paul Graham, taped interview at the IDASA center in Pretoria, September 28, 1999.

9. Sparks, *The Mind of South Africa*, p. xvii.

10. Sparks, *The Mind of South Africa*, p. 5. The historical account that follow draws heavily on Sparks.

11. Sparks, *The Mind of South Africa*, pp. 12–13.

12. Sparks, *The Mind of South Africa*, p. 14.

13. Sparks, *The Mind of South Africa*, p. 20.

14. Henry Lichtenstein, *Travels in Southern Africa* (Cape Town, 1928, Vol. 1), p. 352.

15. Sparks, *The Mind of South Africa*, p. 16.

16. Sparks, *The Mind of South Africa*, p. 228.
17. Sparks, *The Mind of South Africa*, p. 214.
18. Villa-Vicencio, taped interview, October 6, 1999.
19. Sparks, *The Mind of South Africa*, p. 16.
20. Sparks, *The Mind of South Africa*, p. 38.
21. Sparks, *The Mind of South Africa*, p. 24.
22. Sparks, *The Mind of South Africa*, p. 27. He cites Erich Fromm, *The Fear of Freedom* (London: Routledge and Kegan Paul, 1961), pp. 72–79.
23. Sparks, *The Mind of South Africa*, p. 40.
24. Sparks, *The Mind of South Africa*, p. 42. He cites C. W. de Kiewiet, *A History of South Africa: Social and Economic* (London: Oxford University Press, 1941), p. 17.
25. Sparks, *The Mind of South Africa*, p. 40.
26. Sparks, *The Mind of South Africa*, p. 39.
27. Villa-Vicencio, taped interview, October 6, 1999.
28. Sparks, *The Mind of South Africa*, pp. 214–215.
29. Sparks, *The Mind of South Africa*, pp. 20–21.
30. Sparks, *The Mind of South Africa*, p. 40.
31. Villa-Vicencio, taped interview, October 6, 1999.
32. Allan Boesak, *If This Is Treason, I Am Guilty* (Grand Rapids, MI: Eerdmans, 1987), p. 22, quoted in Sparks, *The Mind of South Africa*, p. 218.
33. Sparks, *The Mind of South Africa*, pp. 46–47.
34. Sparks, *The Mind of South Africa*, p. 92. The summary that follows is drawn from p. 106ff.
35. Sparks, *The Mind of South Africa*, p. 125.
36. Sparks, *The Mind of South Africa*, p. 121.
37. Based on Sparks, *The Mind of South Africa*, pp. 88–90.
38. Sparks, *The Mind of South Africa*, p. 146.
39. Geoff Cronjé, *'n Tuiste vir die Nageslag—Die Blywende Oplossing van Suid-Afrika se Rassevraagstul* (*A Home for Posterity*) (Johannesburg: Publicite Handelstretkamediens [Edms.] Bpk, 1945). This was followed by a book coauthored with two Afrikaner theologians, William Nicol, and E.P. Groenewald, *Regverdige Rasse-Apartheid* (Stellenbosch: Christen Studente Vereeniging Boekhandel, 1947). Summarized in Sparks, *The Mind of South Africa*, pp. 175–182.
40. Sparks, *The Mind of South Africa*, pp. 194–196.
41. Sparks, *The Mind of South Africa*, pp. 196–197.
42. Sparks, *The Mind of South Africa*, pp. 200–201.
43. The account of the Congress and the drafting of the Freedom Charter is in Sparks, *The Mind of South Africa*, pp. 240–242.
44. Sparks, *The Mind of South Africa*, pp. 243–244.
45. Sparks, *The Mind of South Africa*, pp. 302–303.
46. Sparks, *The Mind of South Africa*, pp. 285–286. He quotes John de Gruchy, and Villa-Vicencio—*Apartheid Is a Heresy* (Grand Rapids, MI: Eerdmans, 1983), pp. 161–163.
47. Gordhan, taped interview, September 28, 1999.
48. Sparks, *The Mind of South Africa*, p. 315.
49. Sparks, *The Mind of South Africa*, p. 332.
50. Sparks, *The Mind of South Africa*, p. 330.
51. Gordhan, taped interview, September 28, 1999.
52. Sparks, *The Mind of South Africa*, pp. 332–333, 337–338.
53. Gordhan, taped interview, September 28, 1999.
54. Gordhan, taped interview, September 28, 1999.
55. All of the immediately preceding quotes from Pravin Gordhan were recorded in a taped interview on September 28, 1999.
56. Judge Richard Goldstone, taped interview in his Johannesburg office, September 29, 1999.
57. Sparks, *Tomorrow Is Another Country*, p. 34. The account of the beginnings of the secret talks draws on Chapters 2 and 3.
58. Sparks, *Tomorrow Is Another Country*, p. 35.
59. Sparks, *Tomorrow Is Another Country*, pp. 76–87.
60. Sparks, *Tomorrow Is Another Country*, p. 87.
61. Johan Kriegler, taped interview in his Johannesburg office, September 29, 1999.
62. Gordhan, taped interview, September 28, 1999.

63. Kriegler, taped interview, September 29, 1999.
64. The account of these meetings is in Sparks, *Tomorrow Is Another Country*, Chapter 9, especially pp. 112–113 and 115–119.
65. Sparks, *Tomorrow Is Another Country*, pp. 121–124.
66. Steven Friedman, ed., *The long journey: South Africa's quest for a negotiated settlement* (Braamfontein, South Africa: Ravan Press, 1993), pp. 13–14.
67. Friedman, *The long journey*, p. 14.
68. Roelf Meyer, taped interview in his Pretoria office, September 29, 1999.
69. Friedman, *The long journey*, p. 16.
70. This account is based on Susan Collin Marks, *Watching the Wind: Conflict Resolution during South Africa's Transition to Democracy* (Washington, DC: United States Institute of Peace, 2000), pp. 7–8.
71. Meyer, taped interview, September 29, 1999.
72. Marks, *Watching the Wind*, p. 9.
73. Marks, *Watching the Wind*, p. 16.
74. Friedman, *The Long Journey*, p. 16.
75. Sparks, *Tomorrow Is Another Country*, p. 130.
76. Sparks, *Tomorrow Is Another Country*, pp. 136–137.
77. Sparks, *Tomorrow Is Another Country*, pp. 140–146.
78. Sparks, *Tomorrow Is Another Country*, p. 168.
79. Friedman, *The long journey*, pp. 147–148.
80. Sparks, *Tomorrow Is Another Country*, pp. 180–182.
81. Friedman, *The long journey*, p. 152.
82. Meyer, taped interview, September 29, 1999.
83. Friedman, *The long journey*, p. 163.
84. Sparks, *Tomorrow Is Another Country*, pp. 183–186.
85. Sparks, *Tomorrow Is Another Country*, pp. 194–195.
86. Sparks, *Tomorrow Is Another Country*, pp. 226, 228.
87. Gordhan, taped interview, September 28, 1999.
88. Marks, *Watching the Wind*, pp. 13–14.
89. Villa-Vicencio, taped interview, October 6, 1999.
90. Marks, *Watching the Wind*: on p. 191 she cites Meyer's speech at the Young Presidents' Organization conference in Johannesburg, March 1995; on changing the blueprint, she cites Jennifer Bowler, "Changing the Paradigm," *Track Two* (Vol. 3, No. 1, February 1994); her comment on Mandela is on p. 194.
91. Marks, *Watching the Wind*, p. 182.

Chapter Seven   Public Peacemaking and Peacebuilding in Tajikistan

1. Parviz Mullojanov is a participant in the Inter-Tajik Dialogue within the Framework of the Dartmouth Conference and executive director of the Public Committee for Democratic Processes, a nongovernmental organization established in 2000 by members of the Inter-Tajik Dialogue. He is a former international fellow at the Kettering Foundation. At my invitation to be coauthor of this chapter, he wrote a substantial analytical paper reflecting on the Public Committee's four years of experience in organizing Economic Development Committees (EDCs) in Tajikistani communities. Much of the factual description and analysis are his words, but I have placed in quotes those statements of opinion and analysis that deserve to stand out as the reflections of a key participant.
2. See Ramón Daubón and Harold H. Saunders, "Operationalizing Social Capital: A Strategy to Enhance Communities' 'Capacity to Concert,' " *International Studies Perspectives* (Vol. 3, 2002), pp. 176–191 and Ramón, Daubón, "Dialogue for Development," *Kettering Review* (Vol. 22, No. 1, Spring 2004), pp. 47–54. Daubón frequently uses the formulation "missing ingredient in fifty years of economic development theory" in his presentations.
3. This quotation is drawn from an unpublished article by Philip D. Stewart, "Internalizing the Sustained Dialogue Process: One Tajik's Journey." The article was written in November 2002, based on several conversations in Russian in Dushanbe with Ashurboi Imomov, a participant since the

seventh meeting of the Inter-Tajik Dialogue in 1994 and chairman of the Public Committee for Democratic Processes. Stewart was, for 29 years, a tenured professor of political science, a Sovietologist, at The Ohio State University. For 17 of those years, 1972–1979, he was executive director of the Dartmouth Conference as an associate of the Kettering Foundation. He is a member of the Board of Directors of the International Institute for Sustained Dialogue and a senior associate of the Kettering Foundation.

4. See, for instance, Robert D. Putnam, *Bowling Alone: The Collapse and Revival of the American Community* (New York: Simon & Schuster, 2002) in contrast to Carmen Sirianni and Lewis Friedland, *Civic Innovation in America: Community Empowerment, Public Policy, and the Movement for Civic Renewal* (Berkeley: University of California Press, 2001).

5. The remarkable story of this little-known thread in the Cold War is engagingly recounted in James Voorhees, *Dialogue Sustained: The Multilevel Peace Process and the Dartmouth Conference* (Washington, DC: The United States Institute of Peace Press and the Kettering Foundation, 2002). A personal account of the first decade by a Russian who participated in all of the Dartmouth Conference meetings is Alice Bobrasheva, *Thanks for the Memories: My Years with the Dartmouth Conference* (Dayton, OH: Kettering Foundation Press, 2003).

6. Harold H. Saunders, "Thinking in Stages," an unpublished paper presented at the annual scientific meeting of the International Society of Political Psychology in San Francisco in 1991.

7. Gennady I. Chufrin and Harold H. Saunders, "A Public Peace Process," *Negotiation Journal* (Vol. 9, No. 2, 1993). Harold H. Saunders, *A Public Peace Process: Sustained Dialogue to Transform Racial and Ethnic Conflicts* (New York: St. Martin's Press, 1999; Palgrave paperback, 2001).

8. Grant proposal written for the William and Flora Hewlett Foundation in early 1993.

9. The anonymous quotations are taken from a questionnaire administered by Parviz Mullojanov. Respondents did not want their names to be cited.

Chapter Eight   Power and Public Work in West Virginia

1. Jean Ambrose, for ten years director of the Commission for National and Community Service, in a taped interview in her Charleston office July 6, 2004. Her comments throughout this chapter are from this interview.

2. Carmen Sirianni and Lewis Friedland, *Civic Innovation in America: Community Empowerment, Public Policy, and the Movement for Civic Renewal* (Berkeley, CA: University of California Press, 2001), p. 1.

3. Jane J. Mansbridge, *Beyond Adversary Democracy* (New York: Basic Books, 1980), pp. 19–20.

4. Charles A. Reich, *The Greening of America* (New York: Random House, 1970; Bantam Books, 1971), p. 2.

5. I am indebted to my son, Mark Saunders, for this way of framing the dramatic changes of the 1960s and early 1970s. After he had written a novel as his honors thesis at the University of Pennsylvania, a friend of mine asked him, "What does a twenty-two year old in America have to write a novel about?" Mark's quick response: "My generation has inherited the broken pieces of five revolutions. [He named them as I have in the text.] And besides, my mother died when I was seven."

6. See, for instance, Lester R. Brown, *World without Borders: The Interdependence of Nations* (New York: Foreign Policy Association, Headline Series, 1972); Robert O. Keohane and Joseph S. Nye, *Power and Interdependence: World Politics in Transition* (Boston: Little, Brown and Company, 1977); James N. Rosenau, *The Study of Global Interdependence: Essays on the Transnationalisation of World Affairs* (London: Frances Pinter (Publishers) Ltd. and New York: Nichols Publishing Company, 1980).

7. Mansbridge, *Beyond Adversary Democracy*.

8. Mansbridge, *Beyond Adversary Democracy*, pp. 8–9.

9. Mansbridge, *Beyond Adversary Democracy*, p. 13.

10. Mansbridge, *Beyond Adversary Democracy*, pp. 15, 17.

11. Mansbridge, *Beyond Adversary Democracy*, pp. 19–20.

12. A leading figure in developing an academic and active focus on the citizen as a political actor was Harry Boyte whose formative experience in the Civil Rights Movement I noted earlier. For a fuller account of Harry Boyte's contribution, please see Sirianni and Friedland, *Civic Innovation in America*, pp. 245–252. His important books include: Harry Boyte, *The Backyard Revolution: Understanding the New Citizen Movement* (Philadelphia: Temple University Press, 1980); Sara M. Evans and Harry C. Boyte, *Free Spaces: the Sources of Democratic Change in America* (Chicago: University of Chicago Press, 1986); Harry C. Boyte, *Commonwealth: A Return to Citizen Politics* (New York: The Free Press, 1989).

An important milestone for Boyte and the Project for Public Life, which he founded at the University of Minnesota, was his role as a central player in the Clinton administration's emphasis on "the new citizenship" through a sequence of projects starting with the Reinventing Citizenship Project.

13. Daniel Yankelovich, *Coming to Public Judgment: Making Democracy Work in a Complex World* (Syracuse, NY: Syracuse University Press, 1991).

14. For a fuller, more systematic presentation of his thinking, please see David Mathews, *Politics for People: Finding a Responsible Public Voice* (Urbana: University of Illinois Press, 1999). Mathews and Kettering staff worked closely with Daniel Yankelovich, Robert Kingston (who later joined the Kettering staff), and Keith Melville at Public Agenda; often with Harry Boyte; and then with an increasing circle of researchers in this field.

15. The chronological framework and substantive insights provided by Betty Knighton were taped during a visit with her and her colleagues in Charleston, West Virginia, on July 6–8, 2004.

16. Taped interview with Jean Ambrose in her Charleston office, July 6, 2004.

17. Taped interview with Mary Virginia DeRoo in her Council of Churches office in Charleston, July 7, 2004.

18. Taped interview with Julie Pratt in her living room in Charleston, July 7, 2004.

19. Taped interview with Paul Gilmer in his office as manager, community affairs at Columbia Natural Resources in Charleston on July 8, 2004. He had worked as a middle manager at IBM until 1994, then with the City of Charleston, then the Community Council that merged with United Way. He formed a youth track and field club as a NGO.

20. Taped interview with Neal Newfield at the University of West Virginia in Morgantown, West Virginia, on July 8, 2004.

21. Dee Hock, *The Birth of the Chaordic Age* (San Francisco: Berrett-Koehler Publishers), p. 30. For a fuller discussion, see chapter three, in this book, in the section titled, "The Relational Paradigm."

22. Taped interview with Dean Doug Walters in his University of Charleston office on July 7, 2004.

23. Taped interview with Sue Julian in her office on the outskirts of Charleston on July 6, 2004.

Chapter Nine   Citizens Talk about the
Russia–U.S. Relationship

1. Philip Stewart, for 29 years a professor of political science at The Ohio State University, for 17 of those years part-time executive director of the Dartmouth Conference under contract with the Kettering Foundation, was one of the earliest American exchange students at Moscow State University in the early 1960s. In 1989 he resigned his professorship to become an executive with the Kellogg Corporation in Central and Eastern Europe and the former Soviet Union and lived in Latvia during the last half of the 1990s. When he retired, he again became an associate of the Kettering Foundation and of the International Institute for Sustained Dialogue. At the author's request, he began writing from experience a paper on the Russia-U.S. relationship using as his framework the concept of relationship presented in this book. We reviewed his first draft with Russian colleagues. The second and third drafts were the subject of two meetings of the Dartmouth Conference Regional Conflicts Task Force in 2002 and 2003. The second of these drafts incorporated material by then available from the public forums discussed in this chapter. The author has adapted that draft with Dr. Stewart's collaboration to produce this chapter.

2. Igor Nagdasev registered the Russian Center for Citizenship Education in 1993. Denis Makarov registered the Foundation for Development of Civic Culture in 1996.

3. The Russian Center for Citizenship Education headed by Igor Nagdasev, the Foundation for Development of Civic Culture headed by Denis Makarov, and the Library of Foreign Literature headed by Ekaterina Genieva. Nagdasev and Makarov produced the report from the Russian forums.

4. For the story of the Dartmouth Conference, please see James Voorhees, *Dialogue Sustained: The Multilevel Peace Process and the Dartmouth Conference* (Washington, DC: The United States Institute of Peace Press and the Kettering Foundation, 2002).

5. Reports from the forums in both countries were assembled from a variety of sources. Although the pattern varied from forum to forum and certainly from country to country, the following

procedures have been used in various combinations: recorders produced notes capturing the exchanges in forums; a few forums were videotaped or audiotaped; forum moderators produced reports; sometimes moderators and participants were interviewed. From that material, project leaders collaborated to produce composite reports from each country's forums. A draft composite paper by Philip Stewart based on raw materials from both sides and discussed in the Dartmouth Conference Regional Conflicts Task Force was the working paper from which the final U.S. report was written. These reports were the starting point for the "New Dartmouth" meeting in Washington in April 2003. On the basis of that meeting, the first planned publication of the New Dartmouth Conference was prepared and reviewed at a meeting in Moscow in September 2004.

Chapter Ten   Conducting the China–U.S. Relationship: A Diplomat's View

1. Benjamin I. Page and Robert Y. Shapiro, *The Rational Public: Fifty Years of Trends in Americans' Policy Preferences* (Chicago: The University of Chicago Press, 1992), pp. 245–256.
2. First among those nonofficial China-U.S. dialogues has been the regular meetings of the China-U.S. Dialogue sponsored in China by the Institute of American Studies in the Chinese Academy of Social Sciences (CASS) in Beijing and in the United States by the Kettering Foundation in Dayton, Ohio, and Washington, DC. I have also served on the board of the National Committee on U.S.-China Relations and have participated in its programs. Beginning in 2000, the Institute of American Studies and the Kettering Foundation have engaged in parallel research into how Chinese and U.S. citizens form their images of each other. The first year's findings were published in English as Zhao Mei and Maxine Thomas, eds., *China–United States Sustained Dialogue* (Dayton, OH: Kettering Foundation Press, 2001) and in Chinese by the Institute of American Studies. I have also tested the political paradigm and the concept of relationship through interviews, lectures, and seminars in Beijing and at the Johns Hopkins University Center at Nanjing University.
3. Henry A. Kissinger, *White House Years* (Boston: Little, Brown and Company, 1979), p. 754.
4. David M. Lampton, "The U.S. and China: Have They Learned Anything?" *Asian Survey* (Vol. XXXVII, No. 12, December 1997), p. 1110.
5. John Pomfret, "China Shows Less-Than-Warm Response to Disaster in America," *International Herald Tribune from Washington Post Service*, September 14, 2001, p. 9.
6. Pomfret, "China Shows Less-Than-Warm Response to Disaster in America," p. 9.
7. Reported in Zhao and Thomas, *China-United States Sustained Dialogue*, pp. 16–17.
8. Wang Jisi, director of the Institute of American Studies of the Chinese Academy of Social Sciences in private conversation, September 1999. I have paraphrased his comment from memory and checked it with him.
9. Kissinger, *White House Years*, pp. 745–746.
10. James R. Schlesinger et al., "Toward Strategic Understanding Between America and China," A Report on the Project of the National Committee on U.S.-China Relations, Inc. (National Committee China Policy Series, No. 13, December 1996).
11. Lampton, "The U.S. and China: Have They Learned Anything?" p. 1110.
12. George Bush and Brent Scowcroft, *A World Transformed* (New York: Alfred A. Knopf, 1998), pp. 104, 108, 175 quoted in Lampton, *Same Bed, Different Dreams: Managing U.S.-China Relations, 1989–2000* (Berkeley: University of California Press, 2001), pp. 25–26.
13. This account draws heavily on Lampton, *Same Bed, Different Dreams*, especially pp. 30–63.
14. Lampton, *Same Bed, Different Dreams*, pp. 39–40.
15. President Clinton's press conference, May 26, 1994, Office of the Press Secretary, the White House, quoted in Lampton, *Same Bed, Different Dreams*, p. 45.
16. Lampton, *Same Bed, Different Dreams*, p. 45.
17. Michael Barone and Grant Ujifusa, *The Almanac of American Politics*, 1998 (Washington, DC: National Journal, 1997), p. 1020, quoted in Lampton, *Same Bed, Different Dreams*, p. 48.
18. Lampton, *Same Bed, Different Dreams*, pp. 53–54, based on a conversation with Anthony Lake on July 18, 1996.
19. Lampton, *Same Bed, Different Dreams*, pp. 54–55.

20. U.S. House of Representatives, Select Committee, *U.S. National Security and Military/Commercial Concerns*, Vols. 1–3 (Washington, DC: U.S. Government Printing Office, May 25, 1999) cited in Lampton, *Same Bed, Different Dreams*, p. 58.
21. Author's post-meeting record of the conversation.
22. Zhao and Thomas, *China–United States Sustained Dialogue, 1986–2001*, p. 17.

Chapter Eleven   What Difference Does It Make? What Makes This Difference?

1. Harry Boyte's words in describing the aim of the Dorchester School of the Southern Christian Leadership Conference in the 1960s in training rural African Americans to play a role in the voter registration drives in the U.S. South.
2. A citizen of Tajikistan experienced in the development of Tajikistan's civil society. He prefers to remain anonymous.
3. Betty Knighton, taped interview in Charleston, West Virginia, July 6, 2004.
4. Betty Knighton, taped interview, July 6, 2004.
5. Parviz Mullojanov, in his contribution to chapter seven in this book.
6. From a citizen's answer to a questionnaire in one of the Economic Development Committees, quoted in Parviz Mullojanov, from his paper prepared for chapter seven.
7. Parviz Mullojanov, from his paper prepared for chapter seven.
8. Roelf Meyer, taped interview in Pretoria, September 29, 1999.
9. Betty Knighton, taped interview, July 6, 2004.
10. Betty Knighton, taped interview, July 6, 2004.
11. James Voorhees, *Dialogue Sustained: The Multilevel Peace Process and the Dartmouth Conference* (The United States Institute of Peace Press and the Kettering Foundation, 2002), p. 330. Voorhees focuses in depth on how scholars and participants have thought about and assessed the effects of interaction between participants in the Dartmouth Conference and its task forces and the Soviet and U.S. governments. Please see pp. 8–18 and 333–362.
12. Pravin Gordhan, taped interview in his Pretoria office, September 28, 1999.
13. Explained fully in chapter six of this book.
14. Richard Goldstone, taped interview in his Johannesburg office, September 29, 1999.
15. Roelf Meyer, taped interview, September 29, 1999.
16. Marks, *Watching the Wind*, p. 16.
17. Laurie Nathan, taped interview in his Cape Town office, October 6, 1999.
18. Philip D. Stewart, unpublished article, "Internalizing the Sustained Dialogue Process: One Tajik's Journey."
19. Taped interviews in Charleston, West Virginia, July 9, 2004.
20 See chapter one, note 18, in this book.
21. Bohm, *Wholeness and the Implicate Order*, p. xi.
22. Václav Havel, "The End of the Modern Era," *New York Times* (March 1, 1992), p. E15, quoted in David Mathews, *Politics for People* (Urbana: University of Illinois Press, 1994), p. 163.
23. Dwight D. Eisenhower, *Public Papers of the Presidents: 1959* (Washington, DC: Government Printing Office, 1959), p. 625.

INDEX